An Encyclopaedia of Critical Terms :

Eastern & Western Traditions

An Encyclopaedia of Critical Terms :

Eastern & Western Traditions

Volume-1

Dr. Krishna Gopal Srivastava

Formerely
Professor & Head
Department of English & Modern
European Languages
&
Dean, Faculty of Arts University of Allahabad
Allahabad
&
Vice-Chancellor (Interim)
University of Allahabad

RADHA PUBLICATIONS

New Delhi-110 002

First Edition : 2013
ISBN : 81-7487-826-7

ISBN 81-7487-826-2

9788174878267

RADHA PUBLICATIONS
4231/1, Ansari Road, Daryaganj
New Delhi-110002
Phone : 2324 7003, 23254306

Published by Nitin Garg for Radha Publications and printed by Asian Offset Press, Shahadra, Delhi-32

Preface

The guiding principle of the present venture is the conviction that the language of poetry (i.e. the words poets use in their respective languages for purposes of their poems) is universal, for poets across the countries–India, Russia, China, Greece, Italy, England, Syria, Egypt–employ words in as charming a way as possible, no matter whether they are aware of the ways concerned and could name them or not. Homer, for example, uses figures like "arthāntaranyāsa" and "utpreksā" quite like Indian poets even though, to be sure, he did not know the names of the figures concerned. And that is true of all poets in all languages. So in the appreciation of poetry, if critical terms are of any use, these should be used without any racial, national, religious, political or social prejudice. For, poetry must be appreciated as poetry *per se* whether it is in German, Russian, French, Greek, Sanskrit, Urdu or Hindi. So far as critical terms and their niceties are concerned, Sanskrit, beyond doubt, supplies their largest and most detailed accounts; no other language in the world can match it in terms of the categories, kinds, classifications and depth of literary and critical concepts. Take up a simple term such as metaphor which from Aristotle to I.A. Richards has been so popular in the discussion of poetry in the West and has been used extensively down the ages. The West is no doubt far superior to the East (i.e. Sanskrit) in terms of philosophical discourse regarding its nature, function and psychological effect; but so far as its classifications are concerned, Sanskrit is matchless. The varieties of metaphor or “रूपक”–निरङ्गरूपक, परम्परित रूपक, समस्तवस्तुविषयक साङ्गरूपक, एकदेशविवर्ती साङ्गरूपक, मालारूपक and numerous forms of लक्षणा based on it, are, in most cases, unheard of in the Western Criticism. Similarly, another well known figure called simile or उपमा has 32 different varieits, if we could trust the Sanskrit theorist Ācārya Dandī. The same theorist discusses a form of "Pun" called “यमक”, dividing it into 315 varieties. And both classifications, I believe, should be the despair of the West. I agree that Sanskrit ācāryas sometimes indulge in hair-splitting and we can conveniently ignore this bad habit of theirs. But their broad divisions certainly deserve attention and even acceptance. The discoveries of figures like विशेषोक्ति, अर्थान्तरन्यास, काव्यलिङ्ग, उल्लेख, उत्प्रेक्षा, प्रतीप, तद्गुण, मीलित, व्यतिरेक, हेतु, सूक्ष्म, भाविक, to name only a few, for which there are hardly any western equivalents (though Western poetry can supply excellent examples of all of them), can enrich the appreciation of Western poetry; there cannot be an iota of doubt about this. These figures cannot be the monopoly of Sanskrit or Indian poetry; these are the properties of all poetry–Eastern or Western. I see absolutely no harm in using these terms in the appreciation of the passeges of Western poetry where these figures exist. For example, Shakespeare supplies an excellent example of व्यतिरेक in the octave of his Sonnet No. XVIII, beginning with the line 'Shall I compare thee to a Summer's day?'. Now the moot-question is: will English criticism gain or lose by using the term 'व्यतिरेक' in the appreciation of the sonnet concerned? The answer to this question, I believe, will be affirmative. The ethical principle formulated in the following Sanskrit verse, namely,

विषादप्यमृतं ग्राह्यं बालादपि सुभाषितम्

> [Nectar Should be accepted even from poison and good speech even from a child.]

should clinch the matter. I see no harm in pronouncing the beauty of the sonnet's octave as residing in Shakespeare's creative use of व्यतिरेक. Let us cite the relevant lines for our ready reference :

> Shall I compare thee to a Summer's day
> Thou art more lovely and more temperate:
> Rough winds do shake the darling buds of May,
> And summer's lease hath all too short a date.
> Sometiems too hot the eye of heaven shines,
> And often is his gold complexion dimm'd;

Now, in a Simile or उपमा the "उपमान" or 'standard of comparision' is normally superior to "उपमेय" or the thing which is being compared to the "उपमान". But a skilful poet, by means of his imaginative argument, could establish the superiority of the "उपमेय" over the "उपमान" and thus reverse the established order and when that happens, Sanskit theorists hold that the poet has used a trope called "व्यतिरेक". Precisely that is the case with the lines cited above. The sun of the summer season is the standard of comparison here; and the sun is normally superior to any man in terms of shine and glamour. However, Shakespeare has very skilfully established here the superiority of Mr. W.H. (i.e. the "उपमेय" of the passage) by means of a *tour de force* which Sanskrit poeticians have designated as "व्यतिरेक". I am not aware of any term invented by the West for this *tour de force.* So there should be no problem for Western criticism in accepting this term in its critical terminology for the same would be richer and brighter by enlarging its own scope. But "व्यतिरेक" is just an example. Sanskrit theorists have recognized 70 to 90 and some times even 125 or more figures and tropes and each one of them could be illustrated from Western texts as well, apart from Indian texts. Clearly, these terms have a kind of universal applicability. Sanskrit denominations of these figures can be usefully employed in the analysis of Western poetry, provided the analyser himself is familiar with those denominations.

"Kāvyadoṣa" (poetic defects) is another area where Sanskrit poetics has no peer. The West can very conveniently exploit this rich weaponry of Indian poetics in the analysis and appreciation of its poetry. Sanskrit ācāryas have recognized 37 defects of words, 23 defects of sense or meaning and 10 defects of sentiments or "Rasa". All these various defects of poetry can be illustrated from Western poetry. Let us consider the case of the poetic defect called "अप्रतीत" which consists in the use of some technical term of some branch of science, not normally known to people at large. In the following passage from the essay "My Relations" by Charles Lamb, we have this defect in the expression "grand climacteric":

> May they continue still in the same mind; and when they shall be seventy-five, and seventy three years old (I cannot spare them sooner), persist in treating me in my grand climacteric precisely as a stripling, or younger brother!

The expression "grand climacteric" is from astrology and refers to the sixty-third year of a man's life, usually regarded as a very critical year. It must be noted that ninth and seventh years of a man are astrologically regarded as critical years but the number sixty-three which is the outcome of the multiplication of 'nine' by 'seven', is the most dangerous year and so the sixty-third year is regarded by astrologers as a "grand climacteric." But very few people are familiar with this expression.

Thus the quotation from "My Relations" can be subjected to the charge of "अप्रतीत दोष". I am not aware of any corresponding term in the Western tradition. Will not Western Criticism be richer by accepting the Sanskrit concept of "अप्रतीत दोष"? Clearly, yes.

"Nāyaka-Nāyikā-bheda" of the Sanskrit poetics is yet another field which could profitably be exploited by the world, especially the Western world. Some people have the illusions that the Nāyaka-Nāyikā discourse is valid only for Indian literature and that it has no relevance for non-Indian literatures. But this is an entirely wrong notion, having no substance. The classifications of heroes and heroines conceptualized by the Indian theorists are true not only of Sanskrit and other Indian literatures but also of all literatures of the world, at least in their most essential forms. All the heroes and heroines discussed by the Sanskrit ācāryas can be illustrated from Western texts. Take up, for example, the class of heroines, broadly speaking, called मुग्धा who are sexually innocent. A special class of these heroines is called अज्ञातयौवना or ladies unaware of their grown youth. Is not Miranda, the heroine of Shakespeare's last play *The Tempest* an अज्ञातयौवना नायिका particularly when she makes the following speech, addressed to Ferdinand in the first scene of the third Act:

I do not know
One of my sex! no woman's face remember,
Save, from my glass, mine own; nor have I seen
More that I may call men, than you, good friend,
And my dear father : how features are abroad,
I am skill-less of ;

Any sensitive and responsive reader of poetry will agree that the term अज्ञातयौवना is a very helpful term and can be unhasitatingly employed in analysing characters like Miranda.

What is true of "Nāyaka-Nāyikā-bheda" is equally true of the doctrines of "Rasa", "Dhvani", "Vakrokti" and "Aucitya", for all these theories are valid for all literatures and not just for Sanskrit and other Indian literatures. Western poetry can supply examples of all the "Rasas" Indian theorists have dealt with. Whether or not the following passage from Dante's *Divina Commedia* is illustrative of वीभत्सरस well-informed readers of poetry should decide :

A crust of slimy mold
Covered the walls, by exhalations formed
In foulness steaming up from far below,

Disgusting to the eye and nose alike.
So dark the bottom lay beyond our sight
That only when we stood atop the span
Could we discern it. Here we made our way
And peering down we saw souls deep submerged
In filthy dung, as human privies yield.
("Inferno", Canto XVIII 97-106, Translated by Thomas G. Bergin)

Since Western criticism seldom takes account of the emotional aspects of poetry, at least never in the way Sanskrit ācāryas have done, a wholly fresh area of the study of Western poetry can be created by subjecting it to the rigours of the doctrine of "Rasa". And that holds good in respect of the doctrines of "Dhvani, "Vakrokti" and "Aucitya". The theorists of the "Dhvani" doctrine have conceptualized thousands of "dhvani" and I regard that position as absurd; it is hair-splitting, pure and simple. However, the major forms–वस्तुध्वनि, अलङ्कारध्वनि and रसध्वनि, including their broad sub-divisions, are valid and viable. They can illuminate Western poetry a great deal as much as they can illuminate Sanskrit or Hindi poetry. For example, let us take up the following concluding lines from Robert Browning's famous poem "My Last Duchess":

Nay, we'll go
Together down, Sir! Notice Neptune, though,
Taming a sea-horse, thought a rarity,
Which Claus of Innsbruck cast in bronze for me.

This is an excellent example of वस्तुध्वनि for it suggests the speaker's (of the Duke of Ferrara) assumed humility, self-glorification, ostentation, tyrannical attitude and love for art-works–all at once. I agree that Western critics of Browning have illuminating comments of all shades and hues on the passage concerned to offer but they suffer from a lack of critical terminology to pinpoint the sources of the suggested readings they propose. This want is fairly met by the employment of the Dhvani-doctrine. For example, the term of address, namely, "Sir", used in the second line of the quotation, used by the Duke for the ambassador of some Count who has come to the Duke for a marital settlement on behalf of the daughter of the count, can be considered here. The Duke is far far superior to the ambassador in social hierarchy, so he is not expected to use the word 'Sir' for the ambassador and yet he does precisely that, presumably because he is trying to flatter the Count's emissary with a view to winning the highest dowry to be recommended by the emissary to his master (i.e. the Count). Thus, the word 'Sir' is a deliberate design, dictated by the sense of greed of the speaker (i.e. the Duke of Ferrara). No other term of address (e.g. the name of emissary) would serve the purpose. This is an example of शब्दशक्ति-उद्भव-अनुरणन ध्वनि where the suggested sense comes from the word used by the poet alone and where all substitute words are ruled out; only the use of the word 'Sir' can suggest the Duke's inherent purpose and no other word. Similarly, the reference to the art-work displaying the sea-god Neptune, taming a sea-horse is intended to bring home to the ambassador of the Count the thought that the Count's daughter will have to remain contented with a servile position in the home of the Duke of Ferrara for the Duke will remain ever lordly to her, treating her as a very inferior being, expected to obey the Duke's commands at all hours. Here, too, the word 'Neptune' enjoys a sense of inevitability–no other word can suggest the complete sway that the Duke will have over his new bride. This is also illustrative of शब्द-शक्ति-उद्भव-अनुरणनध्वनि as the tyranmical behaviour of the Duke is suggested by the word 'Neptune', the Roman god of the sea who has complete mastery over the waves of the sea and the creatures living therein such as sea-horses and whales. In like manner, the description of the bronze artefact depicting Neptune taming a sea-horse as 'thought a rarity' reveals unmistakably the Duke's indulgence in self-glorification by pointing to his collection of very precious and rare art works such as the one detailed above, showing Neptune, the sea-god taming a sea-horse. That the Duke is given to bluffing is clearly revealed by his reference to a fictitious seulptor Claus of Innsbruck who never existed. Even this is an example of शब्द-शक्ति-उद्भव-अनुरणन-ध्वनि for no other name would do what Claus of Innsbrack does.

Kuntaka's theory of "Vakrokti", too, can help our reading of Western poetry better. The theory explores the causes and sources of the various charms of poetry, inhering in all parts of a poem from individual letters and their artful arrangement to the work as a whole, artistically manipulated. This theory again applies to all poetry and not just to Sanskrit or Indian poetry for, all forms of "Vakrokti" can be illustrated from Western texts. Indeed, Professor Shrawan K. Sharma of Gurukul Kangri University, Hardwar, has applied Kuntaka's theory to English poetry in detail, citing examples of all forms of "Vakratā" from English poems. This he has done in his *Kuntaka's Vakrokti Siddhānta : Towards An appreciation of English Poetry* (Shalabh Publishing House, Meerut, 2004). Here I will discuss only what Kuntaka calls "Paryāya-Vakratā" (i.e. poetic charm by means of skilful use of a particular synonym of a word out of its several possible synonyms available in the language). Great poets, Kuntaka believes, have an innate apprehension of the respective beauty of words; they select spontaneously only those words, out of multiple choices available, that serve their purpose most efficiently and artistically. Consider, for example, Keats's use of the word "embalmed" in the following lines from his "Ode to a Nightingale" (stanza 5) :

> I cannot see what flowers are at my feet,
> Or what soft incense hangs upon the boughs,
> But, in embalmed darkness, can guess each sweet
> Wherewith the seasonable month endows
> The grass, the thicket, and the fruit-tree wild :

If Kuntaka were to analyse the beauty of the lines, cited above, he would come out with the suggestion that the excellence of the verses lies in the poet's choice of the word "embalmed" out of its several possible synonyms available to him: 'fragrant', 'perfumed', 'spiced' 'preserved' etc. Now, the question is : Why did Keats choose "embalmed" and not any other word bearing the same sense? The answer is : "He knew the intrinsic charm surrounding the word 'embalmed'. He wanted to project darkness, not just as something sweet-smelling but also as the preserver and custodian of all basic forms of natural life, the reservoir of all scents and smells, to be distributed, in accordance with season, among plants and trees. The poet knew that no other synonym of 'embalmed' could convey the two ideas of preservation and sweet-smellingness simultancously. So he projected darkness as smelling of all flowers of all times and as the container and preserver of the scents and smells of all Nature, recalling to our mind the Egyption art of preserving dead bodies by means of certain spices that averted decay of those bodies. Thus the word 'embalmed' has an extraordinary charm and makes the entire passage marvellous and examplifies Kuntaka's concept of पर्यायवक्रता at its best.

I have no doubt whatsoever that the critical insights of Kuntaka under the garb of numerous forms of वक्रता will open new vistas of critical thinking regarding Western poetry, or for that matter, any poetry of the world. This is equally true of the doctrine of औचित्य that ācārya Kṣemendra had pleaded for on the ground that the observance of 27 forms of औचित्य guarantees the excellence of poetry. True, the Western world has never been unaware of औचित्य; for, even Aristotle had stressed its importance under the head of 'Prepon' and Horace had stood for 'Decorum'. But

Kṣemendra's theory of औचित्य is far more penetrating and far more broad-based than either of the two Western doctrines of 'Prepon' and 'Decorum'. I am quite sure that by applying the theory of औचित्य to poems like "To a Skylark", "Ode to the West-Wind" and "Adonais" the charges levelled against Shelley by critics like Arnold and F.R. Leavis can be successfully met and justice can be done to the genius of the poet. The theory can also reveal the mystery of Milton's apparently misplaced glorification of Satan in the opening books of the *Paradise Lost.* The application of the theory of औचित्य to the vexed question of several episodes in the great novels of the world can bring out the significance of those apparently irrelevant episodes. Evidently, the theory is very broad and universal in its appeal and can enrich our reading not only of Indian texts but also of non-Indian texts.

The discussion of the 3 powers of words called अभिधा, लक्षणा and व्यञ्जना by the theorists of Sanskrit poetics can also be exploited by the readers of Western poetry in a very positive manner. A reader, well-versed with the concept of लक्षणा and its various forms, can explicate many dark passages of the great literary works of the West and remove the obscurity involved very easily. Let us take the example of the famous lines from the seventh stanza of Keats's 'Ode to a Nightingale':

> The same that oft times hath
> Charmed magic casements, opening on the foam
> Of perilous seas, in faery-lands forlorn.

What precisely is the meaning of the expression "magic casements" English commentaries do not explain. But a fair knowledge of "Lakṣanā" (लक्षणा) can easily clarify the position. There is defintely "arthabādhā" here for 'casements' are, to all intents, inanimate things–they cannot be supposed to be charmed by the song of the nightingale because only animate beings with minds and hearts can be charmed. But when we take into account the word 'magic' with which 'casements' form a compound, we cannot help thinking of some kind of आधार-आधेय सम्बन्ध involved here. This leads us to conclude that 'casements' here mean 'princesses of the fairy-tales, sitting fixed to the 'casements' (window panes) of the castles located in some island, far away from human settltements'; the castles are the piaces where the magicians of the fairy-tales have kept the princesses captives. The picture suggested is that of princesses, magically fixed to the casements, looking despondantly on the waves of the sea, surrounding the castle, cherishing the hope of some saviour-prince's arrival there for their liberation. Thus the expression 'magic casements' clearly means the princesses, fixed to the casements by the magic-wand of the magician who has kept them as captives for the purpose of marrying them some day. The word 'charm' which has given the word 'charmed' as the past tense of its own verb-form compels us to consider the comparative merits of 'charm' on the one hand and of 'magic' on the other. Both are the forms of 'enchantament' but 'charm' is clearly more powerful than magic, at least, in the view of Keats who asserts that the song of the nightingale has the power to undo what magic has done. The magic of the evil magician has rendered the captive princesses senseless and motionless in a state of trance or stupification. But the song of the nightingale could charm the souls of even the princesses, under the spell of the magic of the magician, by nullifying the effects of the magic-words blown on the princesses concerned. Thus the knowledge of लक्षणा can unravel the tangled knots of obscure passages of any language– Sanskrit, Hindi, English and Chinese alike. Similarly, the knowledge of व्यञ्जना could be equally fruitful to the reading of Western poetry. True, Western critics talk of 'suggestion' and 'suggested meaning' quite often. But the Sanskrit ācāryas have probed the matter on a very grand scale. There are 15 different bases of अभिधामूला व्यञ्जना itself, what to talk of the bases of लक्षणाभूला व्यञ्जना. There cannot be any doubt regarding the usefulness of व्यञ्जना and how it functions; its knowledge is sure to enrich our knowledge of any poetry of the world. The symbolist poetry whether of France, Germany, England or America, can be understood better by one who has mastered the व्यञ्जना-व्यापार of words at the feet of ācāryas like Mammaṭha and Viśvanātha. Let us take up the following lines from Sylvia Plath's famous poem "Daddy":

Daddy, I have had to kill you,
You died before I had time–
Marble-heavy, a bag full of God,
Ghastly statue with one grey toe
Big as a Frisco-seal
And a head in the freakish Atlantic
Where it pours bean green over blue
In the waters off beautiful Nauset.

(ll. 6-13)

British and American studies of the poem do not explain the lines satisfactorily but a student of व्यञ्जना and its व्यापार (how it functions) can explicate the lines quite satisfactorily. What is the meaning of the word 'kill' in the first line of the quotationa? Auto Plath, the father of the poet, is already a thing of the past–he had died when Sylvia Plath was barely 7. So the word 'kill' cannot be taken in its usual sense; it has to be taken in the sense of 'getting rid of through some process of exorcism'. The memory of the father is haunting the mind of the poetess all the time and naturally she is feeling suffocated; she, therefore. wants to get rid of her obsession with her daddy–that is what the line: 'Daddy, I have had to kill you' presumably means. But how to interpret the second line: 'You died before I had time–'. The hyphen after 'time' compels us to take time' to mean 'time to kill'. That is to say that the poetess was too young to take an independent course and thus get rid of his influence when her father breathed his last and naturally her obsession with her father continued. The third line of the quotation 'Marble-heavy, a bag full of God' is really very perplexing. It can be taken as a description of the obsession-figure that was the father of the poetess so far her psyche was concerned where he was lurking all the time like a piece of sculpture made of marble. The word 'heavy' points to the undesirability of the father, ever lurking in the mind of the poetess. The father also appeared in the mind of the poetess like 'a bag, full of God'. Evidently, the description is that of absolute reverence the poetess always felt for her father who was a virtual God to her, though that reverence did not have a salutary effect on her growth. This unsalutary aspect of the fatherly obsession becomes clear when the poetess describes her mental figure of the daddy as a 'ghastly statue' . The ghost-like behaviour of the father-fixation is clearly stressed here, requiring to be exorcized–mark the word 'grey' which is suggestive of deathliness, gloominess and cheerlessness. The details of the toe of the fatherly statue can be understood only through the biography of the poetess and that of her father. Auto Plath had hurt his toe accidently and the same had become gangrenous with the result that his leg had to be amputated and he had to wear an artificial leg. This image of the father, in no way, a wholesome image, was imprinted on the daughter's mind which never liked the sight. The adult mind of the poetess is recalling the father's form with an artificial leg having a toe which had struck Sylvia Plath's child-imagination as a big Frisco seal (i.e. a seal of the Frisian sea, known for the largest seals in the world). Here it must be made clear that Sylvia Plath has an ambivalent feeling for her father : she likes his activities in America and detests his European roots–his German ancestry. That is why the toe (i.e. Auto Plath's initial growth, the instrument of his migration from Europe, Polish Corridor, to be precise, to America) is grey and the head (i.e. the centre of intellectual power) pours green bean over blue waters of Atlantic. Here, it must be mentioned that Auto Plath was a professor of Botany at Boston University, Massachusetts, U.S.A., and worked on the behaviour of bees. The reference to the head, pouring 'bean green over blue' suggests the intellectual activity of Auto Plath by way of writing a book on bees. 'Beans' in the poetry of Sylvia Plath, invariably relate to bees. The word 'Nauset' in l. 8 of the quotation makes the favourable American connection of Auto Plath crystal clear. The adjective 'beautiful', used for Nauset, is a pointer to it. Nauset is a sandly place; its modern name is Easthom. The poetess calls it 'beautiful' because its original inhabitants–the Nauset Indians–had saved the lives of their enemies–the Pilgrim Fathers. (who were trying to uproot the natives of the area i.e. Nauset Indians), when the latter had started starving, by providing them corn and bean. The poetess imagines the arrival of the Plaths in the company of the Pilgrim Father in 1620 at Nauset where they settled and one of them, namely, Auto Plath, benefited the new land of their adoption through his botanical researches, 'pouring bean green over blue'. This interpretation of the lines, under discussion, has been possible only through the application of the rules by which व्यञ्जना, both शाब्दी and आर्थी, works. Readers will, I believe, feel fully convinced that the wisdom of the Sanskrit ācāryas contained in their analysis of the powers of the word can be of great help in studying even non-Indian writings of imagination. This is so because the broad view of the ācāryas are the outcome of their deep meditation on how poetic language works whether it is Indian or non-Indian.

However, there is no intention of claiming universal applicability only for the critical doctrines and concepts evolved in India. No; wisdom cannot be the monopoly of any nation or race; by God's grace, it can descend on any people on the earth and become the common property of humanity at large. There is no denying that many concepts of the West–Katharsis, Hamartia, Anagnorisis, Peripety, Unity, High Seriouness, Sublimity, Impersonality, Tension, Paradox, Realism, Naturalism, Expressionism and Impressionism, to name only a few, are not just true of western literature; they are equally true of Eastern literature as well. India and the rest of the world should be prepared to accept these critical terms and employ them freely in the discussion of their respective literatures. This is the age of globalization and the true spirit of globalization consists in bringing all literatures of the world on a common platform without any kind of prejudice or favour in the most objective manner. If the East in its pride of the great antiquity of its critical tradition refuses to accept healthy concepts of the West, it would remain poorer than those countries that welcome and embrace them. Similarly, if the West in its arragance of the advanced technology and prosperity, developed and acquired by it in the modern age, refuses the gifts from India in the form of critical terms unknown to its own tradition, it would be liable to be charged with foolhardiness and self-conceitedness. The healthiest attitude would be that of give and take, fellow-feeling and mutual respect–all in the name of enlarging human vision and understanding. The following statement of Kālidāsa, full of sagacity and practical wisdom, should be our motto:–

पुराणमित्येव न साधु सर्वं, न चापि काव्यं नवमित्यवद्यम्
सन्तः परीक्ष्यान्यतरत्भजन्ते, मूढः परप्रत्ययनेय-बुद्धिः ।।

(मालविकाग्निमित्रम्, 1/2)

> [All that is old cannot be good simply because it is old and all that is new cannot be declared bad simply because it is new. Wise people accept that which is wholesome after examining its merits and demerits and the fools act at the suggestions of others (without applying their minds].

All that is Indian with a long antiquity, therefore, cannot be said to be viable and significant and all that is western cannot be irrelevant and insignificant either. Both East and West must be prepared to hear the voice of sanity and to accept all that is useful and wholesome in either tradition. 'East is East, West is West/The twain can never meet' is a myth which ought to be exploded at the earliest–the sooner the better. At least in the sphere of poetry this dichotomy has no place, for poetry speaks to the heart and human heart is all alike whether it is of the East or of the West. If it were not so, it would be difficult to explain as to how the West danced with joy when it read Kālidāsa's *Abhijnānāśākuntalam* when Sir William Jones published its Latin translation in 1789 and its English translation the following year (i.e. 1790). And equally true is the case of Shakespeare whose plays are enjoyed by all students of English literature throughout the world. Literature defies all barriers–geographical, racial, religious, cultural, ethical, political and even personal.

With that view in mind, the present venture has been undertaken; it is divided into two parts. Part I has two sections A & B. Section A consists of a few essays, dealing with the origin and growth of Sanskrit poetics, its six great schools or sampradāyas and their surveys, and its strengths and weaknesses. Section B is a dictionary of the critical terms of the Eastern tradition, giving lucid explanations of the terms concerned.

In each case illustrations have been given from Indian texts first, followed by examples from the western text. Part II has also been divided into two sections–A and B. Section A contains essays on the origin and growth of Western poetics, its various schools and their surveys, and its critical assessment. And Section B is a dictionary of the critical terms of the Western tradition. In each case, clear-cut expositions of the terms have been provided followed by illustrations first from Western texts and then from Indian texts.

It is the earnest hope of the writer of this encyclopaedia that it will bring about a better understanding between the East and the West by bridging the gap between the two and by highlighting how the creative minds of the two traditions thought and felt alike. May the voice of sanity prevail and divisive forces be quelled for ever!

आ नो भद्रा क्रतवो यन्तु विश्वत :

[May good and auspicious thoughts
come from all quarters of the world!]

A Guide to the Correct Pronunciation of Sanskrit Words Transcribed in Roman Letters

अ	= a		घ	= gha		प	= pa
आ	= ā		ङ.	= nga		फ	= fa oa pha
इ	= i		च	= ca		ब	= ba
ई	= ī		छ	= cha		भ	= bha
उ	= u		ज	= ja		म	= ma
ऊ	= ū		झ	= jha		य	= ya
ए	= ei		ञ	=		र	= ra
ऐ	= ai		ट	= ṭa		ल	= la
ओ	= o		ठ	= ṭha		व	= va
औ	= au		ड	= da		श	= Śa
अं	= nga		ढ	= dḥa		ष	= ṣa
अः	= aḥ		ण	= ṇa		स	= sa
ऋ	= ṛ		त	= ta		ह	= ha
लृ	= lṛ		थ	= tha		क्ष	= kṣa
क	= ka		द	= da		त्र	= tra
ख	= kha		ध	= dha		ज्ञ	= jna
ग	= ga		न	= na		विसर्ग (:)	= ḥ

Part-I : Eastern Tradition
Section A : Essays On Indian Poetics

Indian Poetics :
A History of Its origin and Growth

The history of Indian civilization is shrouded in mystery; it is agless and beyond human measurement of time. And just as Indian civilization is ageless, Indian poetics is also ageless. For, nobody on the earth can pinpoint authoritatively at what particular point of time it was born. This becomes quite clear from the fact that Vedas, being eternal and the source of all knowledge, contain seeds of discourse on poetics and presume a highly developed awarness of poetry and its problems. Those who regard the vedic age as later than the Indus Valley civilization and date the Vedas from 2000 B.C. or 1500 B.C. have not been able to provide any definitive and convincing argument for their assertion. We cannot laugh away the traditional Indian view that the Vedas existed even at the beginning of the creation–even at the commencement of the Kṛta or Satya-yuga crores of years ago. The famous "Puruṣa-sūkta" of the *Ṛgveda* does not share the world-famous Darwinian theory of the gradual evolution of earthly existence : for, it clearly believes in the co-existence of all forms of life from the very beginning of the creation. And the Hindu race has full faith in the vedic view and that has a thoroughly logical and philosophical basis. That view is fully supported by the theory of "karma" according to which all our births are determined by our deeds of previous life. An absolutely rationalistic and pragmatic thinker of modern times–Swāmī Dayānanda Saraswatī–held the Vedas eternal and ageless; the writer of this encyclopaedia finds it impossible to disagree with Swāmījī.

According to the incontrovertible Hindu view, the source of all learning is to be found in the Vedas. And poetics is no exception. Indeed, most of the critical terms used in Sanskrit poetics today–Rīti, Rasa, Alamkāra, Guṇa etc are to be found in Vedic writings. The word "upamā" (उपमा), for example, was defined by the vedic sage Gārgya who is no doubt older than Yāska, the author of निरुक्त ("Nirukta") which was his commentary on निघण्टु ("Nighantu"), the glossary of Vedic words, by some unknwon author, much older than Yāska and even Gārgya. Yāska can be safely placed in the 10th century B.C. and the great commentator cites the view of Gārgya, his predecessor who had defined "उपमा" (or Simile) in the following words :

"यद् असत् सत्सदृशमिति गार्ग्यः"

(निरुक्त 3/3/14)

> [(Upamā) lies in something being presented as similar (though in point of fact) it is not so. That is how Gārgya had defined it.]

And Yāska, in his turn, defines उपमा a little differently :

"ज्यायसा वा गुणेन प्रख्याततमेन वा कनीयांसं वा अप्रख्यातं वा उपमीयते"

> [In a simile (or उपमा) (something) which is inferior or not so famous is compared with something which is superior in quality or with something which is most famous.]

Evidently, the discourse on simile or उपमा is as old as Gārgya and Yāska and Yāska, to all intents and purposes, flourished in the 10th century B.C., as we have maintained earlier. Yāska was very thorough in his treatment of उपमा which he classifies in categories like कर्मोपमा, भूतोपमा, रूपोपमा, सिद्धोपमा, अर्थोपमा, लुप्तोपमा etc. However, the concepts of उपमा and अलंकार (figures of speech) are much older than Gārgya and Yāska. The *Ṛgveda* itself uses the word 'अरंकृति' ("Aramkṛti") as a form of 'अलंकृति' or 'अलंकार' (i.e. ornament) as is clear from the following verse :

'का ते अस्त्यरंकृतिः सूक्तैः'

(ऋग्वेदः 7.29.3)

Again, the same Veda in 8.7.3. has the following words: "आदित्यानामरंकृते" and uses words like 'परिभूषन्ति', 'भूषन', 'परिभूषत' etc. in the sense of 'ornamentation' or 'decoration'.

From the above facts we can rest assured that there had been during the Vedic age some discussion of अलंकार or 'figure of speech' which has been a very significant item of Indian poetics and under whose denomination a whole school of criticism called अलंकार सम्प्रदाय had emerged later. Professor Mahendra Kumar Verma, in his great study called the *Poetic Beauty of the Ṛgveda* asserts, with some solid basis, of course, that the *Ṛgveda* reflects a fairly advanced stage of the knowledge of the critical concepts like 'रस', ध्वनि, 'अलंकार', 'रीति' etc. This view can very easily be confirmed by the fact that extreme care was taken by the Vedic readers of the most ancient days to pronounce even particles of words for the full and favourable effects of Vedic mantras or chants. This was so because :

दुष्टः शब्दः स्वरतो वर्णतो वा मिथ्याप्रयुक्तो न तदर्थमाह।
स वाग्बज्रो यजमानं हिनस्ति यथेन्द्रशत्रुः स्वरतोऽपराधात्।।

(पाणिनीयशिक्षा-52)

[A word rendered bad from the view point of pronunciation of the vowel or any letter in it or used incorrectly does not convey its meaning. The verbal bolt kills the sacrificer (यजमान) as the wrong pronunciation of the expression 'इन्द्रशत्रु' did, involving as it did the criminal pronunciation of अन्तोदात्त instead of आद्योदात्त.]

The verse, cited above, is from तैत्तरीय संहिताब्राह्मण (2/5) as well as शतपथ ब्राह्मण (1/5/2). A sister-verse also appears cited in *Mahābhāṣya* in the same place as the following Vedic injunction :

'एकः शब्दः सम्यक् ज्ञातः सुप्रयुक्तश्च स्वर्गे लोके च कामधुक् भवति।'

(महाभाष्य (1/1/1),

It must be borne in mind that *Mahābhāsya* is a commentary by Patanjalī on the world-famous text of grammar called *Aṣṭādhyāyi* by Pāṇini. We do not know the date of Pāṇini but that of Pātanjali is the second third century B.C. as is proved by Patanjali's use of 'लट्'-लकार (Present Continuous tense) in sentences like 'इह पुष्यमित्रं यजामः ' (i.e. 'here we are sacrificing for Puṣyamitra'). The great Indian Scholar of Sanskrit–Ramkrishna Gopal Bhandarkar–in his brilliant paper entitled "On the date of Patanjali and the King in Whose reign he Lived " (1872), very ably, argued out the contemporaneity of Patanjali with king Puṣyamitra Śunga who reigned from 178 B.C. to 142 B.C. and in whose reign the Bactrian king Menander had invaded Ayodhyā or Sāketa.

Now, the Vedic aphorism, citied by Patanjali, can be translated into English in the following words :

"A single word, well-understood and
well-employed, fulfils all desires in this
world as well as in the heaven."

There is absolutely no doubt whatsoever that the Vedic Indians, well-versed as they were in the celebrations of rituals and sacrifices, were aware of the miracles wrought by words by means of their precise and appropriate use. And this speaks valumes about the level of critical thinking in Vedic times. Finding the justification and function of words indeed constitutes the quintessence of criticism and that being the case here, we are fully justified in claiming for Sanskrit poetics the remotest possible antiquity. Some clear ideas of the existance of poetic theory in India in the most ancient times can be discerned from a careful study of *Aṣṭādhyāyī*, the greatest book of Sanskrit grammar by the sage Pāṇini, for the work uses words like 'उपमा', 'उपमान', 'उपमेय' etc. For example, the concept of 'उपमा' (simile) is implicit in the following sūtra :

तुल्यार्थैरतुलोपमाभ्यां तृतीयाऽन्यतरस्याम् (2.3.72)

> [Optionally the third is used in respect of words bearing the sense of similarity except the words 'तुला' and 'उपमा']

The above assertion can also be confirmed by the fact that the first poet of the Laukika Sanskrit, namely, sage Vālmīki evinces awareness of a highly developed state of thinking about poetry and art-criticism and it must be noted that Vālmīki is anterior to Pāṇini. The tradition places Vālmīki in 'Kṛtayuga' or 'Satyayuga' lacs of years ago. The *Rāmāyaṇa*, the epic by which he is known, claims the author's contemporaneity with the hero of the poem (i.e. Rāma) and uses most of the critical terms of Sanskrit poetics–terms like 'रस', 'अलंकार', 'छन्द', 'महाकाव्य', 'उपाख्यान', 'व्यञ्जना', 'लक्षणा' etc. In the 'उत्तरकाण्ड' of his epic, सर्ग 94, Vālmīki provides us a very advanced state of art-appreciation when he enumerates in verses 4-10 experts of different branches of learning, including connoisseurs of songs and of poetry called 'क्रियाकल्पविद्': नैगम, पण्डित, कलाविद्, स्वरलक्षणज्ञ, गान्धर्वज्ञ, कलामात्रविभागज्ञ, पदाक्षरसमासज्ञ and छन्दोनिष्णात. The context is the proper evaluation of the recitation of Rāmakathā by Lava and Kusha, the two disciples of Vālmīki, who have come to the court of Rāma in the city of Ayodhyā for the purpose :

अथ कर्मान्तरे राजा समाहूय महामुनीन्।
पार्थिवांश्च नरव्याघ्रः पण्डितान् नैगमांस्तथा।।
पौराणिकान्शब्दविदो ये वृद्धाश्च द्विजातयः।
स्वराणां लक्षणज्ञांश्च उत्सुकान् द्विजसत्तमान्।।
लक्षणज्ञांश्च गान्धर्वान् नैगमांश्च विशेषतः।

पादाक्षरसमासज्ञांश्छन्दःसु परिनिष्ठितान् ।।
कलामात्रविशेषज्ञाज्ज्यौतिषे च परं गतान् ।
क्रियाकल्पविदश्चैव तथा कार्यविशारदान् ।।
भाषज्ञानिङ्गितज्ञांश्च नैगमांश्चाप्यशेषतः ।
हेतूपचारकुशलान् हैतुकांश्च बहुश्रुतान् ।।
छन्दोविदः पुराणज्ञान् वैदिकान् द्विजसत्तमान् ।
चित्रज्ञान् वृत्तसूत्रज्ञान् गीतनृत्यविशारदान् ।।
शास्त्रज्ञान् नीतिनिपुणान् वेदान्तार्थप्रबोधकान् ।
एतान् सर्वान् समानीय गातारौ समवेशयत् ।।

[Then the royal work being over, the lion-hearted king (Rāma) invited great sages, kings, scholars of Vedic lore, the experts of the Purāṇas, experts of words, old brahmins, knowers of vowels and their signs, the pundits, full of curiosity, knowers of omens and signs on palms, experts of the science of the gandharvas (i.e. experts of music) specially the experts of the Vedic branch of music, experts of prosody, knowing the arrangements of Pādas, letters and compounds; experts of fine arts, experts of astronomy, knowing that science to its highest limit, knowers of kṛyākalpa (i.e. critics of poetry), art-experts, knowers of languages and signs, specially of the Vedic type, masters of logic and scholars of varied branches and analysers; experts of metres, great brahmins, knowing puraṇas, experts of visual arts and experts of the science of ethics, experts of songs and dances, people learned in śāstrārtha, experts of political science and people having full command over the meaning of Vedānta. Having collected all these people (in the conference hall), he (i.e. king Rāma) introduced the two singers (i.e. Lava and Kusha, who were actually the sons of Rāma and Sītā)].

The mere catalogue of experts, belonging to various sciences, speaks volumes for the level of art, literature and culture India had attained in the age in which the *Rāmāyaṇa* including its "Uttarakānda" was written. The expressions like 'कलामात्रविशेषज्ञान्', 'क्रियाकल्पविदः' 'कार्यविशारदान्' and 'छन्दोविदः' are really very significant and helpful to the determining of the antiquity of Indian thinking on poetry and kindred problems. Another very remarkable point to be noted is the fact that in Vālmīki's view, the critical assessment of the musical epic sung by Lava and Kusha was not just a matter involving the judgment of 'गीतनृत्यविशारद's but also that of the other experts, belonging to cognate branches of learning like Vedic and Paurāṇika lore, linguistics, philology, lexicology and embracing the experts of other sciences like astrology, logic, epistemology, ethics and metaphysics. For our purpose. the word 'क्रियाकल्पविद्' used in the eighth line of the extract is of supreme value. The word conveys the sense of "the judge of creative writings" or "literary critics". The same term, it must be borne in mind, occurs in कामसूत्र 1-3-16 of sage Vātsyāyana. To be very exact, there the term 'क्रियाकल्प' has been used and not 'क्रियाकल्पविद्' but 'क्रियाकल्प' clearly means the science dealing with the working of (poetry); it is almost a synonym of poetics or काव्यशास्त्र. The term 'क्रियाकल्प' succeeds the term 'काव्यक्रिया' (i.e. the art of poetry-making) which has been given the 54th place in the list of 64 arts enumerated by Vātsyāyana. Thus if 'काव्यक्रिया' is the art of composing poems, 'क्रियाकल्प' definitely refers to the science of analysing and judging of poetry. The use of the term 'क्रियाकल्पविद्' by Vālmīki is very significant indeed. It further strengtherns our position, stated earlier, that Sanskrit poetics is ageless. For all practical purposes, Vālmīki is regarded as the 'आदिकवि' of the Laukika Sanskrit literature as distinguished from the Vedic Sanskrit. But he was aware of the tradition of the ācāryas of poetics whom presumably he knew râther well. The way he describes the aesthetic level of singing of Rāmakathā by Lava and Kusha presumes a very high level of art criticism and art appreciation.

> शुश्राव तत्तालयोपपन्नं
> सर्गान्वितं सुस्वरशब्दयुक्तम्।
> तंत्रीलयव्यञ्जनयोगयुक्तं
> कुशीलवाभ्यां परिगीयमानम्।।

> [(Rāma) listened to (the epic poem called the *Rāmayaṇa*) having cantos, couched in sweet and melodious words, being recited with proper tālas and layas (pauses and cadences) and having suggestions prompted by the melody of the vīṇās]

In the third line of the extract, cited above, the word 'व्यञ्जन', on the face of it, bears the sense of consonents but it can also be interpreted in the sense of the verbal power called 'व्यञ्जना' which has a lot to do with the dhvani-school of literary criticism, founded by Ānandavardhanācārya of the 9th Century A.D. If that is the case, the theory of poetic suggestion in some form existed in the age of Vālmīki.

There are certain other details, available in the *Rāmāyaṇa* that establish the existence of a highly developed poetic theory in the age of Vālmīki. That there was a long discussion about poetic genres becomes clear from the way Lava and Kusha give an account of the *Rāmayaṇa* in the 94th 'sarga' of the work's "Uttarakānda" in their reply to the following queries of Rāma:

किंप्रणामिदं काव्यं का प्रतिष्ठा महात्मनः।
कर्ता काव्यस्य महतः क्व चासौ मुनिपुङ्गवः।।

(Verse 24)

[What is the size of this poem? What is the reputation of the great-souled (author of this work)? Where does that great sage (i.e. the author of the work) live?]

The expression 'काव्यस्य महतः' used in the second line of the verse, cited above, conveys the same sense as the term "महाकाव्यस्य" does; in point of fact, it is the break-up of that very compounded expression. We get a fairly good account of Vālmīki's notion of the "epic poem" from the following verses uttered by Lava and Kusha :

संनिबद्धं हि श्लोकानां चतुर्विंशत्सहस्त्रकम्।
उपाख्यानशतं चैव भार्गवेण तपस्विना।।

(Verse 26)

आदिप्रमृति वै राजन् पंचसर्गशतानि च।
काण्डानि षट्कृतानीह सोत्तराणि महात्मना।।

(Verse 27)

कृतानि गुरुणाऽस्माकमृषिणा चरितानि तव।
प्रतिष्ठा जीवितं यावत् तावत् सर्वस्य वर्तते।।

(Verse 28)

[(O King!) In this (poem) composed by that anchorite (i.e. Vālmīki) there are 24 thousands of verses and one hundred episodes. O King! From the beginning (to the end) 500 cantos and six parts (kāndas) have been composed along with the seventh kānda called "उत्तरकाण्ड". All thy deeds have been depicted by our proceptor, the sage (Vālmīki). Whatever be the extent of life, all in present here fully covered.]

This account of the epic, I believe, is unparallelled and unique in the history of the world-criticism. In the first instance, it emphasizes the magnitude (24,000 verses, scattered over 7 kāndas or books. containing 500 cantos and 100 upakhyānas or episodes) and the subject matter or content of the work. Regarding the latter aspect of his poem, Valmīki says : "प्रतिष्ठा जीवितं यावत् तावत् सर्वस्य वर्तते". Clearly, according to him, the epic poem in general and the *Rāmāyana* in particular, takes or ought to take in its sweep the entire extent of human life–all aspects and all phases of human existence–rise and fall, life and death, happiness and unhappiness, victory and defeat, joy and sorrow, prosperity and adversity, laughter and tears, heroism and cowardice, opulence and poverty, vigour and slackness, sunny side and seamy side of the worldly sojourn of man. This account of the Epic poetry is better than any, put forward so for anywhere in the entire world. It is better than Aristotle's, better than that of Dandī, Bhāmaha or Viśvanātha, and even better than that of Northrop Frye, the author of *The Anatomy of Criticism.*

Apart from the discussion on "Mahākāvya", Vālmīki seems to have been aware of the doctrine of Rāsa, formulated by Ācārya Bharata in the famous treatise called the *Nātyaśāstra*. In the 9th verse of the 4th "sarga" of the "Balakānda" of the *Rāmayana*, we come across the following verse, addressed by Brahmā to Vālmīki:

रसैः श्रृंगार-करुण-हास्य-वीर-भयानकैः।
रौद्रादिभिश्च संयुक्तं काव्यमेतद् गायताम्।।

[Sing (O Vālmīki!) this poem, full of all rasas or sentiments–Śṛngāra, Karuṇa, Hāsya, Vīra, Bhayānaka, Raudra etc.]

The above verse leaves us in no doubt whatsoever that the doctrine of Rasa was known to Vālmīki for he refers to all the major Rasas and presumes the rest by using the expression "आदिभिः", clearly implying that there were several other Rasas, not mentioned in the verse.

The age in which Vālmīki flourishad is not known definitively, though all faithful Hindus believe that he was a contemporary of Lord Rāma and thus he flourished, according to this belief, in the Tretāyuga, thousands of years before Lord Krishna of the Dvāparayuga which had come to a close around 3100 B.C. whence the present yuga called Kaliyuga commenced. Ācārya Bharata claims in the *Nātyaśāstra* that he had brought the science of drama (नाट्यवेद) from the heaven sometimes in the Tretāyuga:

पूर्वं कृतयुगे विप्रा वृत्ते स्वायम्भुवेऽन्तरे।
त्रेतायुगे सम्प्रवृत्ते मनोर्वैवस्वतस्य तु।।

(Chapter I. Verse 8)

आज्ञापितो विदित्वाऽहं नाट्यवेदं पितामहात्।
पुत्रानध्यापयं योग्यान् प्रयोगं चापि तत्त्वतः।।

(Verse 25)

[Narrating to sages like Ātreya and others the origin of Drama, sage Bharata says:) "O sages, in the hoary past when Satyayuga had ended at the close of the manvantara of Svāyambhuva Manu and Tretāyuga had started with the commencement of the manvantara of Vaivasvata Manu... having learnt the science of drama from Pitāmaha (Brahmā) I taught the same along with its application in its essentials to my able sons".]

Clearly, the story of the origin of Drama in Tretāyuga, thanks to the labour put forth by sage Bharata, appears to be true for *Nātyśāstra* seems to have influenced Vālmiki's *Rāmāyaṇa* for the epic uses many critical terms of Bharata's *Nātyśastra*–terms like 'Rasa' and its different varieties, mentioned above. There is a view that sage Vālmīki and sage Bharata are the same person. This view can get some support from the fact that the versification of Vālmīki has a very close affinity with that of Bharata in the *Nātyśāstra*. They may and may not be the same person but both definitely belonged to the same age–Tretāyuga and there cannot be any doubt whatsoever about it for Vālmīki claims himself to be a contemporary of Lord Rāma, the hero of his epic called the *Rāmāyaṇa* and Bharata says that he learnt the science of Drama from Brahmā in the Tretāyuga. Interestingly enough, both Bharata and Vālmīki were inspired to do their respective work, namely, of applying the theory of Drama in actual practice and of singing the deeds of Rāma in verse respectively–by Brahmā. Whatever the Western Scholarship might say regarding the dates of the two great personalities of India, we, on our part, take them on their words, taking them to be true sages having no ulterior motive behind the claims they make. In any case, Vālmīki is a very, very old writer who had influenced the Greek poet Sophocles of the 5th Century B.C. through one of his verses, occurring in the 101st "Sarga" of the "Yuddhakānda" of the *Rāmāyana* :

देशे देशे कलत्राणि, देशे देशे च बान्धवाः।
तं तु देशं न पश्यामि यत्र भ्राता सहोदरः।।

> [Lamenting the near-death condition of Lakṣamana, Rāma says:) "Wives can be found in all countries and in all countries can relatives be had; but I do not see a country where one could find a brother from the same womb".]

The thought expressed in the above verse is to be found in more or less the same style, in the following speech of the heroine of *Antigone of* Sophocles :

> Never had I been a mother of children, or if a husband had been mouldering in death, would I have taken this task upon me in the city's despite. What law, ye ask, is my warrant for that word? *The husband lost, another might have been found, and child from another, to replace the first-born, but father and mother hidden with Hades, no brother's life could ever bloom for me again.*
>
> (ll. 905-912)
> (emphasis ours)

The eminent Greek Scholar of the Victorian age and the most famous editor of *Antigone*–Professor R.C. Jebb, in his notes on the lines of the above quotation that I have emphasized, clearly observes that the thoughts expressed therein are un-Greek and seem to have come to Greece in remote antiquity from some oriental scurce. However, he failed to identify the source precisely. In my edition of *Antigone* (Kitab Mahal, Allahabad, 1992, p. 39) I asserted that the oriental source of Jebb's speculation was the verse beginning with the words "देशे देशे कलत्राणि", cited above from Vālmīki's *Rāmāyana*. Now the question arises : how could any Indian thought reach the Greek shores in the 5th century B.C. when, to all intents and purposes, the history of Indo-Greek contact started in 326 B.C. with Alexander's invasion of India? The answer is that the history of Indo-Greek contact is very old. There was Greek script current in India in the age of Pāṇini for the grammarian mentions it in his famous *Aśtādhyāyī* and Pāṇini flourished in 2800 B.C. according to Hindu calculations and in the 6th century B.C. according to British and European calculations. Sophocles's own reference to the pure gold of India in l. 1038 of *Antigone* itself clinches the matter. Jebb's comments on this line of the Greek text informs us that gold used to come to Greece from two sources–Lydia and India. The Lydian gold had a very large amount of alloy in it whereas the Indian gold had a very small quantity of alloy in it. Sophocles mentions in l. 1038 of his work both varieties of gold simultaneously, calling the Lydian gold "the silver-gold" of Sardis, Sardis being the capital of Lydia. Thus if gold could reach the Greek shores in the age of Sophocles, why not the golden thought from India through the merchants of gold? And much before Sophocles the Greek philosopher Pythagoras had brought to Greece a lot of Indian concepts from India with him from his Indian gurus of his age–i.e. the sixth century B.C.– concepts like Metempsychosis and Vegetariansim and above all the geometrical theorem called after his own name–the Pythagorean theorem which he had learnt from the Indian sages, spelling out the rules of mensuration propounded in Śulba-sutras of texts like *Āpastamba-Gṛhyasūtra* and *Baudhāyanagṛhyasūtra.* In this way, Vālmīki's influence on Sophocles becomes quite convincing and fully established. This goes to prove that there had been a very old tradition of poetics in India prior to Vālmīki whose age is shrouded in mystery; but, at all events, he is much, much older than Sophocles. That there had been theorists of poetry before Vālmīki becomes quite clear from his own remark:

तां स शुश्राव काकुत्स्थः पूर्वाचार्यविनिर्मिताम् ।
अपूर्वां पाठ्यजातिं च गेयेन समलंकृताम् ।।

(रामायण, उत्तरकाण्ड, 94/2)

[The scion of Kakutstha (i.e. Lord Rāma) listended to the marvellous song-composition rendered in singing style in accordance with the rules propounded by previous experts of poetics.]

The expression "पूर्वाचार्यविनिर्मिताम्" is very significant for our purpose; it clearly refers to the experts of musicology, dramaturgy and poetics who existed before Vālmīki's appearance on the literary scene of India. In fact, Vālmīki borrows certain technical terms from the treatises of the experts concerned in the verse next to the one we have cited above:

प्रमाणैर्बहुभिर्बद्धां तंत्रीलयसमन्विताम् ।
बालाम्यां राघवः श्रुत्वा कौतूहलपरोऽभवत् ।।

[Rāghava (i.e. Rāma) became wonder-struck after hearing the song-composition, attuned to the melody of vīnā and arranged in various combinations of scales of notes by the two boys (Lava and Kusha).]

The word "प्रमाण" used at the very outset of the above verse is undoubtedly a technical term of musicology and Bharata has dealt with this as he does with terms like 'पाठ्य' and 'जाति' that Vālmīki uses in the verse 2 of the 94th 'सर्ग' of the "उत्तरकाण्ड" of *Rāmāyana* that has been cited above. All these terms have been explained in detail by Bharata in the 31st chapter of the *Nātysāstra.* Thus Vālmīki's indebtedness to Bharata gets confirmed. And curiously enough, Vālmiki as "Bhagavān Vālmiki" has been mentioned by Bharata at the beginning of the 36th Chapter of *Nātyśāstra* in the list of the sages who had made certain enquiries regarding dramaturgy (नाट्यवेद्) and its usefulness.

We do not know when Vālmīki's *Rāmāyana* in its present form was made public but we can assert with confidence that it was as it is today in the 5th century before the Christian era and, as we have argued earlier, it proves the existence of a highly developed poetics, dramaturgy and musicology. It is indeed very pertinent to raise the question of the identity of the experts of fine arts that Vālmiki alludes to in his expression "पूर्वाचार्यविनिर्मिता"; who were these ācāryas? Could they not be Bharata or "Vṛddha Bharata" and his hundred disciples such as Kohal and Dattila? It must be placed on record here that the list of 100 sons or disciples mentioned by Bharata in the *Nātyaśāstra* I.26-40 is not all humbug for treatises by some of them were available to the theorists of drama and poetry of the 10th-12th centuries A.D. Quotations from Ācārya Kohala for example, are to be found in the *Sangīta-Ratnākara* of Śārangadeva and in the commentaries on the same work by Singhabhūpāla and Kallinātha–all of whom flourished between the 12th and 13th centuries. Besides, a few treatises by Kohala, in their incomplete forms, are extant even today, bearing the titles *Kohalamatam* and *Kohalīyam*. Furthermore, the thirteenth chapter of Kohalā's work *Kohalarahasyam* is available in an unpublished manuscript lying in the state Government library of Madras.

However, the earliest extant complete treatise of poetics and dramaturgy is the *Nātyaśāstra* of Bharata, though the tradition of discussion about poetry ramained intact in the *Mahābhārata, Agnipurāṇa, Viṣṇudharmottarapurāṇa* etc–all by Krishnadvaipayana Vyāsa. Even *Śrimadbhāgavatamahāpurāṇa* can supply hints testifying to the existence of a rich drama and poetics tradition of the Aryans in Dvāparayuga which commenced around 3100 years before the Christian era. In its 8th verse in the 21st adhyāya of its tenth "skandha", the great purāṇa asserts:

चूतप्रवालवर्हस्तवकोत्पलाब्जमालानुपृक्तपरिधानविचित्रवेषौ
मध्ये विरेजतुरलं पशुपालगोष्ट्यां रंगे यथा नटवरौ क्व च गायमानौ।।

(वेणुगीत)

[Bearing colourful appearances caused by the dress, studded with garlards, made of mangoleaves, coral, peacock-feathers and lotus-leaves, the two singing sons of Nanda (Krishna and Balarāma) looked in the company of the cowherds *like two expert-actors on the stage (in a theatre)]*

The underlined expressions in the verse cited above is a clear reference to the existence of the theatre, expert actors and the suggested existence of the treatises ḍealing with the theatre and theatrical production in the age in which the *Śrimadbhāgavatamahāpurāṇa* was written. Though the modern historians, following blindly in the footsteps of their Western gurus, think that the *purāṇa* concerned was written quite late in the Christian era, the traiditional scholarship of India firmly holds the view that it was written in 3100 B.C. by the sage Vyāsa who was a contemporary of Lord Krishna whose historicity is now fully established along with that of Vyāsa. I agree that there are certain interpolations in the *Mahābhārata* and the *purānas* but the remote antiquity of these works cannot be questioned at all and since many critical terms are to be found in all these works, we will have to accept the unfathamable antiquity of Indian poetics. That there were *purānas* in existence in the fourth century before the Christian era is clearly confirmed by Kautily's *Arthāśāstra's* statement in the first "adhyāya" called "उपजापः" of the 13th "Adhikaraṇa" entitled "दुर्गलम्भोपाय"

तदस्य स्वविषये कार्तान्तिकनैमित्तिकमौहूर्तिकपौराणिकेक्षणिक गूढपुरुषाः
साचिव्यकरास्तदद्र्शिनश्च प्रकाशयेयुः ।

(Vide the 4th para)

[His advisors and visitors and assistants, soothsayers (कातन्तिक), foretellers (नैमित्तिक), astralogers (मौहूर्तिक), reciters of purānas (पौराणिक), oracles (ईक्षणिक) and spies (गूढपुरुष) should go on propagating the (aforesaid) miracles wrought by the king.]

The word "पौराणिक" used in the quotation is proof positive of the fact that in the age of Kautilya there existed the tradition of organizing the reciatal of purāṇas by their experts called "पौराणिकाः" quite like the modern practice among the Hindus of week-long sessions of *Rāmacaritamānasa* and *Śrīmadbhāgavata,* especially in the country side. And the age of Kautilya is the age of the Mauryan rule in India as Kautilya himself declares at the end of the *Arthaśāstra*:

येन शास्त्रं च शस्त्रं च नन्दराजगता च भूः।
अमर्षेणोद्धृतान्याशु तेन शास्त्रमिदं कृतम्।।

(15.1. last but one verse)

[This science (of political management) has been written by one who salvaged instantly out of sheer anger the science (of political management), weaponry and the earth which had gone in the possession of the Nanda-kings.]

In the last verse of his work, Kautilya makes the question of the work's authorhip clearer still.

द्दृष्ट्वा विप्रतिपत्तिं बहुधा शास्त्रेषु भाष्यकाराणाम्।
स्वयमेव विष्णुगुप्तश्चकार सूत्रं च भाष्यं च।।

[Discerning the differences of opinion among the commentators of sciences that happen rather often, Viṣnugupta (Kautilya) himself has written the sūtra as well as commentary (of his work) all by himself.]

There can be no doubt whatsoever now regarding the antiquity of the purāṇas whose existence in the neighbourhood of 320 B.C. is confirmed by Kautilya's assertion. And regarding the antiquity of Indian poetics, too, Kautilya's can be cited as a clear-cult evidence. The tenth adhyāya called "शासनाधिकारः", प्रकरण no. 26 of the second 'अधिकरण' of the *Arthaśāstra,* that deals with the 'लेखक' of state-documents, presumes a very long tradition of good writing. Kautilya enumereates the qualities of a good writer in the following sentence:

'अर्थक्रमः, सम्बन्धः, परिपूर्णता, माधुर्यमौदार्यं, स्पष्टत्वं, इति लेखसम्पत्।,

[The property of writing consists in (these virtues): orderliness, inter-connectedness, perfection, sweetness, sublimity and clarity.]

The explanations of all these critical terms are also remarkable:

तत्र यथावदनुपूर्वक्रिया प्रधानस्यार्थस्य पूर्वमभिनिवेश इत्यर्थस्य क्रमः।
प्रस्तुतस्यर्थस्यानुपरोधादुत्तरस्य विधानमासमाप्तेरिति सम्बन्धः।
अर्थपदाक्षराणामन्यूनातिरिक्तता हेतूदाहरणदृष्टान्तैरर्थोपवर्णनाश्चान्तपदतेति परिपूर्णता।

सुखोपनीतचार्वर्थशब्दामिधानं माधुर्यम्।
अग्राम्यशब्दामिधानमौदार्यम्।
प्रतीतशब्दप्रयोगः स्पष्टत्वमिति।

[अर्थक्रम or orderliness consists in presenting the content and secondary context in accordance with their order. अर्थसम्बन्ध or the interconnectedness of content or argument implies the expression of the coming chain of thought in a manner that does not harm the present line of idea, upto the close of the document.]

परिपूर्णता or perfection means the avoidance of more or less words than required, the elucidation with the help of analogy and example and dispensing with ineffective words and expressions.

माधुर्य or sweetness consists in the employment of easily comprehensible words and expressions that are elegant and graceful.

औदार्य or sublimity is nothing but the employment of civil or polite words.

स्पष्टता or clarity implies the employment of words of common and current usage.]

Kautilya also discusses in the same place of his *magnum opus* the defects of writing: अकान्ति, व्याघात, पुनरुक्त, अपशब्द and संप्लव along with the explanations of all these terms. (Vide the closing sentences of the "Adhyaya" concerned.)

It appears that Kautilya had benefited here from Vyāsa's treatment of काव्यगुणविवेक and काव्यदोषविवेक, forming chapters 346 and 347 of *Agnipurāṇa*. Whatever be the fact, it is clear that poetics and rhetroic existed in India in the age of Kautilya who was a contemporary of Aristotle, the author of the *Poetics* and that both these sciences had continued from the very beginning of the creation in some form or the other as the Vedic statements, cited earlier, convince us.

Nevertheless, apart from the *Nātyaśāstra* there is no work of dramaturgy or poetics extant today, dealing systematically and exclusively with the problems of creative writing. The text of the *Nātyāśāstra* that we have today, consisting of 36 "adhyāyas" or chapters, may and may not have been the origional text written by sage Bharata or आदिभरत of Tretāyuga. But the text that we have today had already been scribed when Bhāsa appeared on the literary scene of India. That Bhāsa was familiar with the *Nātyaśāstra* is borne out by two points : 1. the Fool or विदूषक in his play अविमारक jokingly describes to the चेटी or maidservant of the heroine Kurangī, daughter of Kunti-bhoja, that there is a नाट्यशास्त्र (णट्टसत्थं) called रामाअण (Rāmāyana) of which he read five verses within a year. 2. most of his plays or almost all his plays end with a भरतवाक्य and that is a clear proof of his acquaintance with Bharata's *Nātyāśāstra*. And since the 4th century B.C. treatise by Kautilya called the *Arthāśāstra* quotes the following verse in the third "adhyāya", "prakaraṇa" 150-152, "adhikaraṇa" X in the account of the kingly exhortation to his soldiers:

नवं शराबं सलिलस्य पूर्णं सुसंस्कृतं धर्मकृतोत्तरीयम्।
तत्तस्य माभून्नरकं च गच्छेद्यो भर्तृपिण्डस्य कृते न युध्येत्।।

This very verse occurs in the 4th Act of Bhāsa's प्रतिज्ञायौगन्धरायणम् as verse no. 2 in the speech of गात्रसेवक, the controller of Vāsavadattā's she-elephant called Bhadrāvatī. Since the verse does not occur in any other ancient text on political science and since it is available only in प्रतिज्ञायौगन्धरायण apart from अर्थशास्त्र, we can rest assured that the original writer of the verse was Bhāsa and not Kautilya who should be ragarded as the beneficiary here for Bhāsa was a very competent and facile writer, requiring no aid from anyone else. And since the age of Kautilya is the fourth century B.C., Bhaāsa has every right to be placed at least in the fifth century B.C. Those who think that Indian drama did not exist in the fifth century B.C. should note that the *Arthāśāstra* refers to नट, नर्तक, कुशीलव and प्रेक्षा several times. The mere use of the word प्रेक्षा leads us to believe that India had theatres in the age of Kautilya. It must be noted that the *Arthāśāstra* is no work of imagination but rather a book of political science, treating of harsh realities in the most pragmatic fashion. Evidently, its references to actors, dancers and the theatre are true of its age. The following statement bears testimony to the existence of professional companies of actors, dancers, singers, story-tellers and performers of physical skills:

सूदारालिकस्नापकसंवाहकास्तरककल्पकप्रसाधकोदकपरिचारकाः
रसदाः कुब्जवामनकिरातमूकबधिरजडान्धच्छद्मानो नटनर्तक-
गायकवादक वाग्जीवनकुशीलवाः स्त्रियश्चाभ्युन्तरं चारं विद्युः
(अर्थशास्त्र प्रथम अधिकरण, प्रकरण 7, अध्याय।। "गूढ पुरुष-प्रणिधिः)

[Simulating the hunch-backed dwarfs, foresters, dumb, deaf, foolish and blind people and feigning to be actors, dancers, singers, vocalists, storytellers and performers of physical skills, women-spies should find out the secrets of officers of the inner circles and so should do the spies called 'Rasada' (i.e. those who, (should there be need), do not hesitate to kill their victims by poison) by assuming the forms of cooks, non-veg cooks, helpers in the bath, massagers, makers of beds, barbers and bringer of water.]

The use of the word 'नट' in the expression 'नटनर्तकगायक - वादकवाजीवनकुशीलवाः' clearly proves that during the Mauryan age there were theatres and companies of actors in India. That there was frequent movement of the companies of actors from place to place is corroborated by the following remark of Kautilya:

तेषां तूर्यमागन्तुकं पञ्चपणं प्रेक्षावेतनं दद्यात्।

(अर्थशास्त्र, अधिकरण 2, प्रकरण 43, अध्याय 27 'गणिकाध्यक्षः')

[The dramatic company coming from outside should pay on each show five "paṇas" as royal tax.]

That there used to be royal company of actors and dancers etc. is borne out by the following statement, placed only a sentence later than the remark just quotal from the *Arthāśāstra.*

गीतवाद्यपाठ्यनृत्तनाट्याक्षरचित्रवीणावेणुमृदङ्गपरिचित-
ज्ञानगन्धमाल्यसंव्यूहनसम्पादनसंवाहनवैशिककलाज्ञानानि
गणिका दासी रङ्गोपजीविनीश्च ग्राहयतो राजमण्डलादाजीवं कुर्यात्।

[The maintenance of people connected with singing, playing on musical instruments, recitation (of passages from great works), dancing, staging, writing, drawing playing vīnā, flute and drum, the art of knowing what is in the mind of the other, the art of preparing perfumes, making of garlands, massaging, fashion-designing and of the people training prostitutes, maidservants and dancers should be met out of the taxes collected from various districts (including cities and villages).]

The words 'प्रेक्षा', 'नाट्य' and 'रंग' used in the above citation are, I believe, conclusive; they proclaim the long tradition of Indian drama in the age of Kautilya.

The history of Indian poetics is usually traced from the *Nātyaśāstra* because no other systematic treatment of the art of poetry prior to it is extant today though the verses that it itself calls "आनुवंश्य" convince us that there existed previous texts also. Bharata deals primarily with dramatic poetry and narrative and lyrical poetry rather casually. But drama and the theatre have been discussed threadbare on an epic scale. No doubt, Bharata's treatment of drama is encyclopaedic for it leaves no department of the theatre unattended; it anticipates all technical innovations introduced by the western dramatists, relying on the latest technological advancement of the modern times, when it asserts:

न तज्ज्ञानं न तच्छिल्पं न सा विद्या न सा कला।
नासौ योगो न तत्कर्म नाट्येऽस्मिन् यन्न दृश्यते।।
सर्वशास्त्राणि शिल्पानि कर्माणि विविधानि च।
अस्मिन्नाट्ये समेतानि तस्मादेतन्मया कृतम्।।

(नाट्यशास्त्र, I–117, 118)

[That is no science, no skill, no learning, no craft, no art that is not to be found in this (sphere of) drama. I have created this (science of) drama because all sciences, skills, acts of all description stand incorporated in it.]

Bharata's *Nātyaśāstra* seems to have influenced the dramatic theory of Aristotle whose definition of Tragedy seems to have been inspired by Bharata's definition of "Nātaka", one of the ten forms of drama, expounded in detail in the 20th "Adhyāya" of the *Nātyaśāstra* (verse 10 &11). It is difficult to assign any date to the Indian text which itself claims to have been written in the Tretāyuga. But in any case, the present text was available to Kautilya of the 4th century B.C. for Kautilya uses many terms used originally in the *Nātyaśāstra*. I have already argued that Bhāsa is prior to *Arthaśāstra* as the latter uses a verse from *Pratijnāyaugandharāyaṇa* and since Bhāsa's plays end with what is technically called "Bharatavākyam", his awareness of the *Nātyaśāstra* becomes certain and thus he clearly belongs to an age that preceded that of Kautilya (i.e. the 4th century B.C.). Thus *Nātyāśāstra* could have been one of the sources of Aristotle's *Poetics*. If one of the verses of Vālmīki's *Rāmāyaṇa* could influence the text of Sophocles's *Antigone*, why could not the *Nātyāśāstra* in its essentials reach the Greek shores and influence the formulation of the dramatic theory propounded by Aristotle? We have a Greek source to support this hypothesis. According to the *Praeparatio Evangelica* IX. 3. written in the 3rd century by Eusebius, an Indian delegation of philsophers had visited Athens in 401 B.C., 2 years before the death of Socrates. There had been a "Śāstrārtha" or wit-combat between the Greek philosophers on the one side and Indian philosophers on the other. The Indians first asked their Greek counterparts to spell out the chief subject of their speculation. When came the answer that man was their main subject, Eusebius says, the Indian philosophers burst into laughter, saying; 'How can you study Man before studying the maker of man?' It must be noted that no Indian had bribed Eusebius to record the above event to which he says Aristobulus was a witness and Aristobulus had narrated it to Aristotle. I believe that the event recorded by the Palestine historian, nick-named 'the Christian Herodotus' is a fact of history and should never be ignored. I further believe that Bharata's dramaturgy had reached the Greek shores through this very delegation of Indian philosophers and since this dramaturgy is quite universal, it found favour with Aristotle who adopted most of its ideas. Aristotle's indebtedness to Bharata cannot be slighted at all.

We know absolutely nothing about the life of Bharata but *Matsyapurāna* (Adhyāya 24, verses 24-32) mentions him with great respect. Bhāsa, the oldest dramatist whose works are extant today, ends, as has been observed earlier, his plays with "Bharatavākya" and thereby pays his homage to the memory of the great sage who had brought drama to the earth from the heaven. And the first century B.C. master of Sanskrit drama, Kālidāsa, pays a very high tribute to him as the originator of the dramatic art in the following words :

मुनिना भरतेन यः प्रयोगो भवतीष्वष्टरसाश्रयो नियुक्त :।
ललिताभिनयं तमद्य भर्ता मरुतां द्रष्टुमनाः सलोकपालः ।।

(विक्रमोर्वशीयम् 2/17)

[(An angel is reporting to the heavenly damsels)"The lord of the gods-Indra-along with the presiding deities of the directions, wishes to witness today the enacting done artistically, of the play, containing 8 sentiments, which has been taught to you by sage Bharata."]

It must be placed on record that Kālidāsa belived the story of the birth of drama in the heaven and Bharata's experiment with it there in which the heavenly damsels had taken part as the *Nātyāśāstra* asserts. Indeed, in the eyes of Kālidāsa, Bharata deserves all the prasises that India has showered on him down the ages and that the sage belonged to the age in which the affair of Pururavas with Urvāsī had taken place and Kālidāsa represents the highest intelligence of India. Thus we do not have any right to bisbelieve Bharata's story pertaining to the birth of drama that he narrates in the *Nātyāśāstra*. The present reference to Bharata clearly proves that the *Nātyāśāstra* was available to Kālidāsa in the first century B.C. and that he had read it thoroughly which fact is borne out by Kālidāsa's reference to 'अष्टरसाश्रयः', that is, to the fact that the total number of 'rasas' (sentiments) that the *Nātyāśāstra* approves is eight. Those who place Kālidāsa in the Gupta age seem to be oblivious of the following statement of the poet placed in the mouth of the "Sūtradhāra" in *Abhijnānāśākuntalam:*

> आर्ये। इयं हि रसभावविशेषदीक्षागुरोर्विक्रमादित्यस्याभिरूपभूयिष्टा परिषद्।
>
> [Madam! This assembly of Vikramāditya, the patron of the artists excelling in the evocation of 'Rasas' (Sentiments) and 'Bhāvas' (feelings), is decorated by many scholars!]

Here the proper name of the king of Ujjain, namely, Vikramāditya, has been used and this name, in all probability, does not give us any hint that it is the title of the king concerned. The Gupta king who bore the title of 'Vikramāditya' was Chandragupta II. Clearly, the word 'Vikramāditya' as used by the Sūtradhāra is the real name and not the title of the king of Ujjainī who is associated with an era which started in the year 57 B.C.. I think this evidence clinches the matter and Kālidāsa emerges as a first-century B.C. poet who was in the court of the great king Vikramāditya, the founder of the 'Vikrama-era'.

The significance of Bharata's *Nātyśāstra* lies in the fact that the Sanskrit drama, by and large, adheres to the rules propounded by the sage in this work, and all the theorists of poetry and drama–Bhāmaha, Dandī, Ānandavardhana, Abhinavagupta etc. refer to him reverentially. Indeed, Bharata is the last word in matters concerning dramatic poetry. No item of drama and of the theatre has been left untouched in the pages of the 36 chapters (and some scholars make 2 chapters of chapter no. 36) of the *Nātyaśāstra*. However, Bharata is not an authority on non-dramatic poetry though the theory of "Rasa" propounded by him applies to non-dramatic poetry also. No doubt, Bharata does discuss items like 'alankāras', metres, heroes and heroines, styles of poetry under the head of "Pravṛttis" (which were called Rītis later) but his discussion is drama-oriented and not poetry-oriented, if by that term we mean non-dramatic metrical composition. It was left for ācārya Bhāmaha, the author of a book of poetics called *Kāvyālamkāra* which studies non-dramatic poetry in detail and ignores dramatic poetry altogether, presumably because in the eyes of its author Bharata had already said the last word on drama Vide the word "अन्ये" in 1/24 of that work).

Bhāmaha flourished, in all probability, in the sixth century A.D. for he is an immediate successor of the poet Bhatti or Bhattiswāmi, the author of the epic entitled *Rāvaṇavadha*, popularly known as *Bhattikāvya*. This is clear from the following verse of *Bhattikāvya*:

> व्याख्यागम्यमिदं काव्यमुत्सवः सुधियामलम्।
> हता दुर्मेधसश्चास्मिन् विद्वत्प्रियतया मया।।
>
> (22/34)

> [This poem is graspable only through the explication (by experts and (provides) great festivity to the scholars. Moreover, on account of my love for scholarship the dull-minded are (sure to be) undone in it.]

Bhāmaha seems to have been inspired by this verse of Bhatti and recast it in the 20th verse of the second "Pariccheda" of *Kāvyalamkāra*:

> काव्यान्यपि यदीमानि व्याख्यागम्यानि शास्त्रवत्।
> उत्सवः सुधियामेव हन्त! दुर्मेधसो हताः।।

> [In case these poems, too, were comprehensible only through commentaries in the fashion of science books, they would be the delight only of scholars; (for then) the unscholarly ones would be undone, how sad it is !]

Since Bhatti was an established poet and his epic had become famous in ancient India and not Bhāmaha, it is clear that the latter is the borrower, for a poet of Bhatti's status could not be thought to be in any need to borrow from some theorist of poetry. I think it would be really reasonable to regard Bhāmaha to be reacting to the view of his predecessor on poetry, deliberately made difficult and scholarly. Now, Bhatti was the court-poet of king Śrīdharasena of Ballabhī who had reigned from 470 to 500 A.D. Roughly, therefore, Bhatti flourished in the 5th century of the Christian era. Bhāmaha, naturally, is liable to be placed in the sixth century. This becomes more strengthened by the fact that the early 7th century prose-master of Sanskrit, namely, Bāṇabhatta, echoes Bhāmha's illustration of the figure "Tulyayogitā" forming the 28th verse of the third "Pariccheda" of *Kāvyālamkāra* in his historical work *Harṣacaritam*. Bhāmaha's verse runs thus :

> शेषो हिमगिरिस्त्वञ्च महान्तो गुरवः स्थिराः।
> यदलङ्घितमर्यादाश्चलन्तीं बिभ्रथ क्षितिम्।।

> [Some poet is paying compliments to his patron-king:) "(O my master!) Śesanāga, Himālaya and you–(all three) are great, glorious and firm for (all of you) sustain the moving earth without ever violating the set norms".]

The line of Bāṇa in the *Harṣacaritam* that echoes the above verse of Bhāmaha has the expression "धरणीधारणाय अधुना त्वं शेषः" ["(O King!) for the purpose of supporting the earth thou art Śeṣanāga."] (Vide षष्ठ उच्छ्वास). According to ācārya Ānandavardhana, Bāna echoes Bhāmaha in the expression, just cited. (Vide Ānanda's own elucidation of kārikā 4.4. of *Dhvanyāloka* and he must have been backed by the tradition, then prevalent. Thus, Bhāmaha is in between Bhatti and Bāṇa and most safely can be placed in the 6th century A.D.

Kāvyālamkāra contains six chapters called "Paricchadas" and deals with non-dramatic poetry at great length in 399 verses. The topics treated by Bhāmaha in his poetics are : the purpose of poetry, its nature, its causes, its forms, its language and diction, its virtues and its blemishes and above all its embellishments called "alamkāras" or figures of speech. Bhāmaha is a formalist critic, exclusively concerned with the external properties of poetry. Naturally, he pays no attention to its inner prowess called "Rasa". Perhaps he believed that "Rasas" are to be found only in dramatic poetry. This explains why he did not deal with "rasas" though in the defintion of "Mahākāvya" (Epic Poetry) he asserts that it must have all "rasas": युक्तं लोकस्वभावेन रसैश्च सकलैः पृथक् [(Epic poetry) contains the nature of the public and is pervaded by all "Rasas"] (Vide काव्यालंकार (I.21). However, Bhāmaha recognizes "Rasas" in the form of certain figures of speech called "Rasavad-Alamkāras" (Vide काव्यालंकार 3/5,6,7)–Preyas, Urjasvī, "Samādhi" etc. He is avowedly the pioneer of the school of literary criticism called "Alamkārasampradāya." His declaration and assertion in the 13th verse of the first "Pariccheda" of *Kāvyālamkāra,* namely, "न कान्तमपि निर्भूषं विभाति वनितामुखम्" ["A women's face, even though it is beautiful, does not look lovely in the absence of ornaments"] has become the watch-word of that school.

Bhāmaha does not suffer from the common weakness of Sanskrit poeticians concerning classifications which often become absurd; he believes in the maximum utlization of minimum classifications. For example, Bharata had discussed 10 guṇas but Bhāmaha restricts the number of guṇas to 3 : माधुर्य (Sweetness), ओज (Gusto) and प्रसाद (Plainness).

Bhāmaha evinces originality, good sense, respectful treatment of the tradition, independence of thinking, liberal outlook and straightforwardness–qualities that ensure critical greatness. There seems to have been a long and unbroken history of poetics in India as is clear from Bhāmaha's reference to ācārya Medhāvī twice in the second 'Pariccheda' of *Kāvyālamkāra.* But since the works of pre-Bhāmaha theorists are not extant today, we regard him as the आद्याचार्य–the earliest thinker who theorizes about non-dramatic poetry systematically and competently, becoming the best model for the subsequent scholars in the field of literary criticism. His contribution to Sanskrit poetics is incalculable, not only historically but also intrinsically. Most of his views were approved even by theorists belonging to opposite camps. For example, his delimiting of the number of "guṇas" from 10, proposed by Bharata, to three, was upheld by a theorist of the eminence of Mammatha. His stand on the figure अतिशयोक्ति paved way for the entire facade of "Vakrokti-sampradāya" founded by ācārya Kuntaka. His assertion on the subject is worth quoting :

सैषा सर्वैव वक्रोक्तिरनयार्थो विभाव्यते।
यत्नोऽस्यां कविना कार्यः कोऽलङ्कारोऽनया विना।।

काव्यालंकार 2/85

[This very figure (i.e. अतिशयोक्ति or what the west calls Hyperbole is the (quintenssence of) "Vakrokti" or unstraight statement. (Poetic) meaning derives all its charms from it. Poets should make efforts towards effecting this. 'Which figure of speech (in the world) is without this?']

Thus Bhāmaha asserts that the poeticality of poetry resides in Hyperbole for Hyperbole makes poetic statements charming and that no device invented by the poet can be without it.

Though he is basically quite liberal in his view, his uncompromising view on "Kāvyadoṣa" (poetic blemishes) is really bold and admirable. Bad poetry (कुकविता), in his considered view, is the spiritual death of the poet:

नाकवित्वमधर्माय व्याधये दण्डनाय वा।
कुकवित्वं पुनः साक्षान्मृतिमाहुर्मनीषिणः।।

(काव्यालंकार, 1/12)

[Non-writing of poetry does not violate 'dharma' (at all), nor does it contract disease or invite punishment. 'But bad poetry-writing is virtual death' thus have declared the men of taste.]

Bhāmaha's opposition to the denominations of poetic styles or paths (कविमार्ग) on the basis of the names of the places to which the poets belong and not on the basis of their intrinsic merits is the measure of his critical boldness and independence. To call all poets of Vidarbha good and all poets of Gaudadeśa bad is unjust and irrational; the essential merits of the work concerned should be decisive rather than the place-name of the author:

वैदर्भमन्यदस्तीति मन्यन्ते सुधियोऽपरे।
तदेव च किल ज्यायः सदर्थमपि नापरम्।।
गौडीयमिदमेतत्तु वैदर्भमिति किं पृथक्।
गतानुगतिकन्यायान्नाख्येममेधसाम्।।

(काव्यालंकार 1/31-32)

[Other scholars (i.e. scholars other than Bhāmaha) hold that the Vaidarbha (path of poetry) is the unique (path). That alone indeed is the best, and any other path (such as Gaudīya), despite its being full of high content, is not good at all. This is Gaudīya, this is Vaidarbha–is this kind of compartmentalization (of poetry) possible? This kind of classification (of poetry) is that of the unintelligent (and that, too) owing to adherence to tradition.]

There are of late certain voices of dissent against the literary criticism in ancient India. There are many scholars today doubting the existence of criticism in Sanskrit. Can a theorist like Bhāmaha be called a literary critic? My answer to this is : 'Yes, Bhāmaha is a critic in his own right'. Those who want to see his criticism in action are advised to read his assessment of a poet like Rāmaśarmā and the suggested criticism of works like *Aśmakavanśa*. Let us see what criticism he has to offer in respect of a poet like Rāmaśarmā. In the 19th verse of the second "Pariccheda" of *Kāvyālamkāra,* Bhāmaha attacks the obscure puns called "Yamaka" and points to a work "अच्युतोत्तर" by Rāmaśarmā:

नानाधात्वर्थगम्भीरा यमकव्यपदेशिनी।
प्रहेलिका सा ह्युदिता रामशर्माच्युतोत्तरे।।

[A poem, difficult to understand on account of words formed from (rarely used and uncommon) roots, trying to distinguish itself by means of "Yamakas" is (nothing but a) puzzle. Such a poem is to be found in the form of अच्युतोत्तर by Rāmaśarmā.]

In the preceding verse Bhāmaha praised the use of "yamakālamkāra" if it is based on popular and common words. Here he is disapproving of difficult and obscure puns which, he asserts, stand fully illustrated in the 'अच्युतोत्तर by Rāmaśarmā who appears to be a near-contemporary of Bhāmaha. In the assessment of Bhāmaha, *Acyutottara* is not a poetic work; it is rather a puzzle-book only, having an intellectual rather than emotional appeal.

The critical level of Bhāmaha is that of the Victorian poet-critic Matthew Arnold who had declared poets like Dryden and Pope to be poetasters and no poets at all. अच्युतोत्तर of Rāmaśarmā is not extant today but Bhāmaha quotes one of its verses as an illustration of the poetic blemish called उपमानाधिकत्वदोष in the 58 verse of the second "Pariccheda" of *Kāvyālamkāra*

> स पीतवासाः प्रगृहीतशार्ङ्गो मनोज्ञभीमं वपुराप कृष्णः ।
> शतह्रदेन्द्रायुधवान्निशायां संसृज्यमान श्शशिनेव मेघः ।।
>
> [Wearing the yellow shawl and holding the bow called Śāranga the body of Krishna looked both lovely and terrible quite like the cloud, grasped thoroughly by the moon in the night and possessing the lightning and the rainbow.]

After quoting the above verse from Rāmaśarmā's *Acyutottara,* Bhāmaha, in the succeeding two verses (i.e. verse no. 59 and 60 of the second "Pariccheda" of *Kāvyālamkāra* analyses the technical weaknesses of Rāmasarma's verse and that demonstrates his critical acumen. This is a great testimony to his practice of what the Cambridge scholar George Watson calls 'descriptive criticism'. This is sufficient to absolve ancient Sanskrit poetics of the western charge of 'lack of really critical act'. It would be quite interesting to see on what grounds Bhāmaha criticizes the *Acyutottara* verse. His point is that there are three features (technically called 'धर्म') in the major term (उपमान) which is the cloud–the moon, the lightning and the rainbow, whereas in the minor term (उपमेय) which is 'Krishna', only two attributes (धर्म) have been enumerated–yellow shawl and the bow "śāranga". Thus there is a kind of imbalance between the 'उपमेय' and 'उपमान' of the verse, under discussion. The poet could very easily have set it right by adding the word 'जलज' as a feature of Krishna's body in the sense of conchshell (शंख) for one of the several senses of 'जलज' is 'शंख' which is a product of the water. There is no doubt whatsoever about the critical brilliance of Bhāmaha. But his treatise suffers from an irritating lack of system and coherence. Sometimes he introduces a concept abruptly and sometimes he gives an illustration of a term without ever bothering to define it. What seems quite odd is the disorganization of the material. For example, he discusses poetic blemishes between verses 37 and 53 of the first 'Pariccheda' of his poetics and then devotes the whole of the fourth 'Pariccheda' to the discussion of poetic flaws. However that may be, Bhāmaha, the son of Pt. Rakril Gomin, as the author maintains at the end of the Sixth and last chapter of his treatise, emerges as a fine critic with a liberal outlook and a judicious discrimination who has enjoyed a very high reputation among the theorists of poetry down the ages. We cannot afford to ignore him even in the 21st century.

The next theorist of poetry worthy of our attention in this survey of Sanskrit poetics is ācārya Dandī, the author of *Kāvyādarśa.* Earlier, it was believed that he was earlier than Bhāmaha but now Bhāmaha's priority over Dandī stands fully established. However, Bhāmaha is not very considerably senior to Dandī who emerges as a near contemporary of the former. In our discussion on Bhāmaha, we have shown that he was a little older than Bāṇa for the latter has been inspired by one of the former's images in his *Harṣacaritam* whereas there is a perceptable impact of Bāṇa on Dandī's 197th verse of the second "Pariccheda of *Kāvyādarśa* in the description of the folly of the young which clearly echoes Bāna's description of the same subject in *Kādambarī* ("Śukanāsopadeśa"). Thus roughly, there is a gap of 40 years between Bhāmaha and Dandī. That Dandī is later than Bhāmaha is proved by the fact that Dandī's discussion of आख्यायिका in the first "Pariccheda" of *Kāvyādarśa* (verses 23-28) is a virtual rejection of the views of Bhāmaha on the same subject; without mentioning Bhāmaha, Dandī rejects his views expressed in *Kāvyalamkāra* (1.25-29). Thus, late seventh century is the age of ācārya Dandī.

Dandī's reputation, like that of Bhāmaha, is that of an alamkāravādīn, though he pays a very high regard to "Rasa" in poetry by declaring rasa-based alamkāras (Rasavat) to be the kings of alamkāras. His respects for Rasas are also clear from the fact that he devotes liberally several verses to the discussion of "kāvya-guṇas" in the very first "Pariccheda" of *Kāvyādarśa*, recognizing 10 guṇas : श्लेष, प्रसाद, समता, माधुर्य, सुकुमारता, अर्थव्यक्ति, उदारता, ओज, कान्ति and समाधि. But alamkāras find the largest space in his great poetics and that makes him an "alamkāravādin" [apostle of figures of speech in poetry].

It is true that Dandī discusses, as he clearly states, the body of poetry only, neglecting its soul (i.e. Rasa); that ensures his formalist approach to poetry. To the question 'What constitutes the body of poetry' Dandī says:

शरीरं तावदिष्टार्थव्यवच्छिन्ना पदावली

(काव्यादर्श 1/10)

[Groups of words (पदावली) full of the meanings intended to be conveyed constitute the body of poetry.]

Thus the poeticality of poetry, according to Dandī, resides in the words, used by the poet, but any order or number of words would not do– only those words, which contain the intended meaning of the poet alone are entitled to be regarded as the body of poetry. Words, used by the poet, should have the capability of giving full expression to the intended meaning of the poet. But what is the intended meaning of the poet remains undefined by Dandī for that would have led him to a discussion of the soul of poetry.

Dandī rather bothers too much about the body of poetry–the exterior of poetry and that engages his attention most. The body of poetry should be free from all defects and should have all that could make it beautiful in appearance. Even a single defect is bound to render poetry bad and therefore unworthy of the favourable response from the readers. He asserts:

तदल्पमपि नोपेक्ष्यं काव्यं दुष्टं कथञ्चन ।
स्याद् वपुः सुन्दरमपि श्वित्रेणकेन दुर्भगम् ।।

(काव्यादर्श 1/7)

[Not an iota of defect should be ignored in poetry. For even an otherwise beautiful body is rendered ugly by just a white spot of leucoderma / leprosy.]

The question of how to make poetry look as appealing as possible receives the greatest attention of Dandī who believes that it is ornaments that lend real charm to the human body and the ornaments of the lady of poetry are called alamkāras. He, naturally, therefore, declares in the very first verse of the second 'परिच्छेद' of *Kāvyādarśa* :

काव्यशोभाकरान् धर्मानलंकारान् प्रचक्षते ।

[Features that cause the beauty of poetry are called alamkāras or figures of speech.]

By the word "शोभा" Dandī means aesthetic excellence achieved by poetry and that is attained primarily by figures of speech. The great ācārya devotes to it several verses of the first "pariccheda", all the verses of the second "paricched" and most of the verses of the third "paricched" of his poetics. He deals with 35 figures of sense (अर्थालङ्कार) in the second "pariccheda" of his work. These are : 1. स्वभावोक्ति 2. उपमा 3. रूपक 4. दीपक 5. आवृत्ति 6. समासोक्ति 11. अतिशयोक्ति 12. उत्प्रेक्षा 13. हेतु 14. सूक्ष्म 15. लेश 16. यथासंख्य 17. प्रेय 18. रसवत् 19. ऊर्जस्वी 20. पर्यायोक्त 21. समाहित 22. उदात्त 23. अपह्नुति 24. श्लेष 25. विशेषोक्ति 26. तुल्ययोगिता 27. विरोध 28. अप्रस्तुत प्रशंसा 29. व्याजस्तुति 30. निदर्शना 31. सहोक्ति 32. परिवृत्ति 33. आशीः 34. संसृष्टि and 35. भाविक. The third 'परिच्छेद' of *Kāvyādarśa* has been devoted to a few figures of words and to poetic defects and the ways of setting them right. Dandī discusses 4 figures here : 1. यमक, 2. आकारबन्ध, 3. चित्रबन्ध and 4. प्रहेलिका. Wherever Dandī discusses alamkāras, he goes very deep into the matter, dwelling at great length at the divisions and sub-divisions of the figures, often giving the impression of hair-splitting. For example, during his treatment of the figure "Upamā" or Simile, he points out 32 varieites of the figure in the second "Pariccheda" of *Kāvyadarśa*. Similarly, the first 77 verses of the third "Pariccheda" of *Kāvyādarśa* treat of "Yamaka" and its innumenable varieties, calling them "अत्यन्तबहवः" (Very many indeed).

Dandī gave recognition to हेतु, सूक्ष्म and लेश—which had stood rejected by Bhāmaha. Moreover, he invented a figure called दीपकावृत्ति and acknowledged स्वभावोक्ति as a figure in its own right.

From the verse no. 171 of the third "Pariccheda" of *Kāvyādarśa,* we come to know that the great ācārya had written a book ("pariccheda") called "Kalāpariccheda" for *Kāvyādarśa* which is missing from the present extant text, having only 3 books or "paricchedas" in which his poetic theory has been expressed as clearly and as voluminously as possible, incorporating whatever he had to say on the nature, objective, causes and kinds of poetry and how it can be pleasing to the maximum in 660 verses. His contribution to Sanskrit poetics being that of the second father of the criticism of non-dramatic poetry, the first father of which was ācārya Bhamha.

To the question of Dandī's status as a literary critic, my asnwer is that the doubter must read Dandī's analysis of the famous Sanskrit verse, presumably of the dramatist Bhāsa, 'लिम्पतीव तमोऽङ्गानि वर्षतीवाञ्जनं नभः', which analysis is quite extended, running between verse 226 and 233 of

Kāvyādarśa's second "pariccheda" and then decide for himself whether Dandī supplies or not literary criticism in the western sense of the expression. The doubter should also be referred to the great ācārya's effort to obliterate the traditional and baseless distinctions between the two prose-forms of Sanskrit, called "kathā" and "ākhyāyikā", given between verses 25 and 30 of the first "pariccheda" of *Kāvyādarśa.* Both of these discussions put forward by Dandī are eye openers and redeem Sanskrit poetics which is supposed by the thoughtless to be deficient in practical and analytical criticism, popular in the West today. It is remarkable that though verse is the medium of Dandī's critical analysis, and not prose-throughout the *Kāvyādarśa* we never come across any prose-passage anywhere-, Dandī manages to be crystal-clear, displaying good sense and candour of the highest order, though we all know that he had produced excellent prose-works like *Dāśakumāracaritam* and *Avantisundarīkathā.*

The next ācārya worthy of our attention is ācārya Vāmana, author of a text of poetics called काव्यालंकारसूत्रवृत्ति. Vāmana flourished in the latter half of the 8th and first half of the 9th centuriees of the Christian era. He was a minister in the court of king Jayāditya of Kashmir to which fact Kṣemendra in his *Rājataranginī* makes a clear reference :

मनोरथः शंखदत्तश्च चरकः सन्धिमांस्तथा।
वभूवुः कवयस्तस्य वामनाद्याश्च मंत्रिणः।।

(राजतरंगिणी 4/497)

[The poets in the court of (king Jayāditya) were–Manoratha, Samkhadatta, Caraka and Sandhimān and (his) ministers were Vāmana etc.]

Since the age of Jayāditya's rule was from 789 to 813 A.D., the above observation regarding the age of Vāmanācārya stands fully established. Thus roughly speaking, Vāmana wrote his poetics around 800 A.D.

The poetics of Vāmanācārya is entitled काव्यालंकार-सूत्रवृत्ति divided into 5 "adhikaraṇas", each "adhikaraṇa" having several "adhyāyas", totalling 12. The whole work has been written in sūtra-style. There are altogether 319 sūtras or kārikās. Each kārikā has been followed by a brief explanation (भाष्य), technically called वृत्ति which contains illustrations also.

The first "adhikaraṇa" is called शारीराधिकरण having three "adhyāyas". The fist "adhyāya" discusses the signs of poetry (काव्यलक्षण), the relationship between poetry and "alamkāras" or figures of speech, and the purpose of poetry. The whole argument is based on the definition of the nature of poetry given in the very first kārikā :

'काव्यं ग्राह्यमलंकारात्'

> [Poetry becomes admirable and acceptable on account of its association with alamkāras or figures of speech.]

From this kārikā we are given to understand that Vāmana belongs to the alamkāra-school of criticism. But that view gets rectified by Vāmana's observation in the sixth kārikā of the second adyāya of the first "adhikaraṇa"

'रीतिरात्मा काव्यस्य'

> [The soul of poetry is its rīti or special combination and arrangement of words and expressions.]

Thus the word "alamkāra" does not really mean "figure of speech" but rather "beauty" in a very wide sense. This becomes clear when Vāmana defines the word alamkāra in the second kārikā of the first chapter of the first "adhikaraṇa"

"सौन्दर्यमलंकारः"

[Alamkāra is nothing but beauty.]

Clearly, the sense of the word 'अलंकार' as used in the first kārikā does not mean 'figure of speech' in its usual sense conveyed by the English expression 'figure of speech'; the word has rather to be taken in its broader sense of beauty. And beauty resides not only in the ornaments that a human form wears but also in the inner qualities that underlie that form. Thus the factors of poetic beauty are not only the figures of speech but also the "guṇas" such as plainness and sweetness. But the soul of poetry, as Vāmana says in the sixth kārikā of the second "adhyāya" of the first "adhikaraṇa", is the peculiar combination and arrangement of words used in the poem, broadly called 'रीति'.

The second chapter deals with the qualifications of the makers of poetry, two varieties of poets and the relationship between the poet and his critic (भावक). In this very chapter. "Rīti" has been established as the soul of poetry. After defining "Rīti" as the peculiar or special combination and arrangement of words, Vāmana discusses with examples the three varieties of Rīti–Vaidarbhī, Gaudī and Pāncālī.

The third chapter ("adhyāya") deals with 3 causal factors of poetry : "Loka", "Vidyā" and "Pratībhā". Each of these factors plays its role in the poetic creation. By the term "Loka" Vāmana means "Lokajnāna" which comes from a close observation of the conduct of the people and different beings of the world, precisely what the West in the neo-classical period understood by the term "Nature". By the term "Vidyā" ācārya Vāmana means the poet's acquired knowledge from different branches of learning like grammar, dictionary-consultation regarding etymology and correct usage, prosody, fine-arts like music, dance, sculpture, architecture, geography, climatology, history, sexology, political science, great classics by other poets, attendance at the feet of the teachers of poetry and poetics and close study of the respective powers and weaknesses of words. However, according to Vāmana, the most important factor of the creation of poetry is "Pratibhā" or poetic powers and impressions formed in and acquired from previous births. But "Pratibhā" is only an element of the third factor of poetic creation called "Prakīrṇa". though it is the most significant member of it, other elements or members of "Prakīrṇa" being concentration of the mind and cultivation of sensibility. After describing the factors of poetic creation, Vāmana discusses various forms of poetry whether in verse or prose, unified and connected or independent and unconnected. In this discussion of the forms of poetry, the most remarkable point that Vāmana makes is that the 10 forms of drama are the source of all poetic forms. He declares this in the 32nd kārikā of the third "adhyāya" of the first "adhikaraṇa":

ततोऽन्यभेदक्लृप्तिः

[Other forms of poetry like "kathā", "ākhyāyikā", "mahākāvya" etc. are the extensions of the ten-form Drama (Rūpaka).]

The second "adhikaraṇa" of *Kāvyālamkārasutra* is called "Daśadarśanādhikarana". It consists of 2 adhyāyas. Both treat of poetic defects (काव्यदोष) rather elaborately: असाधु, श्रुतिविरस, ग्राम्य, अप्रतीत, अनर्थक, अन्यार्थ, नेयार्थ, गूढ़ार्थ, अश्लीलार्थ, क्लिष्टार्थ are the पददोष's treated by Vāmanācārya. The defects of sentences (वाक्यदोष) have been discussed in the second "adhyāya". These are : भिन्नवृत्त, यतिभ्रष्ट, विसन्धि, सन्दिग्धवाक्यार्थ, अपक्रम, लोकविरुद्ध वाक्यार्थ, कलाशास्त्रविरुद्ध वाक्यार्थ etc.

Poetic virtues (काव्यगुण's) have been dealt with by Vāmana in the third "adhikaraṇa" of his poetics. This "adhikaraṇa", too, contains 2 "adhyāyas". The poetic virtues discussed by Vāmana are : ओज, प्रसाद, श्लेष, समता, समाधि, सौकुमार्य, उदारता, अर्थव्यक्ति, कान्ति, माधुर्य. These virtues have been explained and illustrated in the first "adhyāya" of the third "adhikaraṇa" called "Guṇavivecanādhikaraṇa". The second "adhyāya" of the same "adhikaraṇa" discusses the same "guṇas" from the point of view of meaning.

The fourth "adhikaraṇa", containing three "adhyāyas", has been devoted by Vāmana to a discussion of alamkāras. That is why this "adhikaraṇa" has been designated "ālamkārikādhikaraṇa". The alamkāras discussed by him are : यमक, अनुप्रास, उपमा, प्रतिवस्तूपमा, समासोक्ति, अप्रस्तुतप्रशंसा, अपह्नुति, रूपक, श्लेष, वक्रोक्ति, उत्प्रेक्षा, अतिशयोक्ति, सन्देह, विरोध, विभावना, अनन्वय, उपमेयोपमा, परिवृत्ति, क्रम (यथासंख्य), दीपक, निदर्शना, अर्थान्तरन्यास, व्यतिरेक, विशेषोक्ति, व्याजस्तुति, व्याजोक्ति, तुल्ययोगिता, आक्षेप, सहोक्ति, समाहित, संसृष्टि, उपमारूपक, उत्प्रेक्षावयव।

The last "adhikaraṇa" of काव्यालंकारसूत्र in two "adhyāyas" discusses certain issues of practical nature. So Vāmana calls this "Prāyogikādhikaraṇa". Vāmana discusses certain norms established by the tradition which the would-be poet should keep in mind in order to avoid poetic pitfalls.

Vāmana is probably the first ācārya who proposes an aesthetically oriented approach to poetry and declared rather boldly : सौन्दर्यमलंकारः (काव्यालंकारसूत्र 1/2) [Figures of speech are the (quintessence) of beauty.] He is also a great formalist, emphasizing the formal qualities of poetry for he paid very little attention to the internal quality of poetry called "Rasa", "Bhāva", "Rasābhāsa", "Bhāvābhāsa etc. though in his discussion of the poetic virtue called "Kānti" he seems to be discussing "Rasa", for the verse that he cites to illustrate the "Kānti" guṇa in poetry is also an example of संयोगश्रृंगार (Vide काव्यालंकारसूत्र 3/2/15). The word 'Rasa' has been used in the 'kārikā'. Thus "Rasa" assumes the status of a 'guṇa' in the poetic scheme of Vāmana. The treatment of the question of what constitutes poetry, as given in Vāmana's *Kāvyālamkārasūtra*, first "adhyāya", first "adhikaraṇa" (vide the "vṛtti" of the first "kārikā"): काव्यशब्दोऽयं गुणालंकारसंस्कृतयोः शब्दार्थयोर्वर्तते [Words and their meanings refined by "guṇa" and "alamkāra" constitute poetry.] had an enduring quality because it was echoed and re-echoed in the poetics of the succeeding critics especially of Mammathācārya.

Another theorist of the art of poetry in the age of Vāmana was ācārya Udbhata who wrote a poetics entitled काव्यालंकारसारसंग्रह. He was a younger contemporary of Vāmana. Udbhata was in the court of Jayāpīda, king of Kashmir from the year 836 to 870 of the Vikrama-era. He was a courtier of Jayāpīda; this is clear from the following verse of *Rajatarangiṇī* by Kalhaṇa:

विद्वान् दीनारलक्षेण प्रत्यहं कृतवेतनः
भट्टोऽभूदुद्भटस्तस्य भूमिभर्तुः सभापतिः ।।

(राजतरंगिणी 4/495)

[The chairman of the court of that king (Jayāpida) was the learned Udbhata Bhatta who had been appointed on a salary of one lac of dīnārs per day.]

Udbhata is said to have written a commentary on Bharata's *Nātyśāstra* as well as a critique of Bhāmaha's *Kāvyālamkāra* under the title *Bhāmahavivaraṇa.* However, these works of Udbhata are not extant. His entire fame rests today on his poetics *Kāvyālamkārasārasangraha* which cites 100 verses from the author's own poem *Kumārasambhavakāvya* which, too, is not extant today.

Udbhata is an "alamkāravādin" (i.e. a follower of the alamkāra-sampradāya, according to which figures of speech are the soul of poetry). His poetics is naturally devoted to figures and tropes exclusively. The author divides all the figures into 6 groups or "vargas" and deals with them all in 79 kārikās. For each "varga" one full chapter has been used. The fourth "varga" discusses 5 figures: प्रेय, रसवत्, ऊर्जस्वि, पर्यायोक्त and समाहित. The theorist quotes for illustrations one hundred verses from his *Kumārasambavakāvya.*

Udbhata had used Bhāmaha's *Kāvyālamkāra* for his purposes rather profusely but he manages to be independent and original. For example, Udbhata does not recognize the figures "upamārūpaka" and "utpreksāvayava" that Bhāmaha had clearly recognized. The great "alamkārin" that he was, he invented new figures like पुनरुक्तवदाभास, संकर, काव्यलिङ्ग, दृष्टान्त and छेकानुप्रास. Although Bhāmaha and Dandī both had discussed figures like प्रेय, ऊर्जस्वि, समाहित etc., neither had been able to clarify their characteristics clearly but Udbhata explained these figures lucidly and precisely. He was the first to discuss "kāvyavṛttis" like "paruṣā", "komalā" and "upanāgarikā" as the varieties of the figure "anuprāsa" which the West calls "Alliteration." The figure "Lātānuprāsa" had just been mentioned by Bhāmaha but Udhbata defined and illustrated the figure quite precisely. The two varieties of the figure "Śleṣa"–"Śabdaślesa" and "Arthāślesa"–are the creations of Udbhata. Though his range was limited, Udbhata was quite perceptive and reasonable and deserves a place of honour in the history of Sanskrit poetics for his having systematised the figures of speech through classification in the style of a biologist or a botanist to be more specific.

A contemporary of Udbhata was the theorist Rudrata, author of a poetics called *Kāvyālamkāra.* Early 9th century is the period that has been allotted to him. According to Namisādhu, Rudrata's commentator, Rudrata was also called शतानन्द and his father was Bhattavāmuka.

Unlike Udbhata, Rudrata does not confine himself to "alamkāras" exclusively; he also discusses signs of poetry, purpose of poetry, factors responsible for the creation of poetry, various forms of poetry, alamkāras, poetic defects, and varieties of heroes and heroines. Thus his field is quite large–larger than that of Bhāmaha, Dandī, Vāmana or Udbhata.

He has sympathies with the alamkāra-sampradāya but does not ignore the internal quality of poetry (i.e. Rasa). He discusses all the 8 Rasas mentioned by Bharata not in relation to दृष्टकाव्य but rather to श्रव्यकाव्य. Thus he is a "Rasavādin" also apart from being a lover of alamkāras. This is something unique and worthy of critical notice.

His division of alamkāras is quite scientific; the four-fold division of the figures is based on each alamkāra's link with the following 4 categories of their essences: वास्तव्य (truth to life), औपम्य (similarity), आतिशय्य (excessiveness) and श्लेष (pun). He is credited with having invented figures like मत, विहित and साम्य।

It must be clearly made clear here that there was another theorist in the 9th century, bearing the name of Rudrabhatta. Our Rudrata should not be confused with Rudrabhatta, the author of शृंगारतिलक having 3 "Paricchedas", devoted to 'Rasa'. He is a "Rasavādī" critic.

Our next theorist is ācārya Rajaśekhara who was a creative writer besides being a critic. He wrote 3 plays : *Bālarāmāyaṇa*, *Bālamahābhārata*, *Biddha-śālabhanjikā* and above all *Karpūramanjarī.* Ācārya Rājaśekhara was the teacher of king Mahendrapāla as well as of his son king Mahīpāla, of the Pratihāra-dynasty. The fist of these-Mahendrapāla–reigned upto 907 A.D. and the second–his son Mahīpāla-from 907 to 917 A.D. Thus Rajaśekhara flourished in the 10th century A.D. He belonged to a family of kṣatriyas called "Yāyāvara" of Mahārāṣtra.

The poetics of Rājasekhar is entitled काव्यमीमांसा *(Kāvyamīmānsā).* The real significance of Rajāsekhara's *Kāvyamīnānsā* lies in its detailed discussion of many topics of criticism that had remained untouched by the predecessors of its author–topics like the poet and his categories, Pratibhā or poetic genius, the process of poetry-writing, the history of the origin of poetics, "kāvyapāka" or poetic excellence and maturity, readers and their categories (bhāvakas), kinds of literary theft (plagiarism) such as Sabdaharaṇa, arthaharaṇa and "kavisamayas" (i.e. certain established beliefs and norms that have been upheld down the ages in the literary world without any verification whatsoever). Thus *Kāvyamīmansā* has a great popular interest and deserves to be studied by all serious readers of literature–Eastern as well as Western.

Rājasekhara may have been a scholar born and brought up in Mahārāstra but Kannauja was his refuge where his literary activity flourished. He belonged to a family of established literary personages. His grand-father was Akālajalada whose verses stand anthologised in सूक्तिमुक्तावली and his father's name was Durdaka who was a minister of some king. His mother's name was Śīlāvatī. He had married a girl of the great Cahvaṇa family of rulers; her name was Avantisundarī who had staged her husband's drama *Karpuramanjarī*, written in the Prākṛta language.

Kāvyamīmāṇsā is really an encyclopaedic work on the art of poetry, written in eighteen "adhikaraṇas". However, today we have only the first "adhikaraṇa" containing eighteen "adhyāyas". If the remaining lost portions of the work could ever be retrieved, *Kāvya-mīmansā* would be the poetics counterpart of the dramaturgical work of Bharata called *Nātyśāstra* and thus the largest text on the art of poetry not only of India but rather of the whole world. That the work in its entirety once did exist can be discerned from the fact that at the end of its 12th "Marīci" the author of *Alamkārāśekhara* cites a passage of Rājāśekhara concerning "upamā; the verse concerned runs as follows:

> अलंकारशिरोरत्नं सर्वस्वं काव्यसम्पदाम्।
> उपमा कविवंशस्य मातैवेति मतिर्मम।।
>
> [The quintessence of all poetic properties and the crown gem of "alamkāras" (i.e. figures of speech) is "upamā" (simile) (which) in my view is the mother of the family of the poets.]

This verse is not to be found in the extant pages of *Kāvyamīmānsā*. In case the verse concerned is from some chapter of *Kāvyamīmānsā* and not from any other work of Rājasekhara, then we can rest assured that the whole of the text or at least the portion, containing the verse, under discussion, was available upto the time of the author of *Alamkārāśekhara.* However that may be, we have to form our impression of Rājaśekhara's criticism on the basis of the extant pages of *Kāvyamīmānsā* and his critical statements scattered in his creative works.

Rājaśekhara is important to us for having stressed the remotest antiquity conceivable of Indian poetics and for highlighting the divine connection of Bharata, the author of the *Nātyaśāstra*. According to Rajasekhara, poetics was first taught by Śrīkantha (i.e. Lord Vishnu) to his 64 disciples including Parameṣthī (i.e. Brahmā) and Vaikuntha. Lord Brahmā, in his turn, taught the art of poetry to his disciples who had supernatural births and were not born of any womb (अयोनिज), the best of whom was the sage Kāvya-puruṣa who asked his disciples–Sahastrākṣa, Uktigarbha, Suvarṇanābha and Bharata–among others–to study the various aspects of poetry-writing to be completed and compiled in 18 "adhikaraṇas" by himself (i.e. Kāvyapuruśa). However, since each disciple of Kāvyapurusa had his separate work on the aspect of poetry-writing entrusted to him, the works were lost in due course of time, presumably with the exception of the *Nātyśāstra* of Bharata who had been asked to write a dissertation on "drama" or "rūpaka". Those who regard this narration of Rājaśekhara as fanciful will have to explain how the *Nātyśastra* (that had been written, as claimed by Rājaśekhara), still exists and how the work on "Rasa" by Nandikeshvara was available to ācāryas like Abhinavagupta who quote from that work. Does not it follow that the works by Sahastrākṣa, Uktigarbha, Suvarṇanābha etc. were also in existence once upon a time but were later lost? The story confirms the claim of Vālmīki that in the court of Lord Rāma the experts of poetry-writing were present to adjudge the worth of the poem sung by Lava and Kusha. I do not see any reason to disbelieve the history of poetics given by Rājaśekhara at the very beginning of *Kāvyamīmansā*. Let us wish and pray for the recovery of other works by the disciples of Kāvyapuruṣa, including that of Nandikeśvara.

The extant text of *Kāvyamīmānsā* itself entitles Rājāśekhara to an exalted position in the history of Sanskrit poetics for it speaks volumes about his very wide reading and experience and of his liberal outlook. The critic's approach to poets and poetry in this work is not bookish but practical and pragmatic. For example the following advice to the would-be poet is really very practical :

जानीयाल्लोकसाम्मत्यं कविः कुत्र ममेति च।
असम्मतं परिहरेन्मतेऽभिनिविशेत् च।।

(काव्यमीमांसा अधिकरण।, अध्याय 10)

[The poet ought to know what the public opinion is and what is in agreement with him. (He) should give up (the point of view) that does not have public approval and should enter into agreement with the public.]

Again, his advice that 'न नवीनमेकाकिनः पुरतः । स हि स्वीयं ब्रुवाणः कतरेण साक्षिणा जीयेत' [A new poem should not be recited to someone who is alone for if he starts claiming to be its author, where will you find a witness (i.e. of the poem being your original product)] is equally very practical and sane. Rajaśekhara's independent-mindedness is writ large on every page of *Kāvyamīmānsā* wherever the critic after quoting the previous authorities on a given point, expresses his own view by the expression 'इति यायावरीयः' [So says (Rajaśekhara), a descendent of the Yāyāvarīya family.] Rājaśekhara has a modern outlook which can be perceived in numerous statements, scattered all over his poetics. For example, the question of obscinity in poetry has been handled very wisely by him in the sixth "adhyāya" of *Kāvyamīmānsā* where after citing two passages depicting "viparītarati" (reversed pose in the sex-act) which in the view of the common readers are uncivil and therefore unacceptable, Rajāśekhara expresses his considered view : "प्रक्रमापन्नो निबन्धनीय एवायमर्थः" [Such subjects ought to be dealt with if the situation demands so] and in his defence he quotes passages from Vedic texts, depicting similar obscene pictures dictated by the demand of the occasion. Likewise, in respect of a passage, satirising the pious institution of marriage, placed in the mouth of a prostitute who is addressing her daughter, Rājaśekhara defends the passage concerned on the ground that the command of the passage is prohibitive and not imperative in nature – अस्त्ययमुपदेशः किन्तु निषेधत्वेन न विधेयत्वेन". (i.e. its impact is that it prevents the readers from the evil path by enlightening them on the ways of the prostitutes). I think Rājaśekhara is very relevant even for the readers of poetry in the 21st century.

It is high time we discussed the work of ācārya Ānandavardhana, a near predecessor of Rājāśekhara and author of the most famous critical text of India–*Dhvanyāloka*. Ānandavardhana is famous as the founder of a new school of poetics called "Dhvani-sampradāya"–the school that regards "dhvani" or suggestion as the be-all and end-all poetry. The great theorist belongs to the 9th century for he flourished in the court of the king of Kashmir–king Avantivarmā. This is clear from the following verse of Kṣemendra's *Rājataranginī:*

मुक्ताकणः शिवस्वामी कविरानन्दवर्धनः ।
प्रथां रत्नाकरश्चागात् साम्राज्येऽवन्तिवर्मणः ।।

(राजतरंगिणी 5/4)

[During the reign of Avantivarmā (people like) Muktākaṇa, Śivaswamī, the poet Ānandavardhana and Ratnākara achieved (great) name and fame.]

Now, king Avantivarmā reigned over Kashmir from 855 to 884 A.D.. So we can conveniently place ācārya Ānandavardhana in the latter half of the ninth century A.D.. Ānanda has referred to Udbhata and Rājaśkehara has mentioned him and has quoted from *Dhvanyāloka*. This fact also goes to support the 9th century existence of Ānandavardhana, the poet who had written works like *Arjunacarita, Viṣamabāṇalīlā* and *Devīśatakam* besides his work on the art of poetry called *Dhvanyāloka.* He also wrote a commentary called "Dharmottamā" on Bauddha philosopher Dharmakīrti's *Pramāṇaviniścaya.*

Dhvanyāloka consists of "kārikās', 'vṛttis' and examples. Some scholars believe that the 'kārikas' of the work were by some ācārya called Sahṛdaya and Ānanda had written only the 'vṛttis' or explanations of those 'kaārikas'. However, we believe that the whole work–kārikas, vṛttis and examples–all were by Ānanda, most of the examples being the work of others cited by him for purposes of illustration.

The earlier doctrines regarding the appreciation of poetry were formalist in their approaches to literature but with the advent of Ānanda there came into existence an approach which was very broad and comprehensive, concerning the internal as well as external character of poetry. This new approach to poetry came to be known as "Dhvani" or suggestion.

Ānanda had full sympathy with what Bharata had called "Rasa" but reviewed the nature and status of "Rasa" afresh. He studied the nature of poetry in depth and found that its soul was suggestion–suggestion either of thought (वस्तुध्वनि), or of figure (अलंकारध्वनि) or of emotion (रसध्वनि). Thus by declaring "dhvani" as the soul of poetry (काव्यस्यात्मा ध्वनिः) and by conceiving of its three basic forms– वस्तुध्वनि, अलंकारध्वनि and रसध्वनि, the highest of these no doubt being the third, namely, रसध्वनि, Ānanda broadened the base of criticism by encompassing in it "Rasa" and all beautifying elements of poetry–guṇa, rīti, alamkāra, propriety & vakrokti and by allotting these elements their proper places. He came out with the view that "Rasa" was the chief intrinsic element in poetry but it was something suggested rather than stated and therefore under the broad head of "dhvani". This is why in his estimate a poem having "Rasa-dhvani" is the highest form of poetry. Words and sentences are the body of poetry, "guṇas" are its inner qualities and alamkāras are the external means to make it look beautiful and charming. Just as in real life, the characterstic features of an individual are to be located in the qualities of the individual's soul such as bravery, charity, catholicity etc., the poetic virtues called "guṇas" like "prasāda", "mādhurya", "oja" etc. are the qualities of the soul of poetry. And just as ornaments like rings, lockets, crowns etc are the beautifying external devices that enhance the beauty of the person of the individual, alamkāras of words as well as of sense, serve as the beatifying agents of the body of poetry, constituted by the words used in it. Thus "guṇas" and "rītis" are, in the considered view of Ānanda, intrinsic to poetry whereas alamkāras are its external elements; they may and may not be in it (i.e. poetry can exist even without alamkāras but without "guṇās" and "rītis" it can never exist). Since "dhvani" cannot be absorbed into any other component of poetry but can absorb any element of poetry, it stands established as the soul of poetry, its very prime mover.

Dhvanyāloka is also known as *Sahṛdayāloka* and sometimes as *Kāvyāloka*. It has 4 parts called "udyotas". In the very first "udyota" the glory of "Dhvani" or suggestion has been established. Varieties and sub-varieties, numbering more than ten thousand, have been discussed in the remaining "udyotas", thereby establishing the broad-basedness of "Dhvani" or "Suggestion" in poetry or imaginative literature as a whole.

The term "Dhvani" has been defined in the 13th "kārikā" of the first "udyota" in the following words:

यत्रार्थः शब्दो वा तमर्थमुत्सर्जनीकृतस्वार्थौ
व्यंक्तः काव्यविशेषः ध्वनिरिति सूरिभिः कथितः।।

["Dhvani" denotes a special kind of poetry in which the word or sense becomes the deserter of its commonly understood meaning and all this is suggested (rather than stated).]

In this "kārikā" the word 'शब्द' refers to 'words' having commonly fixed meaning called 'वाचक शब्द's or words which instantly denote something commonly accepted. Similarly, the word 'अर्थ' refers to the commonly accepted and comprehended sense of a given statement (वाच्यार्थ). Thus "dhvanikāvya" means a poem in which either words leave out their primary senses and convey senses other than their commonly understood meanings or the sense of the whole statement conveys a sense other than its normally accepted idea or meaning. In this way "dhvani kāvya" can reside in a certain word or words conveying meanings other than those that are normally denoted by them, It can also reside in the entire statement that conveys ideas other than its normally comprehended sense. But this kind of poetry is not to be found in an ordinary poet; it is to be found in the poetry of great masters like Vālmīki, Vyāsa, Kālidāsa, Dante, Shakespeare, Milton, Yeats and Eliot:

प्रतीयमानं पुनरन्यदेव वस्त्वस्ति वाणीषु महाकवीनाम्।
यत्तत्प्रसिद्धावयवातिरिक्तं विभाति लावण्यमिवाङ्गनासु।

(ध्वन्यालोक 1/4)

[The thing called "dhvani" or "pratīyamana" is something extraordinary to be found in the utterances of great poets. It sparkles like the loveliness of well-bodied beautiful women, which (loveliness) transcends (the beauty contained) in the famous limbs (of their bodies such as eyes, hair, breast, etc].

Evidently, the "dhvani" of Ānandavardhana's formulation is something where 'more is meant than meets the eye', to use a famous line of the English poet John Milton in "Il Penseroso". But the theory propounded is so broad that it can subsume any theory of poetry–formalist, moralist, structuralist, poststructuralist, aesthetic, etc.

Ānanda is a very profound critic, full of insight and originality and an ardent advocate of these features in the assessment of poetry and poets. He is, in all probability, the greatest exponent of genius (प्रतिभा) in the history of Indian poetics. His treatment of "Prātibhā" recalls to our minds the theory of "Imagination" propounded by the English critic of the Romantic Age, namely, S.T. Coleridge. According to him, a poet endowed with "Pratibhā" can create charming poetry on subjects already dealt with exhaustively by the masters of the past:

ध्वनेरित्थं गुणीभूतः व्यङ्ग्यस्य च समाश्रयात्।
न काव्यार्थविरामोऽस्ति यदि स्यात् प्रतिभागुणः।।

(ध्वन्यालोक चतुर्थ उद्योत, कारिका।।)

[Provided a poet has "pratibhā", by means of "dhvani" and "guṇībhutavyangyya", he can create charming meanings and will not allow poetic creation to come to a stop.]

And he expands his ideas, contained in the above kārikā, by making the following observation:

सत्स्वपि पुरातनकविप्रबन्धेषु यदि स्यात् प्रतिभागुणः।

[Notwithstanding there being (innumerable) poetic compositions by the poets of the past (on a particular situation) excellent poetry could be created provided there is "pratibhāguṇa" in the (new) poet.]

But what is that power called 'Pratibhā'? In answer to this question, Ānandavardhana observes:

सरस्वती स्वादु तदर्थवस्तु निःष्यन्दमाना महतां कवीनाम् ।
अलोकसामान्यमभिव्यनक्ति परिस्फुरन्तं प्रतिभाविशेषम् ।।
(ध्वन्यालोक, प्रथम उद्योत, कारिका 6)

[Oozing out the enjoyable liquid in the form of the suggested sense or "dhvani", the speech of great poets manifests the effulgent special genius of the poet which is extraordinary and marvellous.]

Thus the creation of newer and never charming meanings called "dhvani" is the function of the mental faculty called "Pratibhā" which is very very rare in this world; it is to be found only in great masters like Kālidāsa, Bhāravi, Shakespeare, Milton, Gray, Wordsworth, Yeats and Eliot, and not in ordinary poets who are, at the best, fanciful or picturesque.

Ānandavardhana is further to be credited with having broken the former boundaries of poetic appreciation. The previous ācāryas illustrated their critical concepts by citing examples from purely Sanskrit texts, giving the impression that only Sanskrit verses were worthy of the critical discourse; the languages of the masses, in their view, it appears, did not deserve to be cited in scholarly and critical discussions of the learned. Ānanda believed otherwise; he held that non-Sanskrit texts could also supply examples of great poetry. This is clear from the numerous examples to be found in *Dhvanyāloka* collected from the poets, using "Prakṛta" as the medium of their expression. This gōes to prove his liberal outlook as a critic, ready to acknowledge beauty even in non-Sanskrit texts, if it was there. He clearly anticipated Sir Philip Sidney, the 16th century English critic, who had no inhibitions in admiring the Border ballads in his famous essay entitled "An Apologie of Poetry" at a time when ballads were unworthy of formal critical attention. This was indeed a very bold step taken by Ānanda and that shows his catholicity of critical outlook and his modern sensibility. He was no doubt a critic of very great eminence who raised the level of Sanskrit criticism quite considerably. There had been no discussion of the total impression of an extended long poem in the history of Indian criticism earlier but Ānanda was an exception to this; he demonstrated his keen interest in the whole view of a long poem like the *Mahābhārata* by way of discussing the chief Rasa (अङ्गी रस) in the work, identifying it as "Śantarasa" in the fourth "udyota" of his poetics (Vide his long discussion in the Vṛtti on kārikā no. 109). In this long discussion Ānanda indirectly discusses the "unity of impression" so important to ensuring greatness to a given work of art. His statement is really remarkable: प्रबन्धे चाङ्गीरस एक एवोपनिबध्यमानोऽर्थविशेषलाभं छायाऽतिशयं च पुष्णाति [In an extended long poem only one principal 'rasa', wonderfully organized, reveals some special idea (of the poet's mind) and accomplishes the aesthetic excellence of the work.]

Ānanda's sharp critical mind is fully revealed in the third "udyota" of *Dhvanyāloka* where he discusses the existence of "vyanjanā" as an independent verbal power, not to be subsumed in "abhidhā" or "lakṣanā" (vide his long extended "vṛtti" on kārikā no. 89). The critical acumen displayed here is worthy of being placed in the list of ten most profound critical discussions of the world of all times.

Ānandavardhana, however, did not go unchallenged in spite of his very able and strong defence of "dhvani". There arose several critics who denied the very existence of "dhvani" and pleaded for its inclusion in "abhidhā". Two of these detractors of the "dhvani"-school of Ānanda were very distinguished critics of their times–Mukulabhatta and Mahimabhatta. Mukulabhatta was almost contemporaneous with Ānanda; he was the son of Bhattakallata who flourished during the regin of king Avantivarmā of Kashmir, Ānanda's patron. Evidently, Mukulabhatta must have been a younger contemporary of Ānanda. Thus his age is the end of the ninth century and the beginning of the 10th. Mukulbhatta wrote a book of poetics entitled *Abhidhāvṛttimātṛkā,* containing in all 15 "kārikas", establishing one and only one power of words called "Abhidhā". He tried to argue that "Lakṣanā" and "Vyanjanā" both could be easily absorbed in "abhidhā" which he divided into 10 forms. The other detractor of the "dhvani" school of Ānanda was Mahimabhatta, the author of a poetics entitled *Vyaktiviveka*, devoted exclusively to the problem of expression in poetry. Mahimabhatta's full name was Rājānaka Mahimabhatta. Śrīdhairya was the name of his father and the name of his teacher was Śyāmala. He flourished in the 11th century. He was basically a philosopher, belonging to the Nyāya school and a staunch advocate of "anumānapramāṇa". Naturally, he tried to prove that "dhvani" was a form of "anumāna" or inference and that there was no need to recognize it as an independent category. His book is divided into 3 parts called "vimarśas". All the examples of different forms of "dhvani" that Ānanda cites in *Dhvanyāloka* have also been cited by Mahimabhatta in the second "vimarśa" of his poetics as illustrative of "parārthānumāna". In the considered view of Ānanda, "Rasa" is something suggested (व्यंग्य) while according to Mahimabhatta, it is "anumeya" (inferable). He has no objection to "Rasa" being regarded as the soul of poetry provided it is accepted as inferable rather than suggestable as Ānanda had argued.

Mahimabhatta holds quite firmly that "Rasa" is "anumeya" (inferable) under all circumstances. In other words, "Rasa" is a matter of experience and not of analysis.

There is no doubt that Mahimabhatta is a very ardent follower of the Rasa-school of Sanskrit criticism; he is a "Rasavādī "critic, pure and simple. But his theory of "Rasa" is "anumiti" or "anumāna"-oriented. In point of fact, he seeks to reiterate the position of Ānanda under the garb of his "anumitivāda" by annahilating the very existence of "dhvani". His proclaimed aim has been stated without mincing any words whatsoever:

अनुमानेऽन्तर्भावं सर्वस्यैव ध्वनेः प्रकाशयितुम् ।
व्यक्तिविवेकं कुरुते प्रणम्य महिमा परां वाचम् ।।

(व्यक्तिविवेक 1/1)

[(The critic) Mahimabhatta writes (his treatise) *Vyaktiviveka* after saluting the great (goddess of) speech, with a view to establishing the absorption of all forms of "dhvani" or suggestion (formulated by Ānandavardhanācarya)] in "anumāna" or inference.]

Like Ānanda, Mahimabhatta is a very subtle and profound critic. Perhaps his extreme subtlety was responsible for his having remained obscure and ineffectual, bereft of followers or supporters. His critical acumen in clearly revealed in his arguments couched in beautiful prose throughout his treatise. His mastery over the Nyāya-philosophy is writ large on each argument made in his poetics. A good example is the prose-passage between the 66th and 67th "kārikas" of the first "vimarśa" of *Vyaktiviveka*, beginning with the words 'विषं भक्षय मा चास्य गृहे भुक्थाः'. His astute critical sense is fully revealed in his attack on ācārya Kuntaka's theory propounded in the following verse:

शब्दार्थौ सहितौ वक्रकविव्यापारशालिनि ।
बन्धे व्यवस्थितौ काव्यं तद्विदाह्लादकारिणि ।।

(वक्रोक्तिजीवित 1/7)

Without mentioning Kuntaka, Mahimabhatta cites this kārikā of Kuntaka and demolishes the theory propounded in it in the prose-passages before the 59th kārikā of the first "vimarśa" of his poetics. The way Mahimabhatta argues his case out is simply marvellous; it places him on a high pedestal of literary criticism in the world.

Mahimabhatta had written, as he himself claims in kārikā no. 119 of the second "vimarśa" of *Vyaktiviveka*, that he had written another critical text entitled *Tattvoktikośa* containing a long discourse on genius ("Pratibhā"). It is really very unfortunate that we do not have it today, But it must have been a very profound discussion of genius. We get a foretaste of its profundity from what he says in "kārikas" 117 and 118 of the second "vimarśa" of *Vyakti-viveka*:

रसानुगुणशब्दार्थचिन्तास्तिमितचेतसः ।
क्षणं स्वरूपस्पर्शोत्था प्रज्ञैव प्रतिभा कवेः ।। ।।7
सा हि चक्षुर्भगवतस्तृतीयमिति गीयते ।
येन साक्षात्करोत्येष भावांस्त्रैकाल्यवर्तिनः ।।

[That mental faculty of the poet is called 'genius' or 'Pratibhā' which is born of the momentary touch with the real form (of things) when he (i.e. the poet) becomes stable-minded in the course of his thought regarding the (choice of) words and ideas suitable for 'Rasa', underken to be expressed. This very 'Pratibhā' is virtually the third eye of Lord Shankara by means of which he perceives all thoughts and ides of all the three times–past, present and future.]

Mahimabhatta deserves to be studied in depth, word for word, kārikā by kārikā, used in the *Vyaktiviveka* for he can yield food for thought even in the 21st century when criticism has made laudable strides, especially in the West. He is a critic par excellence though without much following.

Our next critic is ācārya Kuntaka, who in point of time, was quite senior to Mahimabhatta but proved to be considerably of greater influence. Kuntaka's temporal seniority is clear from a reference to him by name in the following kārikā no. 29 of the second "vimarśa" of Mahimabhatta's *Vyaktiviveka:*

काव्यकाञ्चनकषाश्ममानिना कुन्तकेन निजकाव्यलक्ष्मणि ।
यस्य सर्वनिरवद्यतोदिता श्लोक एष स निदर्शितो मया ।।

[I have cited the same verse as had been regarded as flawless by Kuntaka in his book of poetics (i.e. *Vakroktijīvita*)–the Kuntaka who thinks he is the touchstone of the gold called poetry.]

From the tone of the verse, cited above, we can infer that Kuntaka was still alive when *Vyaktiviveka* was being written. Since Mahimabhatta flourished in the 11th century we can assign the same century to Kuntaka or a little earlier by a generation or so. This is proved by the fact that Kuntaka mentions Rājaśekhara several times, especially in his discussion of *"Vicitramārga"* in his *Vakroktijīvita* and Rājaśekhara flourished in the age of Mahīpāla of Kannauja (early 10th century). Roughly, the latter half of the 10th and the early part of the 11th century is the period of Kuntaka.

Kuntaka appeared on the critical scene of India when the "dhvani" theory of Ānandavardhana was almost established as a force to reckon with. Kuntaka liked many of the ideas that Ānanda had made current but with a view to making his own presence felt in the circle of the ācāryas of the day, he restated Ānanda's view-points in the garb of "vakrokti", declaring it to be the be-all and end-all of poetry, its life-force (जीवातु), though he believes that the "vakrokti" or verbal charm regarded as a whole philosophy of poetry was his discovery, unknown to the previous experts of the art of poetry. In the second "kārikā" of the first "Unmeṣa" or chapter– there are, in all, 4 "unmeṣas"–of Vakroktījīvita, he makes his intention clear :

लोकोत्तरचमत्कारकारिवैचित्र्यसिद्धये।
काव्यस्यायमलंकारः कोऽप्यपूर्वो विधीयते।।

[This very unique and hither-to unheard of work on the art of poetry is created with a view to establishing wondrousness (of speech) as the (ultimate cause of) the extraordinary charm (that poetry yields).]

He presumes that poetry worth its name provides or ought to provide a miracle in the minds of the aesthetes by means of the nectar that it effects and that miracle is something unspeakable. But what is the causal factor of that miracle remains a mystery. Earlier experts of poetry had located that factor in figures of speech (i.e. alamkāras), rīti (रीति) or the manner of combining words and expressions, "dhvani" or suggestion, according to their respective findings. Kuntaka finds all those explanations of poetic miracle unsatifactory. In his turn, he locates it in "vakrokti" or out of the ordinary speech that skilful poets employ. In the tenth kārikā of the first "unmeṣa" of *Vakroktijīvita* he defines "vakrokti" in a very lucid manner:

उभावेतावलंकार्यौ तयोः पुनरलंकृतिः।
वक्रोक्तिरेव वैदग्ध्यभंगीभणितिरुच्यते।।

[A special kind of words and a special kind of ideas, forming

> the body of poetry are the things that have to be beautified and "vakrokti" is their lone beautifier which is none other than a speech containing the finesse of skilful wit.]

Clearly, by the term "वक्रोक्ति" Kuntaka does not mean the figure that had been called "vakrokti" by Bhāmaha and Dandī but any element of speech which is so fine, so very wonderful and so skilful that it wrights miracles and overwhelms the experts of poetry by its wondrous subtlety. Thus the range of "Vakrokti" is very wide, beginning with words and their parts and ending with the entire body of the text, taken as a whole. However, Kuntaka has conceived of 6 broad forms of "vakrokti" : 1. वर्णविन्यासवक्रता 2. पदपूर्वार्द्धवक्रता 3. प्रत्ययाश्रयवक्रता 4. वाक्यवक्रता 5. प्रकरणवक्रता and 6. प्रबन्धवक्रता. All artistic designs and manoeuvrings and dexterities, the human imagination can conceive of, can be covered in Kuntaka's doctrine of "vakrokti", provided it provides the experts of poetry an inexpressible joy (सहृदयाह्लादकारित्व). "Vakrokti", in a nut shell, is the lifeblood of poetry:

> शरीरं जीवितेनेव स्फुरितेनेव जीवितम्।
> बिना निर्जीवतां येन वाक्यं याति विपश्चिताम्।।
>
> (वक्रोक्तिजीवित प्रथमोन्मेष, कारिका 17-39)

> [As the body without breath and as breath without a stir (cannot be conceived of, so poetry without "vakrokti" cannot be conceived of) for in its absence the statements of the wit become lifeless.]

Kuntaka deserves a very high place in the history of world-criticism. The distinction between a poetic statement and a scientific statement that he provides is matchless in world literature. It anticipates De Quincey's distinction made in the essay on "Literature" between literature of knowledge, on the one hand, and literature of power, on the other and is at the back of I.A. Richard's distinction between referential language and emotional language.

Moreover, it is more clear-headed and more lucid than either. His power of critically analysing a given piece is marvellous indeed; it is beyond the reach of the New Critics and Newer Critics of the West. It is fuller and more penetrating than that of Ānanda and Mahimabhatta, though they are remarkable in their own ways. His critical comments, for example, on Kālidāsa's verse beginning with the words भर्तुर्मित्रं प्रियमविधवे etc. from the "उत्तरमेघ" of *Meghadūtam* occurring as citation no. 32 after "kārikā" No. 9 of the first "Unmeṣa" of *Vakroktijīvita* are simply exhilarating. India can feel proud of critics like Kuntaka.

Kuntaka founded a new school of criticism called "Vakroktisampradāya" with a view to eclipsing the Dhvani-school of Ānanda but his efforts were frustrated by a very ardent defender of the latter–Abhinavagupta. It is true that Abhinava has no independent work of his own on poetics, yet he is recognized as a very sharp and brilliant critic in his own right by virtue of his most scholarly and quite original commentaries on Bharata's *Nātyśāstra* called "*Abhinavabhāratī*" and on the *Dhvanyāloka* of Ānanda called "Locana". These commentaries by Abhinavagupta enjoy the status of original books of criticism owing to their critical insights and solutions to age-old critical puzzles.

Abhinavagupta flourished in the court of king Lalitāditya of Kashmir and thus he belongs to the early eleventh century A.D. This is clear from the fact that he has stated that he wrote his ईश्वरप्रत्यभिज्ञा-विवृत्ति-विमर्शिणी in the 4115 th year of Kaliyuga (i.e. 1015 A.D.). His grandfather was Varāhagupta and father Curavala. His mother's name was Vimalā or Vimalakalā. The name of his younger brother was Manorathagupta.

Abhinavagupta is credited with having written 41 books, including his commentaries on Bharata and Ānanda. Most of these books are on religion, tantra and philosophy. He was a great exponent of Pratyabhijnā branch of Śaiva philosophy and tantra. Bhattendurāja and Bhattatauta were his teachers whom he very respectfully quotes in his works.

As an authority on Bharata's *Nātyāśāstra*, he is famous as the most authoritative and reliable interpreter of the "Rasa-Sūtra" of Bharata. He took an expressionist stance on the question of "Rasa-Niṣpatti" He is, therefore, famous as the exponent of "abhivyaktivāda", the vulgate version of the "Rasa-Sūtra", according to which "Rasa" is not something that is expressed as Bhatta Nāyaka had held; it is rather something that is suggested and not stated. His theory, in a nutshell, is that the "sthāyībhāvas" such as "Rati", "Courage", "Wonder" etc are already present in the minds of the enlightened spectators. Owing to suitable "ālambanas", "uddīpanas", "anubhāvas" and "sancārīs", the "sthāyibhāva" comes out of its dormancy and gets activated in the foreground of the minds of the spectators who experience it as "Rasa" through suggestion. The views of Abhinavagupta on "Rasa" are very profound and have a great modern appeal. Indeed, the portion of "Abhinavabhārati" dealing with "Rasa-Niṣpatti" should find place in the top ten critical classics of the world.

Abhniavagupta's contribution to the strengthening of the "dhvani" theory of Ānandavardhana also deserves full recognition. He very ably and boldly defended Ānanda's position against the onslaughts launched by Ānanda's detractors like Bhattanāyaka and Mukulbhatta and later by Mahimabhatta. He is one of those who provided the "dhvani" theory a very great intellectual support at a very critical stage of its growth. His defence of "dhvani" was highly spirited and philosophically based and can provide food for thought to us in the 21st century. His original thinking on all problems of literature entitles him to be regarded as a savant of Indian criticism. He has a very great historical significance, too, for it is through his *Abhinavabhāratī* alone that we get to know the earlier commentators on Bharata's *Nātyāśāstra* such as Śankuka, Lollata and Bhattanāyaka whose views he cites in his works. But for him, these ācāryas would have remained in oblivion.

A little senior contemporary of Abhinavagupta was ācārya Dhananjaya, the author of *Daśarūpaka*, a book of dramaturgy, who lived in the age of king Munja of Dhārā. Munja had reigned from 974 to 996 A.D.. Thus Dhananjaya was a late tenth century writer who may have survived in the 11th century. His brother was Dhanika who wrote a commentary on *Daśarūpaka*. The significance of Dhananjaya in the history of Sanskrit poetics lies in the fact that he made the dramatic theory of Bharata very popular by simplifying and abridging it.

Dāsarūpaka is in 300 kārikās, divided into 4 "prakāśas" or parts. Though the work is devoted to the explication of the rules governing drama, yet it, by the way, treats of subjects like "dhvani", power of words, kinds of heroines (Nāyikābheda) and other kindred matters. Dhananjaya is one of those ācāryas who held "Śāntarasa" as unsuitable for the stage. His brother Dhanika wrote a book of poetics called *Kāvyanirṇaya* which has only historical significance, having nothing original about it.

Another dramaturgical text of the 11th century is the *Nātakalakṣaṇaratnakoṣa* by ācārya Sāgaranandī. It is significant because it refers to the dramaturgical texts by Kātyāyana, Garga, Aśmakutta, Nakhakutta, Vādarāyaṇa etc, now lost.

The successor of king Munja on the throne of Dhārā, king Bhoja, his nephew, was a great poet and scholar. Evidently, Bhoja flourished in the 11th century A.D. He is famous in the history of Sanskrit poetics as the author of two books on the art of poetry: *Śṛngāraprakāśa* and *Sarasvatīkanthābharaṇa.* The first links him with the "Rasa"-school of criticism while the second work expresses his views on different aspects of poetry under the broad head of "alamkāra" of which he takes a very liberal view, bringing "guṇas", rītis" and "rasas" under its umbrella. He is well-known to the students of Sanskrit poetics for his having declared

"Śṛngārarasa" as the only "Rasa", the remaining other "rasas" being the extensions of "Śṛngāra":

श्रृंगार-वीर-करुणाद्भुतरौद्रहास्य-
वीभत्सवत्सल-भयानकशान्तनाम्नः ।
आम्नासिषुर्दश रसान्सुधियो वयं तु
श्रृंगारमेव रसनाद्ररसमामनामः ।।

[Aesthetes have discussed the ten "rasas"—श्रृंगार, वीर, करुण, अद्भुत, रौद्र, हास्य, वीभत्स, वत्सल, भयानक and शान्त but we regard only "Śṛngāra" as "Rasa" on account of its delectability.]

The eleventh century scholar of Kashmir–ācarya Kṣemendra–has gone down in the history of Sanskrit poetics as the founder of a new school of criticism called "Aucitya-Sampradāya". In his book on the art of poetry–*Aucityavicāracarcā*–he tried to establish the supremacy of "Aucitya" or propriety whose violation destroys the spirit of poetry. His other works of criticism are *Kavikanthābharaṇa* and *Suvṛttatilaka*, the first of which deals with various problems of poetry in 55 "kārikas", spread over 5 "Sandhis"; in 3 "vinyasas" and the second gives an account of metres and stanza-forms. *Aucityvicāracarcā* in 39 "kārikas" establishes propriety as the soul of poetry. Kṣemendra discusses 27 forms of propriety, beginning with "padaucitya" and ending with "āśīrvādaucitya." His theory of aucitya" gets fully revealed in the "vṛtti" of the sixth kārikā:

कण्ठे मेखलया नितम्बफलके तारेण हारेण वा,
पाणौ नूपुरबन्धनेन चरणे केयूरपाशेन वा ।
शौर्येण प्रणते रिपौ करुणया नायान्ति के हास्यताम्,
औचित्येन विना रुचिं प्रतनुते नालंकृति र्नो गुणः ।।

[Which are the people who do not become the butt of laughter by (wearing) a girdle in the neck, or a long necklace on the buttocks; (by wearing) anklet in the arms or armlet in the foot; (by showering) compassion on the foe, subdued by valour. Neither a figure of speech nor a guṇa increases lustre in the absence of propriety.]

Clearly, in the absence of propriety, in the view of ācārya Kṣemendra, no "alamkāra", no "rīti", no "guṇa" and no "vakratā" can be of any avail. Indeed, propriety is the very life-blood of poetry and poets are, therefore, well advised to observe propriety at all costs at every stage of their composition. Though "aucitya" had been treated by all ācāryas in the past, right from Bharata down to Mahimabhatta, no ācārya had dared to allot it the status Kṣemendra did. He can be called the Horace of India–Horace, the Latin critic at the beginning of the Christian era, the apostle of "Decorum" in poetry, who had enjoined on all poets through his *Ars Poetica* the imperativeness of "Decorum" or "Propriety". And Aristotle himself had pleaded for the observance of "Prepon" (Propriety) in his *Poetics* (chapter. 17). Kṣemendra was a disciple of Abhinavagupta but the tradition of the guru, namely, the tradition of defending "Dhvani" as the element of the supreme importance in poetry as done in the guru's commentary called "Locana" on Ānandavardhanācārya's *Dhvanyāloka*, was given a great impetus by ācārya Mammatha, the author of *Kāvyaprakāśa*, the most perceptive poetics ever written if we go by the number of commentaries on it by the most erudite of critics of Sanskrit down the ages. The great scholar Māheśvara Bhattācārya, who wrote the commentary "Ādarśa" on Mammatha's *Kāvyaprakāśa* remarks and correctly so:

काव्यप्रकाशस्य कृता गृहे-गृहे टीकास्तथापि एष तथैव दुर्गमः

[Though there are commentaries on *Kāvyaprakāśa* in every (scholarly) home, yet it is as difficult as ever.]

Since Mammatha quotes a verse about the proverbial charity of king Bhoja as an example of the figure "Udātta" in the 10th chapter of *Kāvyaprakāśa* (kārikā 176) and since Rājānaka Ruyyaka (1128-1149) mentions him and *Kāvyaprakāśa* in his poetics called *Alamkārasarvasva*, he must have flourished in the latter half of the eleveth century because king Bhoja was alive until 1054 A.D. and at least twenty to twenty five years must have elapsed for Mammatha to utilize a eulogy of the king in his poetics.

Kāvyaprakāśa is divided into 10 "ullāsas" and discusses all traditional problems of non-dramatic poetry but its chief aim seems to be the vindication of the "Dhvani" doctrine of Ānanda against the erudite opposition to the doctrine at the hands of Mukulabhatta and Mahimabhatta and their tribe. Mammatha's mastery over grammar, Nyāya, Mīmansā, Sāmkhya, Vedānta and Bauddha philosophy is marvellous. His critical power is revealed in his vindication of Ānanda's position on the status of independent existences of the two powers of words called "Lakṣanā" and "Vyanjanā" which scholars like Mukulabhatta had thought were subsumed in "Abhidhā". The way Mammatha demolishes the theory of Mukulabhatta in the second "Ullāsa" of *Kāvyaprakāśa* is marvellous; it brings into limelight Ācārya Mammatha's perceptive mind and his argumentative capacity. But it is a pity that his remarks are highly cryptic and call for lucid elucidation by experts. A whole thesis could be written on each sentence used in the "vṛttis" of the "kārikas" themselves, what to talk of the "kārikas". Had Mammatha been as clear and lucid as Kuntaka, he would be placed far above the most famous names in Western Criticism; it is his obscurity that does not permit us to form a judicious assessment of the great ācārya, nicknamed "Vagdevatāvatāra" (i.e. the very incarnation of the goddess of learning in a male form).

Mammatha represents the crystalization of the critical tradition of India which is rooted in the Vedas. His respective ranking of "Rasa", "Guṇa", "Dhvani" and "Alamkāra" proved to be almost definitive and final. Since he was a follower of Ānanda, he regarded "Dhvani" as the soul of poetry. According to him, the first rate poetry is the poetry based on "Dhvani" and even among the forms of "Dhvani"-"Vastu", "Alamkāra" and "Rasa"-it is the last that makes poetry the best of its kind. That is to say that the poetry designated as "Rasadhvanikāvya", in the considered view of Mammatha, is the highest kind of poetry, Thus the great ācārya recognized the value of "Rasa" in poetry, though technically speaking he belongs to the "Dhvani"-school of criticism and not to the "Rasa"-school. He gave "guṇas" or poetic virtues their due by asserting them to be the integral and inevitable and naturally inherent attributes of poetry for without "guṇas" poetry cannot be conceived of. He recognized "alamkāras" as the external and not inherent attributes of poetry because poetry can manage to be without them, though their presence is sure to enhance the beauty of poetry. This hierarchy of "Rasa", "Guṇa" and "Alamkāra", fixed by Mammatha, was recognized by the scholars of the 20th century and those of the 21st century. "Guṇībhūtavyangya poetry" is the second or middle-order poetry ("Madhyama Kāvya). The third rate or "Adhama" poetry is the poetry in which the whole attention of the poet is on creating wonder by means of manipulating words, letters and expressions; Mammatha called this kind of poetry "Citrakāvya". Mammatha's discourse on the defects of poetry. available in the seventh "ullāsa" of *Kāvyaprakāśa* is the measure of his critical power and critical acumen. This discourse can be exploited by the critics of the world at large, supplying them as it does new insights and proper scope for understanding poetry.

After Mammath, the late eleventh century Jain theorist of poetry-ācārya Hemacandra should find mention in this survey of Sanskrit poetics. Hemacandra Sūri was the teacher of the famous Calukya king–Siddharāja who had reigned from 1093 to 1143 A.D.. Hemacandra had written a book of grammar called *Siddhahema* at the request of his disciple (i.e. king Siddharāja) and it was very famous in its day. However, he is to be remembered in the history of Sanskrit poetics for his *Kāvyānūśāsana* which continunes to be popular among the students of Sanskrit literature. It is divided into 8 "adhyāyas" and treats of the common topics of Sanskrit poetics—काव्य हेतु, काव्य-प्रयोजन, काव्यलक्षण, रस, गुण, दोष, नायक-नायिका-भेद, अलंकार etc. Hemachandra is not an original or profound thinker but an excellent summariser of the views of earlier theorists in a very lucid fashion. Thus as a compendium of the existing tradition of poetics, *Kavyānuśāsana* must be accorded a due place in the history of Sanskrit criticism. Hemacandra was nicknamed 'कलिकालसर्वज्ञ'—'knower of everything in Kaliyuga'.

The 12th century scholar ācārya Ruyyaka, author of the 88-sutra poetics called *Kāvyālamkārasarvasva* attracts our attention. Ruyyaka, like Mammatha, was the follower of the "Dhvani"-school of criticism but he is famous for his scientific classification of alamkāras. He divides all figures of speech into 5 groups on the basis of the following 5 features: 1. साम्य' (Similarity) 2. विरोध (Antithesis), 3. शृंखला (Interconnectedness forming a string) 4. न्याय (Logic) and 5. गूढार्थप्रतीति (Perception of Inner Meaning). Under the above-mentioned 5 Categories, he discusses 6 figures of words (शब्दालंकार) and 75 figures of sense (अर्थालंकार). "Pariṇāma", "Ullekha", "Vikalp" and "Vicitra" are the alamkāras invented by Ruyyaka. In respect of "guṇa", "rasa", rīti" and "dhvani" he reiterates the position of Ananda and of Mammatha.

More or less contemporaneous with Ruyyaka is the Jaina theorist of poetry Vāgbhatta, author of the five-"pariccheda" poetics *Vāgbhatālamkāra,* containing 260 verses altogether. He was the prime minister (महामात्य) of the Chālukya-king. Jaisiddharaja. Like *Kāvyānuśāsana* of Hemacandra Suri, *Vagbhatālamkāra* too treats of all well-known topics of Sanskrit poetics–the nature, function and signs of poetry, its different forms, its relevance to the world of common affairs, poetic virtues and poetic flaws, rasa, alamkāra and powers of words. Quite like him was Śobhākara Mitra, the author of *Alamkāraratnākara* in which the author invented 41 new figures of speech.

We now come to a very popular theorist of poetry, belonging to the "ālamkāra" school of poetry, namely Pīyūṣavarṣa Jayadeva, author of a very famous play *Prasanna Rāghava.* He should not be confused with Jayadeva, the author of *Gītagovinda* but should be identified with the author of *Prasanna Rāghava.* Since he quotes Ruyyaka in his discussion of the figures invented by the former and cites the former's definitions of the figures concerned verbetim, he must be after Ruyyaka or contemporaneous with Ruyyaka. But since ācārya Viśvanātha cites one of the verses, of *Prasanna Rāghava.*, namely. 'कदली कदली करभः करभ': in the kārikā of the fourth "Pariccheda" of his poetics, he must be before Viśvanātha who was a contemporary of the sultan Alauddin Khiljī who reigned during 1296-1316 A.D. In other words, Jayadeva flourished in the thirteenth century.

Jayadeva was a Maithila brahmin and a great scholar of Nyāya philosophy, a poet and an expert of figures of speech. His father was an expert of the science of performing "yajna" (sacrifice) and the name of his mother was Sumitrā.

For our purposes, Jayadeva is important because of his poetics *Candrāloka*, divided into 10 "mayūkhas" and couched in 275 kārikas, using the metre called "anuṣtupa". All the traditional topics of the Indian poetics have been dealt with by Jayadeva. He is best known for the fifth "mayukha" which treats of 104 "alamkāras". He belongs to the "alamkāra"-school of criticism, though he discusses "rasas" and "bhāvas" in the 6th "mayūkha" of *Candrāloka.* The following verse expresses his position on "alamkāras" in a bold and clear way:

अङ्गीकरोति यः काव्यं शब्दार्थावनलंकृती ।
असौ न मन्यते कस्मादनुष्णमनलं कृती ।।

(चन्द्रालोक 1/8)

[Why does not the writer (critic or ācārya) who regards a (composition) without alamkāras as a poem, concede that fire could be cold?]

Clearly, in his view, "alamkāras" are the soul of poetry for without them no composition could ever be called a poem at all. Here, he is attacking ācārya Mammatha who had opined in *Kāvyaprakāśa* (Ist "sūtra" of the first "ullāsa") that a poem could be with or without *"alamkāras"*; i.e. poetry could exist even without "alamkāras".

We now come to a pair of "ācāryas" who worked in collaboration with each other–Rāmacandra and Guṇacandra, both of whom were the disciples of Hemacandra Suri and thus belonged to the 12th and 13th centuries.

Their work is called *Nātyadarpaṇa* which in 4 "Vivekas" deals with the various aspects of the art of drama. In the sphere of "Rasa" the tradition of Bharata and his followers had been that all "Rasas" are ultimately joy-ending but *Nātydarpaṇa* came out with the thesis that some of the "Rasas" are also grievous in effect.

We now come to two theorists of poetry from the East and South-Vidyādhara and Vidyānātha–both of whem flourished in the 13-14 th centuries. Vidyādhara is the author of the poetics called *Ekāvalī* having 7 "unmeṣas". All traditional topics pertaining to non-dramatic poetry have been dealt with by Vidyādhara. Illustrations for each concept have been his own, written by way of eulogies to his patron-Narasingadeva, the king of Utkala. Vidyānātha is the author of the text called *Pratāparudrayaśobhuṣana* having 9 "Prakaraṇas" in which the author discusses all items of non-dramatic as well as dramatic poetry, illustrating all his points through his eulogies written on his patron king Pratāparudra of Kākatīya dynasty. This poetics of Vidyānātha was very popular in the south of India.

Almost a contemporary of Vidyādhara and Vidyānātha was the most popular theorist of the whole of India–ācārya Viśvanātha, an Uria poet and poetician, in the court of the ruler of Kalinga whose "Sāndhivigrahīka" he was. He was a polyglot with command over 18 languages as he himself claims at the end of his treatise. His poetics is entitled *Sāhityadarpaṇa.*

Sāhityadarpaṇa, like *Pratāprudrayāsobhusaṇa* treats of the problems of poetry as a whole–both dramatic as well as non-dramatic, including the imaginative writings in prose. Thus it is a very comprehensive and lucid exposition of all the well-known items of Sanskrit poetics. Visvanātha is said to have written a commentary on Mammatha's *Kāvyaprakāśa* but it is not extant today. Thus *Sāhityadarpaṇa* is the only work on which his fame as an ācārya rests. The work is in 10 "Paricchedas", the tenth of which deals with alamkāras in detail. Ācārya Viśvanātha is a "rasavādi" critic for in his view "rasa" is the soul of poetry–रसात्मकं वाक्यं काव्यम् (Poetry is a statement whose soul is rasa.). His critical power is fully illustrated in the very first "Pariccheda" of *Sāhityadarpaṇa* where he attacks the views of Mammatha, Ānanda, Vāmana etc. and establishes his point of view in a very logical fashion.

We have not mentioned a very remarkable poetics of the thirteenth century called *Bhāvaprakāśana* which is devoted exculusively to "Rasa". The author of this work is ācārya Śāradātanaya who has a very great historical significance as he preserves the names and certain valuable details regarding the experts of "Rasa" such as Vṛddha Bharata, Nārada and Kohala. His treatment of "Rasa" is rather exhaustive and valuable for many new concepts. For example, he separates "Rasa" from "Dhvani" completely and provides it an independent status altogether.

Our next theorist is a 14th century Maithil brahmin, Bhānu Datta by name, who wrote two works on "Rasa" and "Nayikābheda"–*Rasamanjarī* and *Rasataranginī.* It is to be noted that the author's sole concern in both works is for "Śṛngārarasa"; other "rasas" have been paid scant regard by him. He is noted for his having invented a new "rasa" called "Māyārasa". He is also noted for his opposition to "Śāntarasa" being treated as fit for drama. In his view the dramatic possibility of "Śāntarasa" is very very small. But in respect of "Nāyaka-Nāyikābheda" he is the greatest authority because no other theorist than him provides so many varieties and sub-varieties of Nāyikas; his *Rasamanjarī* is really the encyclopaedia of "Nāyaka-Nāyikābheda". Bhānudatta should have given illustrations of his concepts from the Sanskrit texts available to him but his weakness (or strength as he viewed it) is that his illustrations are his own inventions. This is so because he was a fecund poet and wanted to give expression to his thinking in the form of the verses composed as examples of the concepts formulated.

The Vaiṣṇava saint and philosopher–Chaitanya Mahāprabhu had a disciple called Rūpagosvāmī, the grandson of Mukunda and the son of Kumāra. By birth Rūpagosvāmi was a brahmin of Karnātaka. His work in the field of 'Rasa' is quite praise-worthy-*Ujjvalaṇīlamaṇi*. Rupagosvāmi was clearly a rasavādį who dealt with the problem of "Rasa" in a very lucid way. He invented a new "Rasa" called "ujjvalarasa" which is nothing but devotion to Rādhā and Krishna. He also gave very good accounts of "Cetī", "Vita", "Viduṣaka", "Pīthamarda" etc. Rupagosvāmī's contribution to Sanskrit poetics is quite considerable indeed. For, apart from *Ujjvalanīlamaṇi,* he had written another work of aesthetics and poetics called *Bhaktiṛasāmṛtasindhu* which is an encyclopaedic treatment of Rasa from the point of view of the philosophy of devotion to Vishnu as developed in Gauradeśa (Bengala); divided in 4 parts, each part containing numerous waves (Laharīs). He had also written a dramaturgy called *Nātakacandrikā* which, in its own way, is very valuable to the students of drama. Rupagosvāmī flourished in the latter half of the fifteenth and first half of the 16th centuries.

In the sixteenth century we come across an ācārya Keshavamishra who had written a book on the art of poetry called *Alamkāraśekhara,* divided into 8 "Ratnas", each "Ratna" containing several "marīci's" (subsections), numbering 22 "marīcīs" in all. The work deals with all the general topics of Indian poetics; "kāvyalaksaṇaṣ", "kāvyahetu", "kāvyaprayojana", "rīti", "guṇa" "śabdaśakti", "kāvyadoṣa" and "alamkāras". In point of fact, it provides a summary of the views of great ācāryas on the problems of poetry.

Another ācārya of the 16 th century was Appayajī Dīxita whose period is between 1520 and 1593 A.D.. He was the son of Ranganāthana Adhvani and he himself was a scholar in the court of king Venkatapati.

His name is sometimes spelt as Appa Dīxita. He was the teacher of the great grammarian of the Middle Ages–Bhattoji Dīxta. He is said to have written 104 books. However, for purposes of our survey 3 books by him are worth mentioning: *Vṛttivārtika*, *Citramīmansā* and *Kuvalayānaṇda.* The first deals with the powers of words in 3 "Pariccedas" and is incomplete. The remaining two deal with figures of speech. *Citramīmānsā,* as the title itself denotes, deals with picture-poetry (citrakāvya). *Kuvalayānanda* is the work on which the fame of Appayajī Dīxita rests. It is exclusively devoted to "alamkāras" and is highly based on the *Candrāloka* of Jayadeva. It treats of 123 figures of speech in all, seventeen of which are the inventions of the author's own. It enjoys immense popularity among the students of poetics. Appayajī Dīxit was a staunch follower of "alamkārasampradāya".

We now come to the 17th century which saw the rise, on the horizon of Indian poetics, of an aesthete who eclipsed by means of his intellectual and logical brilliance all the masters of Sanskrit poetics of the past. This was Panditrāja Jagannātha, a Tailanga brahmin who had been in the most famous courts of India, including that of the Mogul emperor Shahjahan whose rule lasted from 1627 to 1658. He himself declared: 'दिल्लीवल्लभपाणिपल्लवतले नीतं नवीनं वयः' [(My) young age was spent under the shade of the leaves of the hands of the beloved (sovereign) of the Delhi (Court).]

Panditarāja Jagannatha was born in 1620 and he breathed his last in 1670. He was a great poet in his own right and an expert of the art of poetry. He was an advocate of 'Rasa' and his critical master-piece is *Rasagangādhara* which unfortunately is available to us in its incomplete form, with only two "Ānanas". However, it exemplifies Panditarāja Jagannātha's critical acumen and good sense. It is noted for its author's brilliant account of the nature and power of "Rasa" from the view-point of a Vedāntin. He accepts in its essentials the exposition of the nature of "Rasa" as proposed by Abhinavagupta and Mammatha but expresses his difference by asserting the divine nature of conciousness through his citation of certain Vedic injunctions like "रसो वै सः" [Brahma is nothing but joy itself.]. In plain terms, according to Panditarāja, in the aesthetic attitude called "Rasa", the paramount importance is that of "भग्नावरण चित्" (revealed consciousness) whereas according to Abhinavagupta and Mammatha, the emphasis is on the "स्थायीभाव" (permanent emotion). The entire discussion, as it is available in the first "Ānana" of *Rasagangādhara* is, in all probability, Panditarāja's critical master piece. It is worthy of being placed in the list of ten greatest critical discussions of the world.

However, it is very complex and complicated, couched as it is in the rather difficult logical syllogism, typical of Indian logicians. It belongs to the critical category to which Sanskrit critics like Kuntaka and Mahimabhatta belong, for all these three express their critical thought in chaste Sanskrit prose. What strikes the reader most in reading the critical discourses of Panditarāja Jagannātha, is his subtlety of thought which often makes him obscure. But his sharpness and unmistakable profundity can never fail to make a tremendous appeal to his readers. He will always be remembered for his novelties on all aspects of poetry despite his notorious boastfulness and high egotism as indicated by the titles of works such as मनोरमाकुचमर्दनी and चित्रमीमांसाखण्डन, the first of which is an attack on the grammatical texts of Bhattoji Dīxita and the second of which is a rebuttal of the theories propounded in the book of alamkāras written by the poetician Appayaji Dixit.

The 18th century continued the tradition of poetics-writing by ācāryas such as Vishveshvara Pandita. The text *Alamkārakaustubha* by Vishveshvara Pandita is a very mature work, revealing the independent-mindedness of the author at various places of its argument. Vishveshvara challenges even Panditarāja Jagannatha on various issues and corrects him. *Alamkārapradīpa* and *Alamkāramuktāvalī* are the two texts of criticism by Vishveshvara, devoted exclusively to the discussion of "alamkāras" (figures of speech). It must be noted that Vishveshvara Pandita was the last Sanskrit ācārya after whom Sanskrit criticism virtually came to a standstill. It is true that after India became a free democratic republic and Sanskrit departments came into being in Indian universities, many learned scholars of Sanskrit ventured to revive the tradition of the ācāryas like Mammatha and Vishvanatha by writing Sanskrit text-books of "Alamkārāśāstra" but no new theory has been propounded by them, though novelties in their approaches are not ruled out. However, works of criticism by eminent scholars of Sanskrit like V. Raghavan. Bhagīratha Mishra, Baladeva Upādhyāya, Satyavrata Singh, Bholashamkara Vyasa, Chandrashekhara Pandeya, Babu Lālashukla, Badarī Nātha Jhā and Revā Prasada Dwivedī, to name only a few, are quite significant. Ph.D. and D.Litt. theses, on various aspects of Sanskrit poetics, should also be mentioned here because these also reveal great critical thinking of the writers concerned and these are innumerable. We have not mentioned above the learned commentaries on the individual works of poetics by the ācāryas but many of those commentaries are, in no way, inferior to the works on which these were written. We have certainly referred to the commentaries on *Nātyaśāstra* and *Dhvanyāloka* by Abhinavagupta and the commentaries called "Abhinavabhāratī" and

"Locana" are, in all probability, as original as the works that they comment upon. In the line of Abhinavagupta should be placed commentators like Nāgeśa and Vāmana Jhalakīkara, for both are quite original and full of fresh insights.

We have not considered above the numerous ācāryas of kāvyaśāstra in Hindi, who are usually brushed aside by being described as imitators of Sanskrit ācāryas. But their work should not go unnoticed for sometimes they are found to be more illuminating and brilliant than their Sanskrit models. These gentlemen were poets first and ācāryas or critics later. Keśavadāsa, Rahīma, Rasalīna, Bhikhārīdāsa, "Padmākara", "Deva", Matirāma and Cintāmani are some of the Hindi ācāryas who have dealt with the various aspects of poetry-making in their works of poetics. They derive their ideas from the Sanskrit theorists like Bhāmaha, Dandī, Mammatha, Viśvanātha, Jayadeva or even Jagannātha and are therefore not original at all but sometimes they prove to be more helpful guides than their Sanskrit models and on that ground itself deseve critical attention. In any case, the illustrations provided by the Hindi ācāryas are clearer and more expressive than those given by their Sanskrit guides. And apart from Hindi, other regional languages of India like Bengali, Marathi, Punjabi, Tamil, Telagu, Kannada, Malayalama etc. have their own lists of theorists of poetry, of course, inspired by Sanskrit ācāryas. In modern times, practically all parts of India, can be credited with having produced first-rate thinkers and critics of poetry who could compare notes with their western counterparts. Śri Aurobindo, Pt. Rāmacandra Śukla, Hajāriprasāda Dwivedi, Pt. Viśvanātha Prasāda Miśra, Śyāmasundaradāsa, Bābu Gulābarāya, Rāmadahina Miśra, Ānandaprakāśa Dīxita, Dr Nagendra, Nāmavara Singh, Dvijendra Lāla, Dr Vidya Niwas Mishra, Rabīndranātha Tagore, V. Rāghavan, Kumāraswāmī, Kākāsaheba Kālelkara, K.C. Pandey, P.C. Lahiri, S. Kuppaswamy Śastry, K. Krishna Moorthy, M. Hiriyanna, Gaurinath Śastri, Ganganath Jha, Pravāsajīvena Chaudhari, K.S. Ramaswami Sastri, A. Śankarana and P. Pancapageśa Sastri are some of the names worthy of record, for, each of these has added to our knowledge regarding poetic problems and has thrown fresh lights on the issues involved.

From the above survey, it is clear that Indian Poetics has involved itself with the most significant element of poetry–its soul. Some ācāryas located it in what is called "Rasa", others in "Rīti", yet others in figures of speech. So on and so forth. Thus six schools of poetics emerged–Rasa Sampradāya, Rīti-Sampradāya; Alamkāra Sampradāya; Dhvani-Sampradāya, Vakrokti-Sampradāya and Aucitya Sampradāya. We shall now discuss each Sampradāya separately, highlighting its main tenets, as lucidly as possible.

Rasa Sampradāya

(रस-सम्प्रदाय)

Perhaps the earliest school of Indian poetics is the "Rasa"-school or Rasa-Sampradāya according to which the most fundamental and the most essential element of poetry, whether in prose or verse, is "Rasa". The leading exponents of this school are Bharata, Rudrabhatta, Abhinavagupta, Dhananjaya, Dhanika, Bhattanāyaka, Mahimabhatta, Bhoja, Rāmacandragunacaṇdra, Viśvanātha, Śāradātānaya, Singhabhupāla, Rupagosvāmi, Bhānudatta and Panditarāja Jagannātha. It does not mean that other theorists did not attach any importance to it. No, they did deal with "Rasa" but did not agree to the proposition that it is the soul of poetry, the most significant element of poetry, whereas the theorists, mentioned here, were unanimous in declaring "Rasa" to be of paramount importance in all imaginative writing, broadly called poetry– dramatic as well as non-dramatic, written in prose or verse. The following statement of Bharata should be regarded as the representative statement of the entire school:

> तत्र रसानेव तावद् आदौ अभिव्याख्यास्यामः ।
> न हि रसाद् ऋते कश्चिदर्थः प्रवर्तते ।।
> (Vide the prose-portion of the 31st kārikā of the 6th chapter of *Nātysāstra*)
>
> [Then (after having dealt with all the aspects of the theatre) at the very outset we shall expound "Rasas" themselves for without "Rasa" no aspect of the theatre moves an inch even.]

Evidently, the main thing in the theatrical performance is "Rasa" in the considered view of Bharata. But what is "Rasa"? Bharata replies to this query by the expression "आस्वाद्यमानत्वात्" [Dwing to its being relishable.] Evidently, "Rasa" is that which is relished by the spectators in the theatre. But what precisely is to be relished? The answer of Bharata is "स्थायिभावाः" ("permanent emotions"). This is clear from the following statement of the sage:

> यथा हि नानाव्यंजनसंस्कृतमन्नं भुज्जाना रसाना-
> स्वादयन्ति सुमनसः पुरुषा हर्षादींश्चाधिगच्छन्ति,
> तथा नानाभावाभिनयव्यञ्जितान् वागङ्गसत्त्वोपेतान्
> स्थायिभावानास्वादयन्ति सुमनसः प्रेक्षकाः
> हर्षादींश्चाधिगच्छन्ति ।
>
> [Just as men of taste enjoy well-cooked food of various dishes and experience happiness etc. so do the spectators of good breeding relish permanent emotions (स्थायिभावान्), manifested through vocal, physical and mental actings and revealed through the enactment of various feelings (भाव's) (i.e. अनुभाव, विभाव and संचारिभाव) and undergo happiness etc.]

Thus what Bharata implies by "Rasa" is quite close to what the West calls aesthetic experience. In other words, "Rasa" is the overall impression of the tasteful spectators, formed from a critical witnessing of the dramatic roles performed by the *dramatis personae* on the stage in accordance with the principles of dramaturgy, resulting in their experience of joy. Clearly, the business of the poet is to transform स्थायिभाव into "Rasa" and how he does this has been stated by Bharata in his famous formula of "Rasa", popularly called the "Rasa-Sūtra":

> तत्र विभावानुभावसञ्चारिसंयोगाद्रसनिष्पत्तिः
>
> ["Rasa" is accomplished by the artistic combination of "Bhāva", "Anubhāva" and "Vyabhicāribhāva".]

In the above formula, two words are very crucial; these words are "संयोगात्" and "रसनिष्पत्ति" The sage has left both unexplained with the result that commentators found themselves free to explain those words in their own ways. Four commentators–Śankuka, Lollata, Bhattanāyaka and Abhinavagupta–have been most famous for their views, though there had been many others also to whom references have been made in later works of poetics. We shall discuss the views of these four ācāryas quite briefly, beginning with that of ācārya Lollata. Lottata or Bhatta Lollata is famous as the earliest known explicator of Bharata's *Nātya-Śāstra*. He took the word 'निष्पत्ति' of the Rasa-Sūtra in the sense of production and the word 'संयोगात्' in the sense of 'through the association of'. Thus he put forward a productionist theory of "Rasa" according to which "Rasa" is produced when the permanent feelings (स्थायिभाव) such as "Rati" or

'Love' are presented through proper "vibhāvas", "anubhāvas" and "vyabhicāribhāvas". Thus "vibhāvas "anubhāvas" and "vyabhicāribhāvas" are the cause and "Rasa" is the effect of their interplay with the permanent emotion (स्थायिभाव). But where does this transformation of the "Sthāyībhāva" into "Rasa" take place? Lollata's answer is: in the "anukāryā" (i.e. the original hero such as Rāma or Duṣyanta whose deeds are represented in the play concerned). In his view, the relationship between "sthāyībhāva" and "Rasa" is that of the "producer" and the "produce", the former being the "producer" and the latter the "produce" primarily in the original hero of the play and secondarily in the actor performing the role of that hero.

The greatest drawback in the view of Bhatta Lollata is that it ignores the spectators altogether and relates "Rasa" to the "Anukāryā" (i.e. the original hero of the piece primarily and the "anukartā" (the actor performing the role of the hero) only secondarily, the spectator or the "sāmājika" remaining totally neglected.

The second commentator on the "Rasasūtra" is ācārya Śankuka who placed before the reading public an inferential interpretation of "Rasa". In his view the word "निष्पत्ति" in Bharata's "Rasa-Sūtra" means "Anumāna" or "Pratīti" and the word "संयोगात् implies "through perfect execution or arrangement." The sum and substance of his view is that the "anukartā" or the actor enacts "bhāva", "anubhāva" and "vyabhicāribhāva" so well that these appear to be real and true, though in point of fact the entire facade of the representation on the stage of the "bhāva", "anubhāva" and "vyabhicāribhāva" is artificial and showy. By the logic of the horse in the picture (चित्रतुरगन्याय) the "bhāvas" and activities of the actor are taken to be those of the original character. But the question is: 'What gets inferred?' The answer is the "sthāyī bhāva" of the "anukārya" or the original character. And the answer of the question as to where the said inference takes place is in the spectator's mind for it is he who infers the "sthāyībhāva" of the "anukārya" from the enactment by the "anukartā" or the actor of "bhāva", "anubhāva" and "vyabhicāribhāva" and the resulting inference is the source of joy or Ānanda.

The theory put forward by ācārya Śankuka was subjected to adverse criticism by ācārya Bhatta Tauta, the teacher of ācārya Abhinavagupta. Tauta argued that joy comes from some present experience and inference can never yield joy. According to him, Śankuka's theory is flawed because it lays too much emphasis on inference which can never yield the aesthetic experience called "Rasa", though it focussed attention on the spectator and his role in art-appreciation.

The third commentator on Bharata's "Rasa-Sūtra" is ācārya Bhattanāyaka who put forward an interpretation of the term 'निष्पत्ति' in terms of "Bhoga" or "enjoyment". Bhattanāyaka invented two new functions of words in poetry and drama: "bhavakatva" and "bhojakatva". These functions are apart from the three functions of words that the Sanskrit tradition had approved: denotation, connotation and suggestion. Bhattanāyaka finds it difficult to account for the spectator's enjoyment of the experience of the hero or heroine of an art-work with the help of the three recognised powers and functions of words. How is it that we, the spectators in the theatre, identify ourselves with the hero and at the same time relish whatever happens to him, however painful that happening may be? This question seems to have led Bhattanāyaka to conceive a power of words called "Bhāvakatva", reminding us of the Western concept of "Empathy", by means of which the spectators establish an identity with the fate of the hero on the stage by forgetting their own selves and becoming one with the hero, merging mentally with him. This power of "bhāvakatva" in association with the power of "sādhāraṇīkaraṇa" renders the words of the hero enjoyable when the spectators owing to the other power of words called "Bhojakatva" get thrilled by the words of the hero, whatever the content of those words may be–horrifying, painful, boisterous or sour. Thus Bhattanāyaka took the word "संयोगात्" of the "Rasa-Sūtra" in the sense of "भावकत्व" and "निष्पत्ति" in the sense of "भोजकत्व" as explained above. The objection to his interpretation of the "Rasa-Sūtra" is that there was hardly any precedent for the recognition of the terms he invented and therefore it failed to find favour with the subsequent ācāryas.

The last member of the list of commentators on the "Rasa-Sūtra" was ācārya Abhinavagupta who is credited with having proposed an interpretation of the "Rasa-Sūtra" that is logical, practical and quite satisfactory. And since ācārya Mammatha, the author of *Kāvyaprakāśa,* unreservedly acclaimed it as the most mature work of poetics, the theory of Abhinavagupta has emerged as the Vulgate version of the "Rasa-Sūtra". His is an expressionist view of the said sūtra because in this view the word "निष्पत्ति" has been explicated in terms of expression: 'how is the "Rasa" 'expressed' and the term 'संयोगात्' has been regarded as the common word to denote the functions of all the forms of Bhāvas–"vibhāvas", anubhāvas" and "vyabhicārīs" whose functions are : "भावन", "अनुभावन" and "व्यभिचारण" respectively. The three-fold function, namely, "भावन", "अनुभावन" and "व्यभिचारण" collectively accomplish what Bharata had called "संयोग" and all these three functions are directed to "स्थायीभाव" which

Bharata did not mention in the "Rasa-Sūtra" but which has been used by him several times after the "Rasa-Sūtra". We will now be well-advised to explain the three functions: भावन, अनुभावन and व्यभिचारण. To make the "स्थायिभाव" such as "love" worthy of delectation is "bhāvana". To make the "sthāvibhāva" the subject of experience is "anubhāvana" and to make the "sthāyibhāva" and its effect move throughout the body is "vyabhicāraṇa". All these three functions go to make "Samyoga" and it is through "Samyoga" (i.e. "Bhāvana", "Anubhāvana" and "Vyabhicārana") that the "sthāyibhāva", lying latent in the form of "vāsanā" or "sanskāra" (impressions gathered from birth to birth) gets expressed in the form of "Rasa" or aesthetic joy unlimited. But where does all this happen? The answer is: 'in the mind of the spectator of good breeding'. In other words, the "sthāyibhāva", lying dormant in the mind of a tasteful spectator in the form of "vasanā" gets expressed in the form of a delightful and joyous experience when there are appropriate vibhāvas (i.e. "ālambonas" and "uddīpanas"), anubhāvas" (i.e. bodily reactions of the actors on the stage) and "vyabhicāribhāvas" (instant and transcient gestures like "bashfulness", "fainting", "discolouring of the face", "perspiration" etc.) on the stage. Thus the "sthāyibhāva" becomes the source of joy unlimited when it is artistically treated through the interplay of "vibhāvas", "anubhāvas" and "vyabhicāribhāvas" which suggest it through their respective functions–"bhāvana", "anubhāvana" and "vyabhicāraṇa". And when the "sthāyibhāva" gets revealed, it becomes the source of Ānanda or joy unlimited.

But does every work achieve "Rasa" through its manipulation of "vibhāvas", "anubhāvas" and "vyabhicāribhāvas"? "No, not necessarily" is the answer of Abhinavagupta. The following factors create obstacles in the way of "Raṣa-Niṣpatti":

1. Implausibility of the situation depicted in the play: Abhinavagupta's term is "Pratipatti-Ayojnatā" or "Sambhāvanāvirahatā." The situation presented in the play should look probable and should win the confidence of the spectators in itself, failing which there will be serious problems in what Bharata calls "Sanyoga" and thus the "Rasa-Niṣpatti" will be adversely affected whose first condition is closeness to the truth of life.
2. Personal factors of the spectators: These pose a very grave problem to "Rasa-Niṣpatti". "Nija-Sukha-Duhkhādivivaśī-bhāva" is the term that Abhinavagupta uses. His contention is that in case the spectator remains conscious of his personal joys and sorrows, he will not be able to identify himself with

the hero and thus there will hardly be any "sādhāraṇikaraṇa" and no "Rasa-Niṣpatti."

3. The treatment of certain characters as our men and of others as alien to us: If the spectator starts regarding certain personages of the play as his own men and others as outsiders or enemies, he will not be able to relish the work as a whole and the "Rasa-Niṣpatti" will suffer in the same proportion. Similarly, in case the spectator regards the personages as belonging to a particular period or country, he will have grave problems in achieving identification with them. The play must not be time-specific or place-specific; it should defy the limitations of time and space. Otherwise, "sādhāraṇīkaraṇa" will be an impossibility and thus there will be no "Rasa-Niṣpatti". Abhinavagupta's expression is "Sva-Para-Gata-Deśa-Kāla-Viśesāveśatā".
4. Non-Achievement of the confidence of the Spectator in the Story or Characters of the play and the unclarity regarding them. Unless the spectators find the story and characters of the play quite convining, they will not find the play of real worth and the "Rasa-Niṣpatti" will be a remote possibility. Similarly, in case the development of the plot is not clear, even then it would be difficult for the spectators to relish the play. "Pratītyupāyavaikalya-sfutatvābhāva" is the expression used by Abhinavagupta for this.
5. Disregard to the Principal Character or Plot: If the poet indulges in the depiction of things of lesser importance and pays scant regard for the principal character or event, "Rasa-Niṣpatti" will suffer considerably. Abhinavagupta's term for this point is "Apradhānatā".
6. Scepticism of the Spector: If the spectator remains sceptical about the things depicted in the play, it would be next to impossible for him to relish the play. Naturally, the "Rasa-Niṣpatti" will suffer; willing suspension of disbelief, as Coleridge said, should be a prerequisite of "Rasa-Niṣpatti". The obstacle involved has been described by Abhinavagupta as "Sanśayayoga"

So that the process of "Rasa" could be smooth and unimpeded, ācārya Mammatha warned the poets of the following flaws which should be avoided:

1. Svaśabdavācyatā (Mentioning the Rasa or its constituents by its own Name):–If the poet uses 'Rasa', its "sthāyībhāva" or

"vyabhicāribhāva" by mentioning it directly, it would be regarded as a flaw and the "Rasa-Niṣpatti" would get a big jolt. For example, let us take up the following verse

जाता लज्जावती मुग्धा प्रियस्य परिचुम्बने

[The fond lady became full of bashfulness on being kissed by her lover.]

The poet has used the "vyabhicārī" called "लज्जा" ("bashfulness") by mentioning it directly and Sanskrit ācāryas would declare it flawed. Kālidāsa has expressed the "bashfulness" of Pārvatī in the right way in *Kumārasambhava:*

एवं वादिनि देवर्षौ पार्श्वे पितुरधोमुखी
लीलाकमलपत्राणि गणयामास पार्वती।।

(VI. 84)

[The sage Angirā having said so, Pārvatī, standing close to her father with her eyes bent, started counting the sport-lotuses (that she was holding from before.)]

In this verse the "vyabhicārī" ("लज्जा") has not been mentioned directly; only by depicting the effect of Angirā's words on Pārvatī, the poet has suggested her bashfulness. This is an artistic way of describing "vyabhicāris".

2. Difficult Imagining (कष्टकल्पना):–"Vibhāvas", "anubhava" "vyabhicāris" etc. should be organized lucidly. If the reader or spectator is not very clear about the "ālambanas", "uddīpanas", "anubhāvas" etc.," "Rasa-Niṣpatti" becomes a Himalyan task; every element must be clearly indicated.
3. Organization of Vibhāvas etc. Antithetical to the "Rasa" on Hand:– The poet should be very careful regarding the harmony among the "Rasas" and their constituents in his poem. If he introduces the elements of a "Rasa" antithetical to the one on hand, "Rasa-Niṣpatti" will be difficult to achieve and the verse will be flawed. Sanskrit ācāryas call this flaw परिपंथरसाङ्गपरिग्रह. Let us have a look at the following verse:

निभृतरमणे लोचनपथे पतिते गुरुजनमध्ये।
सकलपरिहारहृदया वनगमनमेवेच्छति वधूः।।

[The married lady, sitting among the elders of the family, started planning to go to the jungle, having renounced mentally all things, on sighting her paramour on a way within her sight (going) secretly.]

Going to the forest, it must be noted, is normally the "anubhāva" of Śānta-Rasa and that "Rasa" is the opposite of "Śṛngāra", the "Rasa" involved in the verse. Had the poet described the plan of the lady, going to the forest with the purpose of bringing timber, that would have been in consonance of the spirit of "Śṛngāra". But the introduction of the idea of renunciation, however remote it may be, mars the beauty of "śṛngāra" and the verse is flawed on that count.

4. Repeated depiction of the same "Rasa" again and again: the flourish (Dīpti) of the same "Rasa" repeatedly is not viable; it mars the beauty of the verse and so the repetition should be avoided.
5. Inopportune Introduction of the "Rasa": If "Rasa" is apposite to the occasion on hand, it is quite wholesome and aesthetically satisfying. But if it does not fit the context on hand, it kills the spirit of the "Rasa". Mammatha calls this defect, "akāndaprathana" (अकाण्डप्रथन). On the occasion of the deaths of his own armymen, if a king starts making love to his queen or anyone of his mistresses, "Rasa-Niṣpatti" would be adversely affected.
6. Another defect, allied to the preceding one is called "Akāndaccedana" (अकाण्डछेदन). The defect occurs where a "Rasa", which is growing steadily, gets suddently switched off. This hampers the process of "Rasa-Niṣpatti".
7. Excessive Depiction of the associate "Rasas":– No "Rasa" should be depicted out of proportion; it should be within limits, particularly the associate Rasa (अंगरस). Excessive growth (अतिवृद्धि) of the subsidiary (अप्रधान) "Rasa" is undesirable and harms the chief (अंगी) "Rasa".
8. Forgetting the Chief Rasa:– If the poet indulges in the subsidiary Rasas and forgets the chief "Rasa", the work suffers; its "Rasa-Niṣpatti" gets a rude jolt if the reader has to discover the chief Rasa (अंगीरस). Sanskrit ācāryhas call this "अंगीरसस्यानुसन्धानम्".
9. The Character's Contrariness to its Type or Category:–The poet of a dramatic piece or any other imaginative work should always

bear in mind the category to which a particular character of the piece belongs: दिव्य (divine), अदिव्य (human) and देवावतार or दिव्यादिव्य. No character should be shown as behaving contrary to the category to which he/she belongs, failing which the piece will be charged with the flaw known as प्रकृतिविपर्यय (Prakrtiviparyaya).

10. The Portrayal of a "Rasa" Having no bearing on the subject of the piece:– If a poet introduces a 'Rasa' which has no connection whatsoever with the subject on hand, the piece will suffer from the defect called "Anangavarṇana" (अनङ्गवर्णन).

Apart from these defects or flaws, there are others also which poets should avoid by all means; these pertain to time, place and established norms of the society. No description in a poem should be against the period portrayed in it or against the spirit of the country or place depicted therein or against the established norms of the society portrayed in the piece. Otherwise, the "Rasa-Niṣpatti" of the piece will not be achieved. Clearly, if the theory of "Rasa" is to be applied to a given work, we will have to take into account all the above points, pertaining to obstacles in the way of "Rasa-Niṣpatti" as pointed out by Abhinavagupta or to the flaws of Rasa, discussed by Mammatha and Vīsvanātha under the head of Rasa-Doṣas.

The application of the theory of "Rasa" should not be a mechanical procedure but rather a very serious exercise, requiring a very high degree of intelligence and insight.

"Other Major Problems Discussed by the Theorists Belonging to the "Rasa-Sampradāya"

We have discussed above the main problems tackled by the theorists belonging to the "Rasa-Sampradāya", i.e. the problem pertaining to the true meaning of ācārya Bharata's "Rasa-Sūtra". But other major problems that engaged the minds of these critics were; the exact number of "Rasas" and that of the "vyabhicāribhāvas", the nature of "Rasa" in general; the question whether "Rasa" is the property of dramatic poetry alone or of poetry in general; the relationship of "Rasa" with other elements of poetry like "Rīti", "Dhvani", "Alamkāra" etc.; "Nāyaka-Nāyikās and their kinds and sub-kinds; the question whether "Rasa" can be produced through works written in words having their standard well-known meanings (i.e. "abhidhāmulaka kāvya") or only through works having suggested meanings (dhvani or vyanjanā-dominated works); the concept of "Rasābhāsa" and its various kinds and the question regarding the identity or otherwise of "Rasa" with "Rasa-Dhvani" (i.e. whether "Rasa", as

Bharata had conceived of, is the same thing as the "Rasa-Dhvani" of Ānandavardhanacārya, author of *Dhvanyāloka*.

Regarding the number of "Rasas", the traditional view is that it is nine, though the founder of the "Rasa" school, namely, ācārya Bharata, had used the word "अष्टौ" (i.e. 8) as the standard number of the "Rasas":

श्रृंगारहास्यकरुणा रौद्रवीरभयानकाः ।
बीभत्साद्भुतसंज्ञौ चेत्यष्टौ नाट्ये रसाः स्मृताः ।।

(नाट्यशास्त्र 6/16)

[श्रृंगार, हास्य, करुण, रौद्र, वीर, भयानक, वीभत्स, and अद्भुत–these are the approved "Rasas" in the drama.]

Now, we do not know whether the number "8" is confined to drama or is for imaginative writings as a whole. Perhaps, the number of "Rasas" in non-dramatic poetry, in Bharata's view, is more than eight. And even the restriction of the number of "Nātya-Rasas" to eight is not of Bharata's own formulation but rather of his teacher "Druhiṇa" or Brahmā": "एते ह्यष्टौ रसाः प्रोक्ता द्रुहिणेन महात्मना" (नाट्यशास्त्र, 6/17) and he has just followed "Brahmā", the Creator. However, the greatest commentator on Bharata, namely, ācārya Abhinavagupta, author of the commentary on *Nātyaśāstra* called "Abhinavabhāratī", regards the number of "Nātyarasas" to be nine. He reads the 16th "kārikā" of the sixth chapter of the *Nātyasāstra* as follows:

श्रृंगारहास्यकरुणा रौद्रवीरभयानकाः ।
बीभत्साद्भुतशान्ताश्च नव नाट्ये रसाःस्मृताः ।।

But this reading of the kārikā cannot be regarded as authentic because Bharata gives a list of the "sthāyibhāvas", corresponding to the "Nātyarasas" and in that list the number of the "sthāyibhāvas" is eight and not nine:

रतिर्हासश्च शोकश्च क्रोधोत्साहौ भयं तथा ।
जुगुप्सा विस्मयश्चेति स्थायिभावा प्रकीर्तिताः ।।

(नाट्यशास्त्र, 6/18)

[Rati, Hāsa, Śoka, Krodha, Utsāha, Bhaya, Jugupsā and Vismaya–these are the well-established sthāyibhāvas.]

Those who regard Bharata as the propounder of "Nine Rasas" read the second line of the kārikā, just quoted, as follows.

"जुगुप्साविस्मयशमाः स्थायिभावाः प्रकीर्तिताः"

But I believe there is no authenticity attached to this reading, for Kālidāsa, who was an ardent follower of Bharata, regarded "Nātyrasas" to be "eight". In all probability, Bharata had excluded "Śāntarasa" as unfit for dramatic exploitation for it is imperative for the hero of a play dominated by "Śāntrasa" to be somewhat ambitious for without "ambition" there cannot be any plan for him to realize and failing that there will be no conflict in the play and the drama would not move an inch. Aristotle, it must be remarked here, in like manner, had ruled out any tragedy in the case of a wholly good protagonist (*cf. Poetics* XIII). What is true of a wholly good protagonist is equally true of a man who is dominated by "Nirveda" (i.e. no feeling for wordly things). Naturally, therefore, Bharata had ruled out the possibility of "Śāntarasa" as dramatically viable. But that cannot be said regarding the treatment of "Śāntarasa" in non-dramatic poetry for here it can be expressed very successfully. Bhartṛhari's *Vairagyāśataka* is an excellent example of "Śāntarasa", let loose from beginning to the end, making us feel indifferent to the pleasures of the world for they are tranśient and illusory.

That the number of "Rasas" was eight only at first gets confirmed by the fact that ācārya Dandī discusses eight "Rasavad-Alamkāras" on the basis of the eight "Rasas" recognized by ācārya Bharata. In kārikā no 292 of the second "adhyāya" of his poetics called *Kāvyādarśa* he clearly and openly mentions this:

इह त्वष्टरसायत्ता रसवत्ता स्मृता गिराम्

[Here in the present work the existence of Rasavat Alamkāras has been estalished on the basis of the 8 Rasas.]

From the above statement of ācārya Dandī, it is clear that even in his day, the total number of "Rasas" was eight. It is ācārya Udbhata who recognizes, for the first time, the existence of nine "rasas":

"शृंगारहास्यकरुणरौद्रवीरभयानकाः
वीभत्साद्भुतशान्ताश्च नव नाट्ये रसाः स्मृताः (काव्यालंकारसारसंग्रह 4/4)

[In drama the approved nine "rasas" are: शृंगार, हास्य, करुण, रौद्र, वीर, भयानक, वीभत्स, अद्भुत and शान्त.]

It must be emphasized here that ācārya Udbhata regards "Śānta Rasa" as viable in drama. Perhaps he had been led to the dramatic viability of "Śānta Rasa" by the success of the allegorical drama

Prabodhacandrodaya by Dāmodara Misra. He may also have been influenced by *Agnipurāṇa* which speaks of "Nine Rasas", including "śānta" (Vidyā Adhyāya" 339, verses 8-9). This might create some problem; we might conclude from the reference to "Nine Rasas" in *Agnipurāṇa* (if it was written by the great Sage Vedavyāsa of Dvāparayuga) that there ever had been two views regarding the total number of "Rasas"–one sticking to 'eight' and the other insisting on 'nine', Bharata of Tretāyuga favouring the first and Vedavyāsa upholding the latter view.

But the number of "Rasas" could not be restricted to 'nine'. Rudrata is credited with having added "Preyān" to the list of "Nine Rasas", thus making the total 'ten'. 'Sneha' or 'affection', according to him was the "sthāyibhāva" of "Preyan" (Vide *Kāvyālamkāra*, 15/17). Later king Bhoja of Dhārā brought the number to twelve, adding four "Rasas" namely, "Preyān", "Śānta", "Udātta" and "Uddhata" to Bharata's list of eight "Rasas" on the line of Abhinavagupta who had added" Śānta" and "Laulya" to Bharata's list of eight. Ācārya Viśvanatha added "Vātsalya" to the list of "Nine Rasas" in which the eight "Rasas" of Bharata's formulation and "Śānta" are included, making the total "Ten". But Mammatha had restricted the number to "Nine", regarding "Śānta" as the ninth "Rasa"."शान्तोऽपि नवमो रस." (*Kāvyaprakāsa* 4/47). Bhānudatta pleaded very strongly for two "Rasas"–"Kārpaṇya" and "Māyā Rasa" but all to no avail. However, Rūpagosvāmī's plea for "Bhakti" or "Mādhurya Rasa" did find favour along with "Vātsalya" as suggested by ācārya Viśvanātha, thus the total of recognized "Rasas" today is "eleven", though in the generality of Indian masses the expression "Nava-Rasa" (Nine Rasas") is almost universally recognized.

Just as there has been a controversy regarding the total number of "Rasas" among the critics belonging to the "Rasa"-school, there has been a great difference of opinion among them regarding the kingship of "Rasas". Bhavabhūti had declared "Karuṇa" as the only "Rasa" in the world, recognizing the remaining "Rasas" as the different forms of "Karuṇa", thus allotting it the greatest position. But king Bhoja of Dhārā declared "Śṛngāra" as the "Rasarāja" (king among Rasas).

शृगारवीरकरुणाद्भुतरौद्रहास्यवीभत्सवत्सलभयानकशांतनाम्नः
आम्नासिषुः दश रसान्सुधियो वयं तु शृगारमेव रसनाद्रसमामनामः

[Theorists have recognized ten "Rasas": शृंगार, वीर, करुण, अद्भुत, रौद्र, हास्य, वीभत्स, वत्सल, भयानक and शान्त but we recognize only शृंगार as "Rasa" owing to its (universal) enjoyability.]

Similarly, ācārya Bhatta Tauta, author of the treatise *Kāvyakautuka* (now untraceable) and the teacher of ācārya Abhinavagupta, had given primacy among "Rasas" to "Śāntarasa" because the highest goal of mankind, namely, "Mokṣa" or liberation can be attained only through this "Rasa". However, "Śṛngāra" seems to have got prime position in the books of poetics in Sanskrit or Hindi or, for that matter, any other regional language of India. This is clear from the fact that the item "Nāyaka-Nayikābheda", which logically should apply to all "Rasas", has come to be discussed by all theorists with "Śṛngāra Rasa" in mind and "Nāyaka-Nāyikā-bheda" is a very long discourse which, in certain theorists such as Bhānudatta, emerges as the sole theme of the writer throughout the work. For example, the text called *Rasamanjarī* by Bhānudatta is virtually a book, dedicated to the subject of "Nāyaka-Nāyikā-bheda", though from the title one infers that it is a discussion of "Rasa" in general.

Bhāvas And Their Role in Rasa

The "Rasa-Sampradāya" right from Bharata onward treats of "Bhāvas" and their various forms. But first of all let us be clear about the sense or senses in which the word has been in the discussion of "Rasa" as distinguished from its use in the course of "alamkāras" by a theorist like Rudrata, who in his *Kāvyālamkāra* regards it as a figure of speech. Ācārya Bharata regards "Bhāvas" as the instruments with which "Rasa" is expressed. In the seventh chapter of his *Nātyśāstra* Bharata observes: वागंगसत्त्वोपेतान्काव्यार्थान्भावयन्तीति भावा (i.e. "Bhāvas" are what convey to the spectators the meanings of poetry contained in the various forms of enactment–verbal, physical and mental or psychic). Thus all that evokes the "Rasa" in drama can be called "bhāva": "sthāyibhāva", "vyabhicāribhāva" "vibhāva" and "anubhāva". "Sthāyibhavas" are permanent emotions which lie dormant in each individual's psyche in the form of "vāsanas" or impressions and have to be evoked through the dramatic medium and when that evocation succeeds, we have "Rasa". Are these "Sthāyibhavas" limited in number or are these unlimited? The answer to this question is that the number of "sthāyibhavas" will be determined by the number of "Rasas" that are approved by the ācāryas. Since in drama on the authority of ācārya Druhiṇa or Brahmā, Bharata recognized eight "Rasas" only, the number of "sthayibhāvas" was "eight". If we belive "Rasas" to be 'nine' in number, then the "sthāyibhāvas" will be nine and since today the universally recognized number of "Rasas" is "eleven" with "Śānta", "Vātsalya" and "Bhakti" added to the list of eight "rasas", recognized by Bharata, the number of "sthāyibhāvas", too, is now 'eleven'. This is so because it is the "sthāyibhāva" that assumes the form of "rasa" when it gets fully evoked. For example, "Vīra Rasa" has "utsāha" or 'courage' as its "sthayibhāva" and "Bhayānaka Rasa" has "Bhaya" or 'fear' as its "sthāyibhāva". These "bhāvas" are called "sthāyibhāvas" because these last from beginning to the end of the composition having that "Rasa". Here it must be made very clear that the Indian poetics had the concept of "Angī" and "Anga" Rasas. Suppose. there is a work having several 'Rasas' dispersed here and there in its expanse; its "Angī Rasa" will be that "Rasa" which is the most dominant and in whose favour is the overall impact of the piece. Other "Rasas" of the work will be called "Anga Rasas". Vedavyāsa's *Mahābhārata,* for example has all "Rasas" in it dispersed in its numerous "Parvas" but according to ācārya Ānandavardhana, the "Angī Rasa" of the epic is "Śānta Rasa" and the remaining "Rasas" are "Anga Rasas" of the work. How to verify this view of Ānandavardhana? I believe, today with the help of the computer, this can be verified in a very scientific manner. We will have to make a statistical analysis of all the "Rasas" on each page of the text. The "Rasa" which has been evoked with the largest frequency, on the whole, will deserve to be called the "Angī Rasa" of the work. Ānandavardhana's finding is an assertion and can be called impressionistic, although the statistical analysis might confirm it.

Readers should note that the "sthāyibhāva" of a "Rasa" can serve sometimes as the "sancāribhāva" for another "Rasa". For example, "Jugupsā, which is the "sthāyibhāva" of "Vībhatsa Rasa", can serve as a "sancāribhāva" for "Bhayānaka Rasa" and "Hāsa", the "sthāyibhāva" of "Hāsya Rasa" can serve as a "sancāribhāva" for "Śṛngāra Rasa". But this is possible only among kindred "Rasas". Here, it is note-worthy that certain "Rasas" go with certain others which are friendly to them and cannot go with certain others which are unfriendly, nay, hostile to them. "Sṛngāra" can go with "Hāsya Rasa" rather smoothly but will find "Vībhatsa" to be quite antithetical. Ācārya Viśvanātha has discussed the interpersonal relationships of the "rasas" both in friendly as well as unfriendly terms in the third "ullāsa" of his poetics called *Sāhityadarpaṇa* in kārikās no. 254 to 259. "Karuna", "Vībhatsa", "Raudra" and "Bhayānaka" are the enemies of "Śṛngāra" and "Hāsya" and "Śṛngāra" are hostile to "Karuṇa" "Vīra", "Raudra", "Bhayānaka" and "Śṛngāra and even "Hāsya" are unfriendly to "Sānta Rasa". However, there is a neutral "Rasa" and it is "Adbhuta" for it is acceptable to the company of all "Rasas". And

"Vībhatsa" has only one enemy and that is "Śṛngāra". This inter-personal relationship of the "Rasas" is psychologically quite valid and the Sanskrit theorists should be credited with having discovered these psychological truths several centuries before the birth of modern psychology.

Another category of "Bhāvas" apart from "sthāyibhāvas" consists of "Vibhāvas". The causal factors of "Sthāyibhāvas" are called "Vibhāvas" and these are constituted by human agencies as well as phenamena and objects of Nature–river-side, sea-side, mountains, parks, gardens, tanks, sun-rise, sun-set, moonlit night, dark night, graveyard, cemetary, animals, birds, over-cast sky, rains, drought, mountains etc.

The first category of Vibhāvas, consisting of human agencies, is called "Ālambanas" and the second category, consisting of the objects and phenamena of Nature is known as "Uddīpanas". "Sthāyibhāvas" issue forth from human agents on the stage–the hero-heroines and other actors in whose hearts the "sthāyibhāvas" lie dormant in the form of "vāsanas" or impressions. Since "sthāyibhāvas" are based on the human agencies, the latter are called "ālambanas". "Ālambanas", in their turn, have two forms–"Ālambanas" and "Āśrayas", The first consist of those agencies over whom the "sthāyibhāvas" move and have their being and the latter consist of the agencies in which the "sthāyibhāvas" primarily 'manifest' themselves. In "Śṛngar Rasa", for example, there may be a situation involving the hero and the heroine, the former feeling bewitched by the beauty of the latter. Since the heroine is the basis of the "sthāyibhāva" called "Rati", she should be called "Ālambana" here and the hero in whose heart the "Rati" for the heroine is being felt will be called "Āśraya". The "uddīpanas" in the present case could be : the beautiful attire and the behaviour of the lady and the setting against which she is sighted by the hero–setting like the pond where the heroine has gone in search of water and the time of her activity, say, a vernal morning, the sun sending forth his golden rays in all directions. In another situation the hero may be the "Ālambana" and the heroine the "Āśraya" and "uddīpanas" could be the acts of the hero, the place where he is standing at the moment concerned as also the particular time at which he is sighted by the heroine. It must be noted that the "Ālambanas" and "Uddipanas" differ from "Rasa" to "Rasa". If in "Śṛngara Rasa" the hero and the heroine are the "āśraya" and "ālambana" respectively, in "Vīra Rasa", the hero is the "āśraya" and the "anti hero" is the "ālambana" and the activites of the hero along with the battlefield constitute the "uddīpana vibhāva".

"Sancārī" or "Vyabhicārī" bhāvas are also included among "Bhāvas". These are feelings which appear for a while and then disappear and do not remain attached to a particular "Rasa" but keep shifting their loyalty from time to time, now to this "Rasa" and now to that. They are also known as "Vyabhicaribhāvas" on account of their promiscuous behaviour. Their number is limited and according to the age-old tradition it is 33 and these are: निर्वेद, ग्लानि, शंका, असूया, मद, श्रम, आलस्य, दैन्य, चिन्ता, मोह, स्मृति, धृति, व्रीडा, चपलता, हर्ष, आवेग, जडता, गर्व, विषाद, औत्सुक्य, निद्रा, सुप्ति, अपस्मार, निबोध, अमर्ष, अवहित्था, उग्रता, मति, वितर्क, व्याधि, उन्माद, त्रास and मरण. The nomenclatures of these "sancāris" in certain cases are given differently in the works of certain theorists. And a few theorists have tried to enlarge this list of 33 "sancāris". Bhānudatta, for example, regarded "छल" as the 34 th "Sancārī". And some modern theorists have come out with the view that "sancāris" can never be delimited. Their view gets some support from the fact that the "sthāyibhāvas", too, can become "sancāris" in the case of "Rasas" other than the one of which it is the known "sthāyī" as has been explained above.

The last form of "bhāvas" are "anubhāvas" and these have been so named because these are the signifiers of the "bhāvas" or feelings. Traditionally, the "anubhāvas" are categorized as "Vācika" (verbal), Āngika" (physical) and "Sātvika" or mental. Speeches of the actors on the stage are their 'Vācika Anubhāvasa'; their physical reactions such as moving here and there on the stage are examples of "Āngika Anubhāva" and the mental reactions of the actors are their "Sātvika Anubhāvas" such as their feeling cheerful or despondant according to the occasion. The spectotors come to infer the feelings felt by the "Āśrayas" on the stage from their "anubhāvas" which are their external reactions to the feelings felt within. Thus the role of "Anubhāvas" in the production of "Rasa" is very vital. Ācārya Bharata has discussed at great length how the actors should behave on the stage with a view to expressing their innermost thoughts and feelings according to the situations and exigencies involved. The entire discussion from the 8th to the 13th chapters of the *Nātyāśāstra* can be regarded as Bharata's discourse on "Anubhāvas" and how to enact them on the stage under the broad head of "Abhinaya". Since "Abhinaya" is a very significant aspect of drama, the importance of "Anubhāvas" is self-evident; on the success or failure of the "abhinaya" by the actor concerned depends the success or failure of the play. It must be noted here that the way the actors wear their dress is also included in the "Anubhāva", a special kind of "anubhāva" called "Āhārya Anubhāva" and that is of very vital importance in the "Abhinaya". The "anubhāvas" of female characters have been discussed by the followers of the "Rasa" school with especial care. The theorist Śāradātanaya, for example, discusses ten mental and ten physical anubhāvas of heroines. "Bhāva",

"Hāva", "Helā", "Shobhā", "Kānti" "Dīpti", "Mādhurya", "Prāgalbhya", "Dhairya" and "Audārya" are their mental "anubhāvas" and "Līlā", "Vilāsa", "Vicchitti", "Vibhrama", "Kilkincita", "Motāyita", "Kuttamita", "Bibboka", "Lalita" and "Vihṛta" are the physical "anubhāvas" of female characters.

Thus all the elements of the "Rasasūtra" of Bharata have been clarified above. Now comes the turn of the discussion of the nature of the aesthetic attitude called "Rasa". Since the term "Rasa" has been used in Vedas and Upaniṣads and since "Brahma" has been indentified with "Rasa" in statements like "रसो वै सः", the joy accruing to the readers and spectators from reading poems and witnessing plays enacted on the stage, has been regarded as divine. The "ānanda" or joy of poetry and drama and all imaginative writings has been designated as "Rasa" and this is very close to the "Rasa" or "Ānanda" felt by the yogis when they undergo a trance-like state called "samādhi" and experience the fellowship with "Brahma" or the Universal Spirit. The experience of the readers and spectators of poetry and drama is akin to that of the yogīs when the latter realize the Self and are pervaded by God-consiciousness. That is why it has been designated as ब्रह्मानन्दसहोदर (literally, "the real brother of God consciousness"). *Agnipurāṇa* (339-1 to 4), *Sāhitydarpaṇa* (3/3-8) and *Rasagangādhara* (प्रथमानन, paragraph beginning with समुचितललितसंनिवेशचारुणा and ending with भग्नावरणा चिदेव रसः) and above all "Abhinabhāratī" (p. 281 containg the expression "सर्वथा रसनात्मकवीतविघ्नप्रतीतिग्राह्यः भाव एव रसः")–These are some of the most celebrated texts that throw fresh light on the nature of "Rasa" and its divine nature: The upshot of all these discussions, with certain fundamental differences, is that the experience of drama and all other forms of poetry is that it makes the readers and spectators rise above their narrow selves and for a time they assume perfect identification with the hero, the symbol of humanity at large and of God, the universal spirit, and enjoy His fellowship which is another name of bliss or beatific vision. The experience is extraordinary and inexpressible; it can only be felt and not described because it is supra-rational and mystical. Now arises a very pertinent question here: "If 'Rasa' cannot be described, how to know whether a given work is successful or not in achieving "Rasa" which is its true function? For, any work can claim to have achieved what Bharata called "Rasa-Niṣpatti", just by saying that its "sthāyibhāva" is that, "Vibhāras are those, "Sancāris" are these and "Anubhāvas" are these. If that were that simple, the doctrine of "Rasa" as a critical tool would be most mechanical and most impressionistic. Then the claims for "रससिद्ध" poets as in the following verse:

जयन्ति ते सुकृतिनो रससिद्धाः कवीश्वराः, नास्ति येषां यशःकाये जरामरणजं भयम् ।।

> [(Truly) victorious are the good creators, excellent poets who have realized "Rasa" fully and in whose body in the form of fame there is no fear born of old age and death!]

are likely to prove hollow and groundless for then all differences of first rate, second rate, third rate poets would be obliterated. The fact of the matter is that the "Rasa" Theory is a very practical and helpful critical tool for making judgments about given works of imagination–dramatic as well as non-dramatic, written in prose or verse. The अनिर्वचनीयता or in-expressibility of the "Rasa Experience" is only a poetic way of describing and highlighting the high level of art-experience. Philosophers, for that matter, call God "indescribable" and yet theologies are full of accounts of God in all traditions. So far as the success or failure of a given piece is concerned, a critic, applying the test of "Rasa" doctrine to it, should take into account the "Rasa-Vighnas" that ācārya Abhinavagupta had pointed out and see whether the given work has overcome those difficultics or not. The artistic success or failure of the work concerned will be determined by the extent to which the work concerned has been able to surmount the same or not. The critic should also test the work on the touchstone of "Rasa-Doṣas" pointed out by ācārya Mammatha. The excellence of the given work will be determined by the extent of its freedom from those defects. If many of the "doṣas", as pointed out by Mammatha in the *Kāvyaprakāśa* are to be found out in the work, under review, the worth of the piece as a work of art, would suffer in the same degree. Then the critic should also subject to the test of "aucitya" the entire work for, as Ānandavardhana has asserted in *Dhvanyāloka*.

"अनौचित्याद्यृते नान्यत् रसभंगस्य कारणम्"

> [Apart from impropriety, there is no other cause of deviation from the theory of "Rasa".]

And above all, the would-be critics of poetry should consider the term 'संयोगात्' in the famous "Rasa-Sūtra" of Bharata afresh and interpret it in terms of "structuring" and see whether the given text passes the test of proper arrangement of "Bhavas", "Anubhāvas" and "Vyabhicāribhāvas"; in a nutshell, he should see whether all questions of the development of the plot, portrayal of characters, use of "Alamkāras", "Rītis", "Vakroktis". "Dhvanis" etc. have been tackled satisfactorily, for all these are covered up in "Samyoga" or Arrangement–the term is as broad as the Aristotelian term "Mimesis". Thus the test of "Rasa" is no simple matter but rather a very complex affair, involving almost all issues of aesthetics. Moreover, "Rasa" should not be taken just in the sense of 'Nine', 'Eight' or 'Elevan' Rasas such as "Śṛngāra", "Hāsya", "Karuṇa" etc. but as representative also of "Bhāvaśānti", "Bhāva Śabalatā", "Rasābhāsa", "Bhāvodaya" and "Nāyaka-Nāyikābheda". The critic is also called upon to identify the "Angīrasa" of the work, under review, and for that he will be well-advised to take the help of the science of computer for the statistical analysis of the "Rasas" used in the work concerned. The largest frequency alone ensures the status of "Angī" or principal "Rasa"; the other "Rasas", will have to remain contented with the status of "Angarasas"

Alamkāra Sampradāya

As a school of critical speculation of India regarding the composition and evaluation of non-dramatic poetry, "Alamkāra" school is the oldest if we leave the "Rasa" school of criticism aside, as it was in the beginning confined to drama. We must place on record that the earliest exponent of the "Rasa" school, whose text is available today, was ācārya Bharata who had declared "Rasa" to be the chief element of drama and not of poetry in general. Thus he was virtually the founder of the "Rasa" school and the earliest systematic theorist of drama, his *Nāṭyāsāstra* being the virtual encyclopaedia of the science of drama with "Rasa" as the centre of his entire discussion. And Bharata no doubt had discussed "Four" "alamkāras"–उपमा, दीपक, रूपक and यमक along with 36 "Lakṣaṇas" in the 17th chapter of the *Nātyśastra* but these were subsidiary to "Rasa" which was the be-all and end-all of drama. But after Bharata, it was felt that "Rasa" might be regarded as the soul of dramatic poetry but the soul of non-dramatic poetry was "Alamkāra" and soon the entire science dealing with the issues of poetry in general and non-dramatic poetry in particular came to be known as "Alamkāraśāstra" in imitation of "Nātyaśastra"–the science, dealing with the affairs and issues of dramatic poetry.

It must be made clear here that the 6 critical "Sampradāyas" or schools, mentioned earlier, were named on the basis of the element of poetry which the critics of that school used to regard as the soul of poetry. For example, the "Rasa Sampradāya" was so called because the critics belonging to it held "Rasa" as the soul of poetry–रसात्मकं वाक्यं काव्यम् as one critic of the school, namely ācārya Viśvanātha, author of *Sāhitya Darpaṇa*, had asserted. Similarly, the critics of the "Rīti Sampradāya" claimed that "Rīti" (or style in its broadest sense) was the thing of the utmost importance is poetry–its very soul and life. This was true of the critics belonging to the "Alamkāra" too for they all were of the view that without "alamkāras" the very existence of poetry would be ruled out for "Alamkāras" were the soul of poetry.

Though, as we have shown earlier, the history of "alamkāras" starts with the Vedas, the first systematic detailed account of "alamkāras" or figures of speech is that of ācārya Bhāmaha, the author of the treatise called *Kāvyālamkāra.* Majority of the alamkāras recognized today are dealt with first of all in the *Kāvyālamkāra* of Bhāmaha, who flourished in the 6th century A.D. Thus, the first systematic work on the art of poetry, available to us today is Bhāmaha's *Kāvyālamkāra* just as the first systematic work on the art of drama is the *Nāṭyāśastra* of ācārya Bharata. Clearly, Bhāmaha is our earliest critic of non-dramatic poetry, belonging to "Alamkāra Sampradāya" though he mentions a few of his predecessors like Medhāvī in his *Kāvyalamkāra* (2/40 and 2/88). It must be remarked that we should call a critic "Alamkāravādī" or belonging to "Alamkāra Sampradāya" only when he/she regards "Alamkāras" to be the soul of poetry or inevitable to poetry. A critic just discussing "Alamkāras" cannot be called "Alamkāravādī". For example, Mammatha discusses "Alamkāras" in the 9th and 10th "Ullāsas" of his *Kāvyaprakāśa* at great length but he is not an "Alamkāravādī" critic for he does not regard "Alamkāras" as the soul of poetry but rather as agents enhancing the beauty of poetry; in his view great poetry can exist even without "Alamkāras". Bhāmaha, on the other hand, deserves to be called an "Alamkāravādi" critic because he regards "Alamkāras" as of vital importance to poetry. In the 13th kārikā of the first "Pariccheda" of his *Kāvyālamkāra* he proclaims:

न कान्तमपि निर्भूषं विभाति वनितामुखम्

> [Notwithstanding its being beautiful (intrinsically), the countenance of a lady does not look beautiful in case it is devoid of ornamets.]

Clearly, in order to look beautiful a lady ought to wear ornaments for if she is without ornaments, her intrinsic beauty, however great it may be, will lose all its meaning. What is true of the face of the lady is equally true of poetry: in order to be meaningful and really beautiful both externally and internally, it ought to be in possession of figures of speech on which rest the charms of poetry under all circumstances.

The author of *Agnipurāṇa* (in the view of the Indian public Vedavyāsa) is also "Alamkāravādī" because he holds a similar view of "alamkāras": without "alamkāras" poetry would look like a widow despite all her intrinsic charms. Thus "alamkārās" are very essential for poetry whether these are of sense or of words. Indeed, before Bhāmaha appeared on the critical scene of Sanskrit, the "alamkāravādī" critics were divided in two camps, the first emphasizing the importance of figures of sense (Arthālamkāras) and the second stressing the significance of the figures of words (Śabdālamkāras). Bhāmaha, in his turn, took a holisitc view of the matter, highlighting the value in poetry of both kinds of figures: "arthālamkāras" as well as "Śabdālamkāras". This is so because poetry implies essentially the togetherness of words and their senses: without this togetherness poetry cannot flourish in the considered view of Bhāmaha. Though only two of the six "Paricchedas" of *Kāvyālamkāra* have been devoted to "Alamkrti" or figures of speech, Bhāmaha has a very lofty view of "Alamkāras" in poetry. He discusses two figures of words: "Anuprāsa" and "Yamaka" at great length and the "arthālamkāras" or figures of sense that he dwells at are : 1. रूपक 2. दीपक 3. उपमा 4. आक्षेप 5. अर्थान्तरन्यास 6. व्यतिरेक 7. विभावना 8. समासोक्ति 9. अतिशयोक्ति 10. यथासंख्य 11. उत्प्रेक्षा 12. स्वभावोक्ति 13. प्रेय 14. रसवत् 15. ऊर्जस्वी 16. पर्यायोक्त 17. समाहित 18. उदात्त 19. श्लिष्ट 20. अपह्नुति 21. विशेषोक्ति 22. विरोध 23. तुल्ययोगिता 24. अप्रस्तुतप्रशंसा 25. व्याजस्तुति 26. निदर्शना 27. उपमारूपक 28 उपमेयोपमा 29. सहोक्ति 30. परिवृत्ति 31. ससन्देह 32. अनन्वय 33. उत्प्रेक्षावयव 34. संसृष्टि 35. भाविक and 36. आशीः. His discussion is not very methodical and orderly but rather quite arbitrary. According to him, "Alamkṛti" or figurativeness lies in indirectness of speech (वक्रोक्ति) whether the figure is of word or of sense : वक्राभिधेयशब्दोक्तिरिष्टा वाचामलंकृति'. He also holds the view rather firmly that in the heart of indirectness is 'अतिशयोक्ति' or what the West calls "Hyperbole"–a kind of exaggeration. Thus the poeticality of poetry lies in some kind of exaggeration; it is exaggeration that makes a statement poetic. He openly advises the poets:

सैषा सर्वैव वक्रोक्तिरनयार्थो विभाव्यते।
यत्नोऽस्यां कविना कार्यः, कोऽलंकारोऽनया विना।।

(काव्यालंकार 2/85)

[This very figure called "Atiśayokti" is in point of fact

nothing but indirect speech. The meaning of poetry derives its charm from this. The poet should try to cultivati it; which "alamkāra" is without it?]

If the real task of the poet is to make indirect speeches, the importance that Bhāmaha attached to "alamkāras" becomes self-evident– poetry just cannot be conceived of without exaggeration and thus without figures of speech. That Bhāmaha is an "alamkāravādī" critic becomes clear from the last and 58th kārikā of the third "Pariccheda" of *Kāvyālamkāra:*

गिरामलंकारविधिः सविस्तरः स्वयं विनिश्चित्य धिया मयोदितः
अनेन वागर्थविदामलंकृता विभाति नारीव विदग्धमण्डना।।

[I have discussed at great length the method of beautifying poetic statements after making discriminative judgment according to my mind. The statement of the poets (the knowers of meanings), decorated by means of this, looks beautiful as does a lady, making appeal to the men of taste, when she wears ornaments.]

Evidently, in the opinion of Bhāmaha, poetry means the creation of beauty but that aim can never be realized in the absence of figures of speech, the real makers of beauty.

Now arises the question of Bhāmaha's application of "alamkāras" to concrete texts that had been available to him. The answer is: yes, Bhāmaha has used "alamkāras" as critical tools in making judgments on certain poets and poems available to him. In kārikā no. 19 of the second "Pariccheda" of *Kāvyalamkāra* he attacks the poet Rāmaśarmā and his work *Acyutottarā* which is no longer extant. *Acyutottarā* seems to have been an epic poem dealing with the deeds of Acyuta (i.e. Krishna) and his association with Uttarā, the daughter of king Virāta and wife of Abhimanyu, the son of Arjuna. Now, the poem of Rāmaśarma appears to have been full of difficult and obscure "Yamākas": Bhāmaha first expounds the theory of lucidity regarding the use of "Yamakas" by the poets. He says:

प्रतीतशब्दमोजस्वि सुश्लिष्टपदसन्धि च।
प्रसादि स्वभिधानञ्च यमकं कृतिनां मतम्।।

(काव्यालंकार 2/18)

[That "Yamaka" alone finds favour with the men of taste and good sense in which there are words of common usage;

joinings of words are well-done; words are full of clarity and are easily pronouncable.]

The great ācārya, then, applies his theory to the poem *Acyutottarā* by Rāmaśarmā and finds it utterly disappointing because the "Yamakas" used in this poem, so Bhāmaha argues, are far-fetched and obscure. So the great critic declares the whole work a quizz or puzzle, beyond the head of common readers. He remarks:

नानाधात्वर्थगम्भीरा यमकव्यपदेशिनी।
प्रहेलिका सा ह्युदिता रामशर्माच्युतोत्तरे।।

(काव्यालंकार 2/19)

[An obscure text, rich in various root-meanings is distinguished as Yamaka-kāvya only in name; such a work is, at the most, a puzzle as is the *Acyutottarā* by Ramaśarmā.]

Another application by Bhāmaha of the theory of "alamkāra" to poetry is to *Bhattikāvya or Rāvaṇa-vadha* by Bhattiswāmī. The author of the epic feels proud of the obscurity of his poem caused by the introduction of most uncommon grammatical forms in the texture of the piece. He asserts unabashedly:

व्याख्यागम्यमिदं काव्यमुत्सवः सुधियामलम्।
हता दुर्मेधसश्चास्मिन् विद्वत्प्रियतया मया।।

(भट्टिकाव्य 22/84)

[This poem can be comprehended with the help of a commentary, for it is a great festivity for the learned. But alas! the unintelligent will be undone by my love for learning.]

Bhāmaha took exception to this self-glorification of Bhattisvāmī and observed by way of retort:

काव्यान्यपि यदीमानि व्याख्यागम्यानि शास्त्रवत्।
उत्सवः सुधियामेव हन्त! दुर्मेधसो हताः।।

(काव्यालंकार 2/20)

[If like the works of science, even these poems could be comprehensible only with the help of commentaries, there would be festivity only for the learned and the unintelligent alas! would be undone!]

Bhāmaha, in other words, says that if the use of figures of speech were to make the poems heavy readings. the purpose of poetry would be defeated. Clearly, he is all for lucidity and plainness in the use of figures of speech and dead against the practice of the poets like Bhatti and Rāmaśarma. But is he at all appreciative of any poet or critic known to him? The answer is: "Yes, he is all praise for the practice of theorists like Medhāvin, his predecessor; he adopts Medhāvin's views regarding the seven defects of simile: हीनता, असम्भव, लिंगभेद, वचनभेद, विपर्यय, उपमानाधिक्य and उपमानासदृशता. This clearly establishes his openness of mind and readiness for accepting views worth appreciating. He was a bold and fearless thinker who could attack anyone whom he found at fault and admire any one who deserved his words of appreciation.

The next "Alamkāravādī" critic of Sanskrit is ācārya Dandī, author of *Kāvyādarśa.* He probably flourished in the late seventh and early eighth centuries. That he was a follower of the "Alamkāra Sampradāya" is evident from the fact that the now available text of *Kāvyādarśa* is dominated by the discourse on "alamkāras"; it occupies the largest portion of the work. Out of the total number of the verses used in the work (i.e. 860 verses), more than 500 have been devoted to "alamkāras" which occupy some portions of the first and third "Paricchedas" and the whole of the third "Pariccheda", containing 368 verses:

It is true that ācārya Dandī does not claim anywhere in his treatise that "alamkāras" are the soul of poetry but he does claim that the beauty of the body of poetry owes itself to "alamkāras". In the first verse of the second "Pariccheda" of his poetics, Dandī remarks:

> "काव्यशोभाकरान् धर्मानलंकारान् प्रचक्षते"
>
> [The factors responsible for poetic beauty are called "Alamkāras".]

It must be placed on record here that Dandī's is a formalist approach to poetry. In the first "Pariccheda" of his poetics he has dealt at great length with the body of poetry (काव्य-शरीर). Like a materialist philosopher, he seems to be concerned with the body only, ignoring the inner principle called "Atman". Since, the body of poetry constitutes, in his view, the be-all and end-all of poetic pursuit, he concentrates on the means which ensure its beauty; for, the value of poetry will be enhanced to the extent its beauty is incrased. This explains why he attaches so much importance to "Alamkāras"; it is "alamkāras" that make the body of poetry look beautiful just as ornaments make human body charming and attractive.

Now, the body of poetry consists of the words that give expression to the intended meaning of the poet:

"शरीरं तावदिष्टार्थव्यच्छिन्ना पदावली"

(काव्यादर्श 2/10)

[A group of words, containing intended meanings, constitutes the body (of poetry)].

Qualities of poetry (गुण), flawlessness (अदोषता) and figures of speech (अलङ्कार)—all these make the body of poetry (i.e. words with intended meanings) beautiful. But among these three, the most effective means are "Alamkāras". Dandī Discusses 35 "alamkāras" in the second "Pariccheda" of his work along with their numerous varieities. These "Alamkāras" are: स्वभावोक्ति, उपमा, रूपक, दीपक, आवृति, आक्षेप, अर्थान्तरन्यास, व्यतिरेक, विभावना, समासोक्ति, अतिशयोक्ति, उत्प्रेक्षा, हेतु, सूक्ष्म, लेश, यथासंख्य, प्रेयस्, रसवत्, ऊर्जस्वी, पर्यायोक्त, समाहित, उदात्त, अपह्नुति, श्लेष, विशेषोक्ति, तुल्ययोगिता, विरोध, अप्रस्तुतप्रशंसा, व्याजस्तुति, निदर्शना, सहोक्ति, परिवृत्ति, आशीः, संसृष्टि and भाविक. Apart from these 35 "alamkāras", Dandī has discussed अनुप्रास along with its numerous varieties in the first "Paricched" in the course of his discussion of वैदर्भीमार्ग and यमक and its 315 varieties as also varied चित्रालंकार's like गोमूत्रिकाबन्ध and सर्वतोभद्र in the third "Pariccheda" of his work.

Now, the question arises as to how Dandī applies the "alamkāras" as a critical tool to discuss a given text. To all intents and purposes, the examples of "alamkāras" in *Kāvyādarśa* are by Dandī himself. But in the course of his discussion of उत्प्रेक्षा he cites a verse, without mentioning its authorship, which we all know as coming from Bhāsa, the great pre-Kālidāsa dramatist. The verse runs as follows:

लिम्पतीव तमोऽङ्गानि वर्षतीवाञ्जनं नभः ।
असत्पुरुषसेवेव दृष्टिर्निष्फलतां गता ।।

This is the 19th verse of the first Act of *Cārudatta* by Bhāsa. The verse is spoken by the "Vita" of the play. We can render this verse in the following words:

[The darkness is, as it were, besmearing the limbs and the sky were, as though, raining collyrium. The eyesight is meeting failure like service done to an evil man.]

Dandī cites the above verse twice in the second "Pariccheda" of his *Kāvyādarśa.* The first line has been cited in verse no. 226 as an illustration of "अचेतनगतोत्प्रेक्षा" and the whole verse as verse no. 362 of the said "Pariccheda". In the second line of his verse 226, Dandī observes that the line लिम्पतीन तमोऽङ्गानि. is clearly illustrative of "उत्प्रेक्षा":

> इतीदमपि भूयिष्ठमुत्प्रेक्षालक्षणान्वितम्
> [Even this (illustration) is full of the signs of उत्प्रेक्षालंकार.]

And then the great critic takes to task the theorists who regard the verse as an illustration of उपमा. Dandī's discussion is contained in Verses 227-231. The critic's power of critical discrimination is writ large on these verses and the whole argument can be cited as an example of practical criticism of ancient India during the Classical Age. Without specifying the critics, Dandī says that the scholars who find 'उपमा' in the line, under review, on the ground that it contains the word 'इव', forget the age-old rule that the word 'इव' in the sense of similarity cannot be used in ति-ending verbs. Perhaps Dandī is calling attention to Patanjali's rule 3.1.7 Vārtika 14 in *Mahābhāsya.* The verbs 'लिम्पति' and 'वर्षति' are ति-ending and therefore they cannot be used to serve as 'उपमा' and thus the existence of 'उपमा' in the line is ruled out. The figure involved is उत्प्रेक्षा, pure and simple. Dandī's rejection of उपमा in the verse of Bhāsa concerned is quite lively and lengthy and continues upto kārikā no. 231 and demonstrates his power of defending his case against the pleas put forward by his opponents. The verse, in its entirety, is cited by Dandī again in kārikā no. 362 of the second "Pariccheda" of *Kāvyādarśa* as exemplifying the figure संसृष्टि and that shows his fascination for the verse concerned. No doubt, this is proof positive of his critical preference for a text that seems to have made a tremendous appeal to his heart.

The most ardent and outspoken follower of the "Alamkāra" school was the 13th century theorist of poetry–Pīyūṣavarṣī Jayadeva (1200-1300 A.D.), the author of the popular poetics called *Candrāloka*. The great theorist Mammatha of the 12th century A.D. in his poetics called *Kāvyaprakāśa* had slighted alamkāras by saying that they are not an integral element of poetry, for poetry can exist even without them; they are the "anitya dharmas" of poetry whereas "guṇas" are its "nityadharmas" (i.e. part and parcel) of poetry. Incensed by this "unjust" treatment of "alamkāras", Jayadeva burst into the following utterance:

> अङ्गीकरोति यः काव्यं शब्दार्थावनलंकृती।
> असौ न मन्यते कस्मादनुष्णमनलं कृती।। (चन्द्रालोक 1/8)

[The theorist (i.e. Mammatha) who regards words and meanings, devoid of figures of speech, as constituting poetry, should (be prepared) to regard fire as unhot (cold). Why does not he do so?]

Jayadeva clearly refers us to Mammatha's definition of poetry: "तददोषौ शब्दार्थौ सगुणावनलंकृती पुनः क्वापि" (काव्यप्रकाश, प्रथम उल्लास, सूत्र 1) [That (i.e. poetry) is flawless words and meanings, containing guṇas and figures generally but exceptionally even without them.]. In the considered view of Mammatha, poetry is nothing but words and meanings which are devoid of all defects and are full of "guṇas" and figures generally but sometimes existing even in the absence of the latter (i.e. figures of speech). Jayadeva finds this "Sūtra" of Mammatha unacceptable; in his view, it is travesty of facts: how can poetry exist without figures of speech, for it is the figures of speech which go to make words and meanings assume the character of poetry; without figurativeness accruing to words and meanings, no sensible man can conceive of the existence of poetry just as nobody can conceive of unburning fire. Since the existence of fire without its nature to burn is unthinkable, the existence of poetry in the absence of the figures of speech is impossible.

Jayadeva has discussed 104 figures of speech out of which 87 are real and others are only the extensions of उपमा, अपह्नुति, आक्षेप and अतिशयोक्ति. Some of the figures invented by Jayadeva are: उन्मीलित, प्रौढोक्ति, सम्भावना, प्रहर्षण, विषादन, आवृत्तिदीपक, विकस्वर, पिहित etc.

An early "alamkāravādī" critic after Dandī was ācārya Rudrata who flourished in the ninth century A.D. His poetics is called काव्यालंकार which contains 16 "Paricchedas" or chapters. The second, third, fourth, fifth, seventh, eighth, ninth and tenth chapters of *Kāvyālamkāra* of Rudrata deal with "alamkāras". He is credited with having classified the figures of speech on scientific lines, considering them under the following categories: "Vāstava", "Aupamya", "Ātiśayya" and "Śleśa". That he is an "alamkāravādī" critic is clear from the largest attention given to a discussion of "alamkāras" in his poetics–half of it having been allotted to "alamkāras" and the other half to all the remaining issues of poetry–its signs, its true nature, its function, its purpose, its various kinds, its virtues and defects and "Nāyaka-Nāyikābheda". His classification of alamkāras into four groups based on (i) the essential nature of things (वास्तवमूलक) (ii) similarity (औपम्य) (iii) exaggeration (आतिशय्य) and (iv) pun (श्लेष) is quite interesting and speaks of his scientific approach. However, there are only critical assertions throughout Rudrata's *Kāvyalamkāra* and hardly any critical analysis or critical judgment on any poet or work except for citations here and there from Bhavabhūti and Bhāravi etc. and mentioning of *Meghadūta, Kādambarī* and *Harṣacaritam* etc. Clearly, Rudrata is a theorist, pure and simple, and not a literary critic and even when he theorises he never puts forward any philosophical or linguistic reason in support of hiṣ point of view. That is clearly his weakness.

Here, it must be noted that "alamkāra" is a very important item of Indian poetics; all ācāryas, to whichever school or sampradāya they might belong, treat of alamkāras in detail. But we cannot designate them as "alamkāravādi" critics for in their view something other than "alamkāra" is the soul of poetry. Thus the denomination and characterization of an ācārya as a literary critic will be determined by the element which in the view of the critic concerned is the soul of poetry. For example, if the critic concerned regards "Vakrokti" as the soul of poetry. (i.e. the element of the supreme importance in poetry), he will be designated as a "vakroktivādī" critic, though he might discuss "alamkāras" in detail in his poetics. Kuntaka is a "vakroktivādī" critic because he holds "vakrokti" to be the *summom bonum* of the poetic act, although he does not ignore the "alamkāras" and discusses them at great length, emphasizing the element of "vakrokti" in them.

The question arises as to how could we apply the theory of "alamkāras" in poetry whether it is written in German, French, Greek, Latin, Sanskrit, Hindi, Urdu or English. The easiest approach seems to point out the figures and tropes used by the poet concerned in a particular poem or the entire corpus of his poetic writings and find out the predominance of the figure which appears to be his *forte*. For example, Udbhata, it seems, after a thorough analysis of the poems of Kālidāsa, found that his similes (उपमा) were his greatest achievement as a poet– उपमा कालिदासस्य (i.e. Kālidāsa excels in similes). In the same view is the criticism of the poetry of Kālidāsa by the critics who called him "दीपशिख कालिदास" on the basis of the poet's use of the image (उपमा) of दीपशिखा (flame of the lamp) for his heroine of the sixth canto of रघुवंशम्, namely, Indumatī, who passed by all princes collected in her 'Swayamvara' ceremony in the fashion of the lamp-flame that renders all houses on the royal thoroughfare gloomy when its bearer passes by them. The comparison is so apt and composite that the critics under its influence called Kālidāsa "Dīpasikha-Kālidāsa", reminding us of the Greek poet Homer, noted for his apt similes. Clearly the study of the figures of speech of a given poet in any language can provide us clues that can reveal the quality of his mind and the range of his life-experiences.

Another way of how we can put the study of "alamkāras" to a critical use is to find justification of the employment of the figures in the passage or the entire text concerned. In such studies, we have to decide whether the figures are functional or just decorative. In the first case, their employment is praiseworthy and in the second case inartistic and therefore not commendable at all. Figures that help the "Rasa-Niṣpatti" or "Rasa-Paripāka" are admired by the sensitive critics but figures for the sake of figures make the composition inartistic and must be avoided. Sanskrit ācāryas like Mammatha were inclined to place such verses under the poetic category called "citrakāvya" which was another name of "adhama kāvya" or bad poetry, though there is no denying that "citrakāvya" involves a very alert intellectual activity; it is no joke to write verses illustrative of "khadgabandha", "padmabandha", "sarvatobhadra' etc.. This is so because poetry belongs primarily to the heart and then to the intellect.

And yet another way how figures could be put to good critical use is to connect them to the age when the verses using them were composed and to trace the tradition of figures involved. This involves questions like the following: 'Can the religious and cultural developments of the 17th Century England explain the birth of the figures like 'Metaphysical conceit'? Cannot the cultural decline in India in the eighth century A.D. and after explain the tendency among poets like Bhāravi and Māgha to try "Citrakāvya"? Which is the first poet to try his or her hand on "Citrakāvya"? How is it that poets like Kālidāsa do not indulge in "Citrakāvya"? Was Kalidāsa incapable of making picture-poems like "Sarvatobhadra" and "Khadgabandha"? To what extent did the Indian tradition of "citrakāvya" influence the Elizabethan and 17th century tradition of picture-poetry followed by poets like Quarles?" Questions such as these demand for their solution a very perceptive and philosophical mind and deep knowledge of the history of world-poetry, possible only for polyglots, full of insights and acute sensibility: unless the researcher knows Sanskrit, Turkish, Arabic, Hebrew, Latin, Greek, Italian, English etc., he cannot explain the interaction between the East and the West with confidence and a sense of authority. But the questions are significant for a proper understanding of world-poetry.

Rīti Sampradāya

The third notable school of literary criticism in India was that of Rīti whose founder was ācārya Vāmana, author of the treatise called *Kāvyālamkārasūtravṛtti.* written in the ninth century A.D. in the reign of the king of Kashmire–Jayāditya. Kalhaṇa, in his history called

Rājataranginī, refers to Vāmanācārya in the following verse:

मनोरथः शंखदत्तश्च चरकः सन्धिमांस्तथा।
वभूवुः कवयस्तस्य वामनाद्याश्च मंत्रिणः।।

(राजतरंगिणी 4/497)

[(In the court of king Jayāditya) there were poets like Manoratha, Samkhadatta, Caraka and Sandhiman as also ministers such as Vāmana etc.]

The word Rīti is derived from the root "Ringa", implying movement, with the help of the suffix 'क्तिन्', suggesting the word's feminine gender. Thus the word means the gait and movement of the verse which comes from the peculiar combination of words called "Samāsas" in Sanskrit grammar. This is clear from Vāmana's definition of "Rīti":

विशिष्टा पदरचना रीतिः

(काव्यालंकारसूत्रवृत्ति 1/217)

[A very special composition of verse is called Rīti.]

From Vāmana's argument of the nature and function of "Rīti", we come to know that the very special composition of verse that he has in mind comes from the elements of poetry called "guṇas" like "Oja", "Prasāda", "Mādhurya" etc. which, according to Vāmana, are 20 in number, of which ten belong to words and the other ten pertain to the meanings of words. But what are "guṇas"?. Vāmana clarifies in the following words:

काव्यशोभायाः कर्तारो धर्माः गुणाः

(काव्यालंकारसूत्रवृत्ति 3/1/1)

["Guṇas" are the factors effecting the beauty in poetry.]

But "alamkāras" or figures of speech, as their very name indicates, are beauty-producing agents in poetry: "अलंकरोतीति अलंकारः" ("Alamkāra is what renders (poetry) beautiful). If that is the case, then what is the difference between "alamkāras" and "guṇas", for both create poetic beauty? Vāmana's position on this point is that "guṇas" are integral and constant factors of poetry (नित्यधर्म) whereas "alamkāras" are "anitya" or not an integral element of poetry, i.e. poetry can afford to exist even without "alamkāras whereas its life in the absence of "guṇas" is unconceivable. Clearly, guṇas" are integral to poetry whereas "alamkāras" are just incidental to it. There can be poetry without any "alamkāra" whatsoever but there cannot be any poetry, worth its name, without "guṇas". "Guṇas" have the same status in poetry as mental, physical and spiritual qualities have in the making of a man's personality and "alamkāras" are, on the other hand, like ornaments such as armlet, necklace, chain etc. that add to the physical appeal of man. "Guṇas" or poetic merits in collaboration with "alamkāras" or figures of speech produce beauty in poetry by creating a special kind of word-combinations which is, precisely, what Vāmana calls Rīti and in the considered view of Vāmana, the composition, having a very special kind of word-combinations, otherwise known as "Samāsas", is the soul of poetry. Vāmana declares:

रीतिरात्मा काव्यस्य

(काव्यालंकारसूत्रवृत्ति 1/2/6)

(Rīti is the soul of poetry).

If words and their meanings constitute the visible form of poetry, these must be regarded as the body of poetry for we identify people by their bodies. However, the body of a being is really distinguished by its soul which animates it and makes it meaningful; the body of poetry, too, should have a soul to make it alive. But what is the soul of poetry? Vāmana identifies the soul of poetry with Rīti which is "Guṇātmikā Padaracanā", that is, "a composition of verse having its soul in the guṇas". In other words, the soul of poetry is to be located in "Guṇas" and Vāmanācārya should be designated as a "guṇavādī" critic for he is basically an advocate of "guṇas" in poetry, no matter if he swears by "Rīti". This becomes clear from the fact that out of the three forms of Rīti–Vaidarbhī, "Gaudi" and "Pāñcāli"–that he discusses, the first has been described by him as containing all the ten "guṇas" that he recognizes: ओज, प्रसाद, श्लेष, समता, समाधि, माधुर्य, सौकुमार्य, उदारता, अर्थव्यक्ति and कान्ति. Clearly, the presence of all the guṇas in the poetic style designated as "Vaidarbhī" makes a verse composed in that form (or Rīti) illustrative of true poetry. No doubt, "guṇas" constitute the quintessence of poetry–its very soul. Here we should remember that if we were to describe the soul of a man, we would start enumerating the various traits of his personality–his fearlessness, his benevolence, his propensity to help his fellow-beings, his straightforwardness, so on and so forth. So Vāmana rightly locates the soul of poetry in "guṇas" and since these are to be found simultaneously in a poem in "Vaidarbhī Rīti" which represents poetry at its best, "guṇas" emerge as the soul of poetry, though he maintains that "Rīti" is the soul of poetry: "रीतिरात्मा काव्यस्य". In support of our view that it is "guṇas" that constitute the soul of poetry, we can cite Vāmanācārya's own definition of "Rīti", namely, 'विशिष्टा पदरचना रीतिः' (1.2.7) where the term "विशिष्टा" has been identified by him with "guṇātmā" (i.e. that which is marked by "guṇas"). In other words, only that पदरचना (composition of verse) can be called poetry which is pervaded by "guṇas" intrinscially and by "alamkāras" extrinsically. But the moot-question is: "What are guṇas?" Vāmana, or for that matter, no Sanskrit theorist, worth his name, including Ānandavardhana and Mammatha, has defined "guṇas" satisfactorily. However, from a careful analysis of the first three kārikas of the first chapter of the first "adhikaraṇa" of काव्यालंकारसूत्रवृत्ति we gather that Vāmana's concept of "guṇas" is kallistic and aesthetic. This is so because he maintains in the very first kārikā of his work that poetry makes an appeal to us because of its association with beauty–काव्यं ग्राह्यमलंकारात्. Here the word "अलंकार" should not be taken in the sense of figures of speech like उपमा-रूपक-उत्प्रेक्षा etc. but rather in the sense of "beauty". This is quite clear from his second kārikā, namely, सौन्दर्यमलंकारः [The word "अलंकार" means "beauty"]. The matter becomes crystal-clear when in the first kārikā of the first chapter of the third "adhikaraṇa" of his poetics he defines "guṇas":

> "काव्यशोभायाः कर्तारो धर्माः गुणाः"
>
> [The factors responsible for the beauty in poetry are called gunas.]

Evidently, "guṇas" are what make poetry intrinsically and inherently beautiful and animated. But what is the role of "alamkāras" like यमक, रूपक, उपमा etc. in poetry? Vāmana declares: "तदतिशयहेतवस्त्वलंकाराः" (i.e. what make poetry extra-beautiful or extrinsically beautiful are "alamkāras".)

The word 'अतिशय' used in the above kārikā should not be taken in the sense of 'excessive' but rather in the sense of extrinsic. Thus the expression "तदतिशयहेतवः" comes to mean "the external causes of that (i.e. the beauty of poetry) are "alamkāras" or figures of speech. Admittedly, Vāmana is of the view that there are two categories of causes of poetic beauty: extrinsic and intrinsic; "alamkāras" are its extrinsic causes and "guṇas" intrinsic. This is amply clear from the two verses that Vāmana cities in the explication of the kārikā concerned. The verses run as follows:

युवतेरिव रूपमङ्गं काव्यं स्वदते शुद्धगुणं तदप्यतीव।
विहितप्रणयं निरन्तराभिः सदलंकारविकल्पकल्पनाभिः।।
यदि भवति वचश्च्युतं गुणेभ्यो वपुरिव यौवनवन्ध्यमङ्गनायाः
अपि जनदयितानि दुर्भगत्वं नियतमलंकारणानि संश्रयन्ते।।

[Poetry, having just pure guṇas only (and bereft of figures of speech) makes an appeal (to the men of taste) just as a young lady's natural appearance (even without ornaments) appeals profoundly (to the connoisseurs). (But) poetry, having beautiful figures and strange imaginings, if it is without guṇas, makes a very superficial appeal just as the body of a woman, bereft of youthfulness but covered with all kinds of beautiful and various ornaments, touches the connoisseurs only superfically for in the absence of youthfulness even most popular ornaments doubtless become tasteless and futile.]

There is hardly any doubt whatsoever that Vāmana is all for guṇas in poetry; it is guṇas that give life to poetry. Alamkāras are undoubtedly useful to the enhancing of the beauty of poetry but guṇas are inevitable to the matter and guṇas mean avoidence of all kinds of poetic flaws and cultivation of all virtues like ओज, प्रसाद, माधुर्य, अर्थव्यक्ति, कान्ति etc. at one and the same time.

If "guṇas" are central to Vāmana's literary criticism, then the scope of "guṇas" should be broad enough. And that precisely is the case. We have already seen how his definition of Rīti" as "विशिष्टा पदरचना" actually means "गुणात्मिका पदरचना" (composition of verse distingusihed by "guṇas") and the word "गुणात्मिका", it seems, includes "dhvani", "vakrokti", "aucitya" and everything else that could add to the "विशिष्टता" of पदरचना which includes diction, imagery, sentence-structure, prefix, suffix, tense, gender, number, "vākyālamkāra", "Nipāta" and all other elements of creative expression. Some hints of this are available in the way Vāmana treats of "शब्दसमय" and "शब्दशुद्धि" in the first and the second "adhyāyas" of the fifth "adhikaraṇa" of his poetics. In the first chapter of this "adhikaraṇa", in the explication of the tenth sūtra, namely विशेषणमात्रप्रयोगो विशेष्यप्रतिपत्तौ (i.e. if the qualified could be discerned clearly, the adjective alone should be used.), Vāmana cites the following line from the twelfth verse of the first canto of the epic शिशुपालवधम् by Māgha:

गिरेस्तडित्वानिव तावदुच्चकैर्जवेन पीठादुदतिष्ठदच्युतः

[Acyta or Krishna rose swiftly from his high seat (to receive Nārada) like a cloud from a mountain.]

Here the word "तडित्वान्" (literally, "possessing lightning) which is normally the adjective of the word "मेघ" (cloud) has been used without the qualified "मेघ", presumably because the latter can be easily discerned from its adjective itself. The question is: "why should Vāmana plead for the adoption of the rule concerned?" I think, Vāmana is all for brevity and would not tolerate any redundant word used in poetry–a practice followed very ritualistically by the modernists like Ezra Pound and his followers. No doubt, if some adjective or epithet can convey the desired meaning to the reader, the use of the qualified is uncalled for. This seems to have been the practice of all good poets in all languages. The American poetess–Sylvia Plath, for example, demonstrates the rule framed by Vāmana in her anthology-piece "Daddy":

Daddy, I have had to kill you
You died before I had time-
Marble-heavy, a bag full of God,
Ghastly statue, with one grey toe
Big as a Frisco seal
And a head in the freakish Atlantic
Where it pours bean green over blue.

In the above passage the word "blue" has been used; it is normally used as an adjective of the 'sky' or the 'ocean' and is followed by the term qualified by it, exemplified by expressions like 'blue sky', 'blue ocean' etc. However, Sylvia Plath has used it in her poem without its विशेष्य (i.e. the term qualified) because the reader readily realizes that it is for the water of the Atlantic ocean and thus the poetess has rightly observed poetic economy.

That Vāmana regards the doctrine of "Rīti" or "Guṇas" as quite broad is supported by the fact that the "guṇa" called "कान्ति" of his formulation, subsumes all "Rasas" (which have bright colours) such as शृंगाररस. Clearly, he is acquainted with "Rasas" but regards them as covered in what he calls कान्तिगुण. In the 15th sūtra of the second chapter of the third "adhikaraṇa" of काव्यालंकारसूत्रवृत्ति he defines कान्तिगुण as follows:

दीप्तरसत्वं कान्तिः

And in the explication (वृत्ति) of this sūtra he says: दीप्ता रसाऽशृङ्गारादयो यस्य स दीप्तरसः । तस्य भावो दीप्तरसत्वम् [That in which Rasas such as Śṛngāra etc. are effulgent is Dīptarasa. 'Dīptarasatvam' means that state (i.e. of being Dīptarasa).]

And in order to illustrate कान्तिगुण, the great theorist cities a passage from *Amaruśataka:*

प्रेयान् सायमपाकृतः सतपथं पादानतः कान्तया
द्वित्राण्येव पदानि वासभवनात् यावन्न यात्युन्मनाः।
तावत् प्रत्युत पाणिसम्पुटलसन्नीवीनितम्बं धृतो
धावित्वैव कृतप्रणामकमहो प्रेम्णो विचित्रा गतिः।।

[(Some onlooker is commenting on the behaviour of a couple:) A husband, swearing profusely while he had fallen on the feet (of his wife) on being rebuked (by the latter) in the evening, was caught up by her ladyship. When sad and woe-begone he had hardly moved out of the bed-chamber only two or three steps, (the wife) running after him with her hands grasping in its fold the string of her "sāri" slipping from her buttocks made salutations (to her husband). Oh, how strange are the ways of Love!"]

According to Vāmanācārya, the verse from *Amaruśataka*, cited above, contains कान्तिगुण because of the presence of one of the brilliant "Rasas", namely, "Śṛngārarasa" in it which is so marked in it. Clearly, Vāmana's notin of "kāntiguṇa" subsumes the "Rasas" in itself. Similarly, all kinds of "vakrokti" contemplated by Kuntaka are presumed in Vāmana's concept of "Mādhuryaguṇa" which he defines in the following words:

उक्तिवैचिञ्यं माधुर्यम् (3.2.11.)

[Cleverness of speech is (the essence of) what is called the poetic virtue known as "Mādhurya".]

There cannot be any doubt whatsoever that what Kuntaka had formulated under the head of "vakrokti" is precisely what Vāmana canveys through his concept of "Mādhyuryaguṇa". If "Mādhurya", considered as "uktivacitrya", could be equated with poetic beauty, then all "alamkāras" are the different forms of "uktivaicitrya", for, according to the great ācārya, "alamkāras" are the manifestations of beauty, nay, beauty itself– सौन्दर्यमलंकारः. Thus "alamkāras" are also subsumed in Vāmana's concept of "Mādhuryaguṇa". Evidently, Vāmana's doctrine of "Rīti", hardly distinguishable from his concept of "Guṇas", is quite broad-based and liberal, having nothing sectarian about it, taking, as it does, in its sweep all conceivable elements of poetic beauty, be it "alamkāra", "rasa", "vakrokti" or "dhvani", the last being clearly suggested in Vāmana's concept of "Vāsanīya Sūkṣmārtha" (वासनीय सूक्ष्मार्थ), expounded in काव्यालंकारसूत्रवृत्ति (3/2/10)

Changing Faces of the Concept of Rīti

The theory of Rīti was no doubt placed on the pedestal of a "sampradāya" or critical school by Vāman who is thus credited with having founded that school but the concept is very old, as old as the *Vedas*. In Ṛgveda 28.14 the word occurs in the sense of a current. In the same *Veda* the word bears the sense of the movement of thoughts and ideas, a sense which is close to Vāmana's concept of "विशिष्ट पदरचना". However, "Rīti" as a technical term has not been used in the works on the art of poetry before Vāmana though the idea of "Rīti" can be traced to the concept of 'प्रवृत्ति' enunciated in the earliest poetics of India, available today, namely, Bharata's *Nāṭyaśāstra*. In the 14th chapter of *Nāṭyaśāstra* Bharata talks of 4 "Pravṛtti's": आवन्ती, दाक्षिणात्या, पांचाली and उद्रमागधी. Bharata defines the term 'प्रवृत्ति' in the following words:

"पृथिव्यां नानादेशवेषभाषाचारवार्ताः ख्यापयतीति प्रवृत्तिः"

(नाट्यशास्त्र, 14/36 के बाद गद्यभाग)

> [(Since) this declares the various local dresses, languages, manners and habits (of different people) on the earth, it is called "Pravṛtti".]

What is 'this' in the above citation? Clearly, it refers to the depiction of traits of people, belonging to a particular part of the earth. By displyaing the typical characteristics, mores and traits of the people of a particular area, the dramatist lends authenticity and convincingness to the story treated by him in the play. All this–the peculiarities, manners of speech, way of reacting to the phenomena of the world, typical customs and beliefs, peculiar to the area concerned, is collectively called "Pravṛtti". In all probability, Vāmana derived his notion of "Rīti" from Bharata's concept of "Pravṛtti".

After Bharata, Bhāmaha is the first poetician who discusses very briefly what Bharata has called "Pravṛtti" and what Vāmana later called "Rīti" under the head of "kāvyaprakāra", presumably, without precisely stating what he has in mind. This he does in the verses 31-35 of the first

"Pariccheda" of his treatise called *Kāvyālamkāra*. The use of the words "वैदर्भ" and "गौडीय" leads us to believe that the theorist is discussing poetic styles or poetic modes although he finds the terms unsatisfactory and confusing. But it is quite clear that the concept of poetic modes–वैदर्भ and गौडीय, was in existence in the sixth century A.D.. The near contemporary of Bhāmaha, namely, Ācārya Dandī, can be credited with having described the वैदर्भ and गौडीय varieties of poetic expression as the two paths of poetry by the term "मार्ग" in the 40th kārikāa of his treatise काव्यादर्श (प्रथम परिच्छेद):

अस्त्यनेको गिरां मार्गः सूक्ष्मभेदं परस्परम्।
तत्र वैदर्भगौडीयौ वर्ण्येते प्रस्फुटान्तरौ।।

> [Numberless are the (varieties of) the path of poetic speech, having very subtle differences. Among them the two paths–वैदर्भ and गौडीय–having clear-cut differences, are being discussed (here).]

It must be placed on record that Dandī discusses the two poetic paths–वैदर्भ and गौडीय–in the course of his discourse about poetic virtues (काव्यगुण). Thus he is quite close to Vāmana whose concept of Rīti is guṇa-oriented and is on the pattern of Dandī's idea of poetic paths (मार्ग). Clearly, Dandī is virtually discussing "Rīti" in the garb of "kāvyamārga" and is at the back of Vāmana's doctrine of "Rīti".

Rudrata, author of *Kāvyālamkāra,* who flourished in the 9th century A.D. and was a little later than Vāmana, uses the term "Rīti" directly, presumably under the influence of his older contemporary but adds the Rīti "Lātīya" to the twins called "Gaurī" and "Vaidarbhī "plus "Pāncālī" recognized by Vāmana, making the total of "Rīti's" to "four". However, he does not regard "Rīti" as the soul of poetry (as Vāmana does) but he does plead for the use of "Rīti" in accordance with the "Rasa" on hand. He clearly proclaims:

वैदर्भीपांचाल्यौ प्रेयसि करुणे भयानकाद्भुतयोः।
लाटीयागौडीये रौद्रे कुर्याद् यथौचित्यम्।।

(काव्यालंकार 15/20)

> [Vaidarbhī and Pāncālī should be used in the depiction of "Preyās", "Karunā", "Bhayānaka" and "Adbhuta" sentiments and "Lātīya" and "Gaurī", properly speaking, be used in "Raudra".]

In respect of other than the above-mentioned sentiments, Rudrata holds that the poet is free to employ the Rīti that his sense of propriety demands. Thus Rudrata established a very close relationship between "Rīti" and "Rasa" and fixed the compounds or "Samāsas" as the basis of its classification.

A near-contemporary of Rudrata, Ācārya Anandavardhana, like Rudrata, uses the term "Rīti" directly and declares compounds as the basis of its classification. In this sense he seems to have been influenced by Rudrata and like Rudrata he regards the "Rīṭi's" as the handmaids of "Rasas". He uses a fresh term "संघटना" as a synonym of Rīti with a view to making the concept self-explanatory. By 'संघटना' Ānandavardhan implies the use of compounds sparingly or abundantly. And that precisely determines the classification of संघटना as Vaidarbhī, Gaudī or Pāncālī. But since "Rīti" or "Samghatanā" suggests "guṇas" which are the attributes of "Rasas", it cannot be the soul of poetry; in point of fact, "Rīti" is subsumed in suggestion or "dhvani" which alone is fit for being described as the soul of poetry. He clearly poohpoohs Vāmana in the following kārikā:

अस्फुटस्फुरितं काव्यतत्त्वमेतद्यथोदितम्।
अशक्नुवद्भिर्व्याकर्तुं रीतयः सम्प्रवर्तिताः।।

(ध्वन्यालोक 3/47)

["Rīti's" were propagated by those who were unable to expound the essence of poetry which appears to be implicit (and not explicit) as has been demonstrated.]

Ānanda's insinuation is that the concept of "Dhvani" was beyond people like Vāmana who had wrongly advocated the cause of "Rīti", giving it the status of "the soul of poetry". The fact of the matter is that "Rīti" is subsumed in "Dhvani" as is clear from the fact that 'संघटनात्मकता' or the very nature of compound-structures suggests some "guṇa" or the other and "guṇas" are the qualities of "Rasa" which is a form of असंलक्ष्यक्रमध्वनि and the soul of poetry.

After Ānandavardhana, the theorist Rājaśekhara of the 10th century, author of काव्यमीमांसा casually discusses "Rīti" in the third chapter of his poetics where he differentiates among "Vṛtti", "Pravṛtti" and "Rīti". He asserts rather boldly:

तत्र वेषविन्यासक्रमः प्रवृत्तिः, विलासविन्यासक्रमो वृत्ति, वचनविन्यासक्रमो रीतिः।

["Pravṛtti" refers to the way people dress up, "vṛtti" refers to the way they decorate themselves and "Rīti" refers to the way they give expression to their thoughts and ideas.]

Rājaśekhara recognizes 4 "Rītis" without naming them in the third chapter, presumably having "Gaudī", "Vaidarbhi", "Pāncālī" and "Lātīyā" in mind but in the seventh chapter of *Kāvyamīmānsā* he refers to three "Rītis" of human speech–Vaidarbhī, "Gaudī", and Pāncālī and discusses their various deformations or "kāku":

वैदर्भी, गौडीया, पाञ्चाली चेति रीतयस्तिस्रः।
आसु च साक्षान्निवसति सरस्वती तेन लक्ष्यन्ते।।

[Vaidarbhī, Gaudīyā and Pāncālī–these are the three styles ("Rītis) of poetry in which Saraswatī, the goddess of learning virtually lives and through that cause these styles are discerned.]

However, it must be recorded here that Rājaśekhara mentions several forms of poetic speech-"Vaibudha" or of the gods, "Vaidyādhara" or of the demigods called Vidyādharas, Gāndharva or of the Gandharvas, another class of demigods and "Yoginīgata" or belonging to the female Yogis. Human speech has been called by him "Vaiṣṇava speech". The three "Rītis" are the forms of human or "Vaiṣṇava" speech. He not only mentions the forms of speech other than human but also gives illustrations of them all. But Rājaśekhara does not regard "Rīti" as the soul of poetry. In the third chapter of his *Kāvyamīmānsā*, he clearly declares "Rasa" as the soul of poetry and thus indirectly rejects Vamana's view that "Rīti" is the soul of poetry.

The next theorist who discusses "Rīti" is ācārya Kuntaka, author of the critical text called *Vakroktijīvita.* Kuntaka flourished in the 10th century (latter half). In the first chapter (unmeṣa) of his poetics, Kuntaka discusses "Rīti" by name although his own term for the concept is "Mārga" or path. The prose-passage, after kārikā no. 24 discusses the three "Rītis". Kuntaka opposes the naming of poetic styles after certain places and their hierarchy, too. The nature of the poet and the poetry concerned should be the sole criterion of the style to be assigned. Thus the poets the world over could be classified broadly under three heads: सुकुमारमार्ग, विचित्रमार्ग and मध्यममार्ग. Indeed, Kuntaka's observations are quite reasonable and far ahead of Vāmana and Dandī.

The 11th century theorist king Bhoja of Dhārā discussed the concept of "Rīti" under the heads of प्रस्थान, पन्थ, मार्ग and रीति. He increased the number of "Rītis" from 4 to 6 by including आवन्तिक and मागधी in the traditional list of four. However, he has nothing fresh to say on the subject. "Guṇas" and compound expressions (i.e. समास) are the basis of the differentiations among the six "Rītis" of his formulation.

The later theorists such as Mammatha and Vishvanāth down to Panditaraj Jagannathā make very casual remarks on "Rīti" without any fresh views to offer on the subject. Thus "Rīti" emerged as a means of "Rasa-realization" and lost its status as the soul of poetry that Vāmana had allotted to it.

Are there any Parallel Concepts of Riti in the West?

It would be very interesting to explore the presence of the critical concepts in the West to parallel the Sanskrit concept of "Rīti". It is really a matter of pleasant surprise that ancient Greek literature has a twofold division of literary style called "Attic" and "Doric" or "Dorian" to parallel the Sanskrit styles called "Vaidarbhī" and "Gaudī", named after the people of the areas concerned. Just as the region called Vidarbha, now in Mahārāṣtra, was regarded in ancient India as a place having achieved the acme of refinement and elegance and thus having become the characteric of the highest and most excellent kind of poetic expression, the Greek region called Attica in the east central part of the country, including Athens, gave rise to Attic prose style, regarded as the purest Greek prose, marked by sweetness, good sense and candour plus intellectual sharpness. Thus "Vaidarbhī" and "Attic" are the two epithets, signifying more or less the same qualities of literary style in the Eastern and Western traditions respectively. The antonyms of these terms are "Gaudī" in Sanskrit and "Doric" or "Dorian" in Greek. The term "Gaudī" comes from Gauda-desha in ancient India, known for its harshness and lack of refinement of all sorts, the antithesis of all that Vidarbha stood for. And precisely that is the case with the word "Doric" or "Dorian", derived from the region of Greece called "Doris", located between Mt. Parnassus and Mt. Oeta, known for the rustic nature of its people, and hence giving rise to a literary style, marked by a language–awkward, uncouth and unpolished. Thus the Sanskrit "Gaudi" and the Greek "Doric" are quite close to each other.

So far as the question of the soul-status of "Rīti", considered as the order and arrangment of word-groups (विशिष्टा पदसंघटना), is considered, its echoes in Western Criticism can be traced. Aristotle's well-known declaration that "Action" or "Plot" is the soul of Tragedy can very easily be cited in the vindication of Vāmana's point-of-view for "Plot" precisely means the arrangement and ordering of events sequentially. Subtitute the word "Padas" in place of "Events" and realize the significance of what Vāmana says on the role of "Rīti" in the life of poetry. Coming a little closer in respect of time, we can find some support to Vāmana's theory in Coleridge's differentiation between prose and poetry in his *Table Talk* dated 12 July 1827:

Prose / Words in their best order

Poetry / the best words in the best order

Evidently, in the view of Coleridge, the essence or soul of poetry lies in the best ordering of the best words, that is to say, in what Vāmana calls "रीति" or "विशिष्टा पदरचना".

The concept of "Dolce Stil Nuovo" (New Sweet Style) is also close to the concept of "Rīti". The concept of "Dolce Stil Nuovo" was enunciated by Dante, the greatest poet of Italy in the 14th century. Expounding that concept, Professor Lewis H. Gordon, who was a professor of Italian and French at Brown University, U.S.A., observes: "The term was used by Dante, "Purgatory", 24.57, where it is spoken by the poet Bonagiunta Orbicciani of Lucca. Dante's term has considerable validity. The "sweetness" of his style is attained, analysts have discovered, through his *careful selection of words of pleasurable sound and their ordering*". [Vide the entry on "Dolce Stil Nuovo" by him in *Princeton Encyclopedia of Poetry and Poetics* ed. Alex Preminger, Princeton, New Jersey, Princeton University Press, 1965 edition, p. 198.]. The italisized portion of this statement suggests the idea of "Rīti". Thus it is clear that Vāmana's theory of Rīti is quite reasonable and finds its confirmation in Western criticism (theory as well as practice).

Is the Theory of Rīti Universally Applicable?

It is true that at the hands of Ānandavardhana and his followers, the Doctrine of Rīti found a big jolt and "Rīti" came to be regarded as a handmaid of "Rasa", having lost its position as the soul of poetry, i.e., from the position of supreme importance in poetry. However, to my mind, Vāmana had correctly pinpointed the element that assures any writing the status of poetry–big or small, dramatic or non-dramatic, prose or verse. The element that he discerned as linking all imaginative writing, broadly called poetry, he designated as Rīti. We have to see now whether what he called "Rīti" is a critically viable theory, applicable to all imaginative writings world over. I think that if we could leave aside all discourse regarding the three categories of "Rīti" which are Sanskrit-specific and concentrate on the basic idea of the term, the theory will be found to be of universal significance. But the question is: What is the basic idea or inner meaning of "Rīti"? I think the real meaning that Vāmana wanted to convey through the term "Rīti" was the "inevitability" and "proper order" plus "full functionality" of each linguistic element employed by the poet in his composition. If each item in the poet's composition could justify itself by being functional and also its order of placement in the work, whether it is a novel, a short-story, a lyric, a play or even an epic, then clearly the work abides by the doctrine of Rīti. In this inevitability and order and functionality lies the true being of the composition–its soul virtually–its artistry, its aesthetic beauty, its "Saundarya". "विशिष्टा पदरचना रीतिः" "सौन्दर्यमलंकारः" and "रीतिरात्मा काव्यस्य"–all these axioms of Vāmana support the above interpretation of "Rīti". This view of the term makes it really broad and capable of universal application for it subsumes Aristotle's ideas of plot, unity, and organic wholeness of a work of art, each of which involves the question of order and functionality. A composition that claims to have "Rīti" must satisfy the following questions: 1. How is it that it has only that number of sections that are there in it? 2. Why has the poet begun and ended the composition concerned in the manner in which it begins and ends? 3. Why does the poet use a particular category of words and not other than what is there in the poem? 4. Can the meaning of the poem remain unaffected even if the synonyms of the significant words in the poem are used in place of the words that the poet has chosen to use? 5. Why does the poet employ the figures of speech that are there in the poem? 6. Will not the change in the order of the sections of the poem affect the meaning? Clearly, the doctrine of "Rīti" is a thoroughly formalist and structuralist approach to imaginative writing and can be put to practical use for critical evaluation of literature.

Dhvani-Sampradāya

Poetry expresses itself through words and words have meanings but meanings have several levels. In our daily life, too, we use words which instantly tell us certain facts, ideas or things. This is called the literal sense or the dictionary meaning of the words which the common speaker of the language concerned knows and understands, the moment he hears those words uttered by his fellow-beings. To the query of a student, 'Is *Veṇīsamhāra* available?', the book-seller instantly brings out Bhattanārāyaṇa's eminent play annotated or unannotated because the word "Veṇīsaṁhāra" is understood by him as the name of a famous play of the great dramatist Bhattanāryaṇa, having the same title. Here, the words, used in the statement concerned, by and large, bear their literal, conventional or dictionary meaning, are known to the generality of mankind and are technically called "Vācaka śabdas" that convey

"Vācyarthas" or conventional or dictionary meanings. Our science-books, "Śāstras" or what De Quincey, the 19th century English prose-writer, called "books of knowledge" use "vācaka śabdas" for their purpose, for, the statements made in these books are matter-of-fact, having nothing evocative or emotional about them. But poetry, because, by its very nature, is emotional, it cannot afford to remain contented with "Vācaka Śabdas;" it must needs employ words other than "Vācaka" if it wants to touch the hearts of its readers; it must depend on "Lakṣanika Śabdas" and "Vyanjaka Śabdas", leaving "Vācaka Śabdas" for the use of the "Śastras". This is so because its statements are found to be arch, arcane and out of the way, a little illusive and untangible owing to the fact that it (i.e. poetry) is transcendental and extra-ordinary in its appeal. Once we are able to realize this fact, we will readily agree that it cannot achieve its ideal by remaining contented with words that have dictionary or commonly accepted meanings; it must, of necessity, have recourse to words that take the readers beyond their literal sense. Poems, worth their names, should be able to convey to us what remains unstated, what is beyond the layman's reach. Poems, possessing this quality, are called "Dhvani Kāvya" (poetry of suggestion) and the critical school that looks for the unstated and the suggested in true poetry is called the "Dhvani" school or "Dhvani Sampradāya", founded by ācārya Ānanda-Vardhana of Kashmir, the court-poet of king Avantivarmā of the latter half of the ninth Century A.D.. That Ānandavardhana was in the court of Avantivarmā is evidenced by the following verse of Kalhaṇa's *Rājatarangiṇī:*

मुक्ताकणः शिवस्वामी कविरानन्दवर्द्धनः ।
प्रथां रत्नाकरश्चागात् साम्राज्येऽवन्तिवर्मणः ।। 5/4 ।।

[In the reign of Avantivarmā poets like Muktākaṇa, Śivaswāmī, Ānandavardhana and Ratnākara achieved pinnacle of fame.]

Since King Avantivarmā ruled over Kashmir from 855 A.D. to 883 A.D., Ācārya Ānandavardhana can be safely placed in the latter half of the ninth century A.D..

Before the appearance of Ānandavardhana on the critical scene of Sanskrit, leaving aside Bharata who had emphasized the importance of "Rasa" in poetry, especially dramatic poetry, Sanskrit critics like Bhāmaha, Dandī, Vāmana, Udbhata etc. had expressed their preoccupation with the external features of poetry and had ignored its inner life. To Ānanda goes the credit of having brought to the fore the element that pervades the entire body of poetry like the soul that sustains and controls the entire human frame called the body. According to Ānanda, that element is "Dhvani" which is the mastermind of the entire poetic creation, prevailing in all its components and making them animated. He declared: 'काव्यस्यात्मा ध्वनिः' [the soul of poetry resides in "Dhvani"]. But the question is 'What is Dhvani?'. The answer is that the term has been taken from the doctrine of "Sphota" propounded by grammarians like Patanjalī and Bhartṛhari who regard "Sphota" and "Dhvani" as synonyms. Thus, if we want to realize the true meaning of "Dhvani", we must be clear about the doctrine of "Sphota". According to grammarians, a word yields its meaning only after each of its letters has been uttered or sounded. In the process, the individual letters go on dying out until the last is uttered and that is the culmination of the previous letters, which leave their impressions on the succeeding letters and thus reveal the eternal, undying form of the word, technically called "Sphota". In point of fact, "sphota" is that inherent power of words which reveals their true meanings after all the particles of the words have been uttered, the last particle inhering the impressions left by the previous particles. For example, the Sanskrit word 'कमल' consists of six particles: क्+अ+म्+अ+ल्+अ. The meaning of the word (i.e. a flower called 'Lotus' in English) is grasped by the listener only when all the individual particles, ending with the last 'अ', have been uttered, giving rise in the mind of the listener the idea of lotus (which is eternally present there) which is the 'Sphota'–form of the word 'कमल'–its suggested sense. It is said that the moment an individual particle of a given word is uttered, it gets lost. Then the question arises as to how the listener makes out the sense of the word. The answer is that the idea of each word is in the mind of the listener in the form of the 'sphota' of that word and that flashes on the listener's mind on account of the mysterious power of the word, also called 'sphota', inhering in each particle of the word, manifested in the sound of the last particle of the word in a special way. Since grammarians have used the word "Dhvani" in certain places, as a synonym of 'Sphota' rather analogically, the literary critics like Anandavardhana felt encouraged to adopt the word "Dhvani" in poetics to convey the idea of "sphota". Their argument is that just as the individually uttered particles of a given word fail to convey to the listener the idea of the word, the literal sense (वाच्यार्थ) of a given poetic piece can never lead us to its inner and true sense and just as the power called 'sphota' alone, inhering in the individual particles of the word, leads us to the "sphota" or true form of the word, revealing its meaning, the power of words called 'Dhvani' or 'Vyanjanā' alone can enable the reader to get to the core meaning of the piece concerned, the word-powers known as "Abhidhā" and "Lakṣanā" being inadequate for the purpose.

The word "Dhvani" is formed from the root √ध्वन् by adding the suffix 'इ' to it, meaning 'voice'. The ancient grammarians, as has been shown above, have used the word in the sense of the sound that reveals the "Sphota" or the true meaning and nature of that word. Ācārya Mammatha's explication of the term is very pertinent in this connection:

ध्वनति स्फोटं व्यनक्ति इति ध्वनिः। ध्वनति
व्यंग्यार्थं प्रकाशयति इति ध्वनिः।।
(काव्यप्रकाश, प्रथम उल्लास)

["Dhvani" is that which suggests "Sphota". "Dhvani" is that which illuminates the suggested sense.]

It must be noted that the word "Dhvani" in poetics has been subjected to numerous nuances, sometimes numbering 5:

1-2. ध्वनति ध्वनयति वा यः स ध्वनिः व्यञ्जकः शब्दः अर्थश्च ध्वनिः। ["Dhvani" is that suggestive word or meaning which sounds (the unsaid or unstated).

3. ध्वन्यते इति ध्वनिः व्यंग्यरसादिरलंकारः वस्तु च ध्वनिः [The suggested "Rasa" "Alamkāra" and "Vastu" are "Dhvani" as these are all suggested (and not stated).]

4. ध्वन्यते अनेनेति ध्वनिः शब्दार्थयोर्व्यञ्जनाव्यापारो ध्वनिः [The power to suggest something inhering in words and their senses, is "Dhvani" because it is owing to that power that the act of suggestion is accomplished.]

5. ध्वन्यतेऽस्मिन् इति ध्वनिः काव्यम् ["Dhvani" is that poem in which something gets suggested.]

Clearly, the concept of "Dhvani" is very broad and comprehensive, emcompassing everything pertaining to poetry from words and their meanings to the composition as a whole quite like the soul that permeates all aspects of human personality, from the individual limbs to the entire bodily frame, including mind, intelligence and brain. That is why Ānandavardhana calls it the soul of poetry. Just as the quality of the soul is reflected on the face and the over-all grace of the person concerned, the existence of "Dhvani" makes its presence felt without being clearly pinpointed and localized in the poems of great poets. Ānanda states very beautifully:

प्रतीयमानं पुनरन्यदेव वस्त्वस्ति वाणीषु महाकवीनाम्।
यत्तत्प्रसिद्धावयवातिरिक्तं विभाति लावण्यमिवाङ्गनासु।।

(ध्वन्यालोक, प्रथम उद्योत, 4)

[The "Pratīyamana" or "Dhvani" or "Suggestion" is something inexpressible in the speeches of great poets that is quite like the loveliness in well-formed ladies which is something beyond their famous limbs (like eyes, hair, breasts, neck, countenance etc.]

Dhvani, in point of fact, resembles the skylark of the English romantic poet P.B. Shelley, who sings about the bird's unfathomable mystery:

What thou art we know not;
What is most like thee?
From rainbow clouds there flow not
Drops so bright to see,
As from thy presence showers a rain of melody.
X X X X X X
Sound of vernal showers
On the twinkling grass,
Rain-awakened flowers,
All that ever was
Joyous, and clear, and fresh, thy music doth surpass.

The above verses of Shelley can be usefully employed to bring home to a common reader the nature and power of poetry called "Dhvani" which is beyond all analysis and is inexpressible. Duṣyanta in Kālidāsa's *Abhigyānśākuntalam* on seeing his lady-love for the second time in the play, utters the following line:

'अये लब्धं नेत्रनिर्वाणम्' [Oh, I have got the "nirvāṇa" of the eyes.]

The line is regarded as an excellent example of "Dhvani"; it is so because it suggests the idea of the speaker's heightened experience of true beauty–his ecstatic vision of Śakuntalā whose beauty was for his eyes the greatest bliss possible. To a lay reader, the line means: 'I, Duṣyanta, have achieved the state of "Nirvaṇ" for my eyes.' This literal meaning of the line does not quench the curiosity of the reader. But a sensitive reader, acquainted with the concept of "Nirvaṇa" or the beatific spiritual condition attained by the extinction of desires, instantly interprets the expression "नेत्रनिर्वाणम्" in terms of the cessation of Duṣyanta's quest for beauty after sighting Śakuntala, the highest form of beauty conceivable, for, after seeing Śakuntalā, there remains for Duṣyanta no need to move further in his search for beauty since he has come across the highest form of beauty where all possible beauties culminate, for, Sakuntalā is the *Ultima Thule* of beauty. Without saying all this in so many words, Kālidāsa has made Duṣyanta suggest this view of the beauty of Śakuntalā through the use of the expression "नेत्रनिर्वाणम्" which emerges as highly suggestive, for the essence of Suggestion or "Dhvani" lies in saying the unstated whether it is thought, emotion or figure of speech. We can take up an English example of "Dhvani". Consider the following lines from Robert Browning's famous dramatic monologue entitled "My Last Ducless":

> Nay, we'all go
> Together down, Sir! Notice Neptune, though,
> Taming a sea-horse, thought a rarity,
> Which Claus of Innsbruck cast in bronze for me!

The verses, cited above, are the concluding lines of "My Last Duchess" and have been addressed to the ambassador of the Count of Tyrol, sent to the Duke of Ferrara, to negotiate the marriage of the Count's daughter with the Duke. The speaker is the Duke of Ferrara himself who has taken the envoy upstairs for having a look at the painting of his last Duchess made (according to him), by a famous Italian painter Fra Pandolf, admired by the Duke, out of proportion. After having had a visual feast of the said painting, the Duke is coming downstairs with the Count's envoy to meet the rest of the party of the envoy, awaiting their arrival downstairs. While coming down from the picturegallery upstairs, the Duke calls the attention of the envoy to a sculpture in bronze, showing the sea-god Neptune, taming a sea-horse. Ākording to the Duke, this sculpture is by Claus of Innsbruck and is one of the rare art-works in the world. The Duke addresses the envoy, much junior to himself in social hierarchy, as "Sir", the term, normally used by juniors for their seniors. Moreover, the name of the sculptor (i.e. Claus of Innsbruck) is a ficticious one for Claus of Innsbruck is not to be found in any list of painters/sculptors in the history of European Art. But what do the lines, quoted above, actually come to? The paraphrase of the passage, given above, does not appear to be very interasting. However, when we read the passage sensitively, the suggested sense of the passage is found to be enlivening and illuminating. When we read the passage between the lines, we come to know a lot about the character of the speaker (i.e. the Duke of Ferrara Alfonso II, belonging to the House of Este). His address to the envoy as "Sir", against the normal practice, leads us to believe that he is trying to win the heart of the envoy by means of his assumed humility so that the Count of Tyrol could be persuaded by the envoy to give the Duke the highest dowry in the event of his accepting the hand of the daughter or niece of the Count. Thus there is a selfish purpose behind the Duke's seeming but deceitful humility and that makes him quite ignoble. When the Duke calls the attention of the envoy to the sculpture, depicting Neptune, taming a sea-horse, we come to know of some other traits of his personality. In the first place, he wants to pass for an owner of rare artefacts. He asks the envoy not to bother about what the sculptor has depicted (i.e. Neptune taming a sea-horse) but rather to note the fact that the sculpture is a rare piece, hardly to be found elsewhere and it is by no less an artist than Claus of Innsbruck, a great name indeed in sculpture. Since we know it for a fact that Claus of Innsbruck is a fictitious name, we infer that the Duke is a bluff who wants to impress with his great love for art the envoy of the Count through the use of a high-sounding name. Perhaps he takes the envoy to be a man with no knowledge of the tradition of European art and therefore easy to be impressed by names-dropping. And though apparently the Duke asks the envoy not to pay much attention to the subject of the sculpture but to its execution and rarity, he unconsciously wants to bring home to the envoy that the count's niece would be tamed by him–she would not be allowed to lead a life of her own choice. The emphasis on the word 'me', and the mark of exclamation after it, are intended to highlight the Duke's sense of self-pride, implying that Claus of Innsbruck does not make sculptures for all and sundry but rather for a select few like himself, known for their power and pelf. Clearly, the "vyangyārtha" (i.e. the suggested meaning) of the passage makes it very powerful by revealing the real traits of the Duke's personality–his greed, his showiness, his tyrannical behaviour, his deceitfulness, his ostentation and his over-consciousness of his high status. And this is beyond the power of the literal meaning of the passage–its "vācyārtha". The passage is evidently an example of "Dhvani-Kāvya" for, what is unstated here is far more important than what is openly stated.

The concept of "Dhvani" as expounded by Ānandavardhanācārya is very broad and comprehensive. According to him, all elements of poetry—रस, छन्द, अलंकार, गुण, रीति, वक्रोक्ति etc.–come within the perview of "Dhvani", for the best forms of these, without exception, are obtained in their suggested manifestations, and not in their straight and normally accepted expressions. Not only these, but other items of poetry also–case-endings, tense, voice, number, prefix, suffix, comma, full-stop and even exclamations–are covered in "Dhvani" because even these can be suggestive of something unsaid and unstated. In the third "Udyota" of *Dhvanyāloka* Ānanda cites the following verse from Kālidāsa's *Megadūtam* (Uttaramegha) to illustrate how सुबन्त's (i.e. noun-forms in various cases and numbers) can be "vyanjakas" (suggestors) in the explantory portion of the kārikā no. 72:

'तालैः शिञ्जावलयसुभगैः कान्तया नर्तितो मे,
यामध्यास्ते दिवसविगमे नीलकण्ठः सुहृद् वः ।'
'तन्मध्ये च स्फटिकफलका काञ्चनी वासयष्टिः
मूले बद्धा मणिभिरनतिप्रौढवंशप्रकाशैः ।

(उत्तरमेघ 18)

[(The Yakṣa is providing identification-marks of his residence in Alakāpurī to the Cloud, his messanger to his wife in the Himalayan city:) "(on the sport-mountain (क्रीडाशैल) by the side of the pond in front of my house between the two trees of 'Raktāśoka and 'Kesara') there is a perch-stick of gold with a plank of marbles and its base is studded with gems, shining green like young bamboos. (On this perch-stick) at the close of the day perches thy friend, the blue-necked (i.e. the peacock) being made to dance by my wife (the Yakṣiṇī) by means of beating times (ताल) made sweeter by the melodies of her bracelets.]

In the above verse of *Meghadūta,* Kālidāsa has used the word तालैः (beating times), having a plural number. The question is: 'Does this plural form serve any purpose?' For common readers there is no significance attached to the plural form of the word; its singular form would have done the self–same purpose. However, a sensitive reader will realize the significance of the word "तालैः" which leads him to believe that the Yaksiṇī is well-versed in music, mastered, as she has, various "tāla-layas". And this detail regarding the musical expertise of the Yakṣiṇī intesifies the Yakṣa's pangṣ of separation from his fully accomplished sweet-heart. Thus the word "तालैः" proves to be highly suggestive; it makes the whole verse an example of "Dhvani-Kāvya".

Let us take an English example to illustrate the point raised above. The eighth stanza of Keats's "La Belle Dame Sans Merci" reads as follows.

"She took me to her elfin grot,
And there she wept and sighed full sore;
And there I shut her wild, wild eyes
With kisses four.

The last word, namely, 'four', used in the stanza, just quoted, is highly remarkable. The question is: "Is the word to be taken literally in the sense of the number 'Four'? Or does the word signify something else?" The answer is that the word cannot be taken in its literal sense of the number 'Four' because the speaker of the lines is a romantic lover, defying all kinds of limitations. How can one who, while he set his lady-love on his pacing steed, had nothing else seen all day long (Vide stanza 6), be expected to restrict himself to the number 'Four' while he was kissing his sweet heart? Clearly, 'Four' here stands for "countless" or "numberless" and suggests that the Knight-at-arms went on kissing his beautiful beloved beyond all counting. The number 'Four' is suggestive of perfection. In India Hindus imagined 'Four' arms of Lord Vishnu, giver of the fruits of all "purusārthas" conceivable. Indeed, "Four" is the universally accepted number of completeness and perfection, covering the immensity of life–infancy, boyhood/girlhood, youth and old age. Thus the word 'Four' in Keats's poem suggests completeness of kissing indulged in by the Knight-at-arms just as the expression "ten thousand" in the second stanza of Wordsworth's poem "I Wandered Lonely as a Cloud", also called "Daffodils" suggests the numberlessness of the flowers Wordswooth had seen during his walk, described in the poem–the expression, suggesting the enormity of the crowd of the daffodils that had surprised him with joy; "ten thousands", taken in its literal sense, will deprive the poem of its true beauty that lies in suggestion and not exactitude. In the opening verse of the "Puruṣasūkta" in the tenth "Mandala" of the *Ṛgveda*, for example, the word "सहस्त्रशीर्षा" should not be taken as meaning "thousand-headed". used for the "Priemal Man" considered as the universal society incarnate; the term "सहस्त्र" has to be interpreted as meaning "having the infinitude of heads". If the literal sense of the word is taken, the whole beauty of the description will disappear.

We have maintained that any member of a poetic statement can have "dhvani". In the stanza from Keats's "La Belle Dama sans Merci', cited above, apart from the word 'Four', there are other words and expressions, having the power of suggestion. The word 'and', used thrice in the stanza, for example, is quite remarkable. Literally, it denotes the piling up of activities of the lady of the poem. But it is also suggestive of the endlessness of the arrangements made for a successful and satisfying love-making, known naturally to lovers of both sexes. Similarly, the word 'wild'. used twice for the eyes of the lady, is equally very suggestive, especially in its repetition. The word literally means "belonging to the jungle and therefore uncultivated and untamed and uncontrollable". However, the suggested sense of the word is "lacking restraint or prudence–genuinely and innocently loving" The eyes of the lady, in the view of the Knight-at-arms, were full of innocent and genuine feeling of love, unspoilt by prudence or selfishness. And this "vyangyārtha" of the word is for more beautiful than its "vacyārtha". But what is the significance the word's repetition? We can say that since the eyes were two, the lover has used the word twice–one for each eye. But a better reading of the repetition is that the eyes were extremely 'wild' in the sense explained just now; the repetition brings into limelight the intensity of the feeling of the Knight at-arms for the eyes of his sweetheart–excessively and intensely loving, without any thought of loss or gain. It must be placed on record that the suggested sense does not occur to the literal-minded, common reader; it flashes on the minds of sensitive readers of refined taste and knowledge. Ānandavardhana, naturally, proclaims:

शब्दार्थशासनज्ञानमात्रेणैव न वेद्यते।
वेद्यते स तु काव्यार्थतत्त्वज्ञैरेव केवलम्।।

(ध्वन्यालोक, प्रथम उद्योत, 7)

[The extraordinary suggested sense (व्यंग्यार्थ) cannot be grasped by a mere knowledge of words provided in grammar-books and dictionaries; it can be grasped only by the knowers of the essence of the meaning of poetry.]

Ordinary literal sense of poetry is, no doubt, for the lay readers whereas the suggested sense called "ध्वन्यार्थ" or "व्यंग्यार्थ" is the privileged possession of the imaginative and insightful readers who are persons of taste and are trained in the art and craft of poetry.

The Definition of "Dhvanikāvya" Provided by Ānandavardhana:–

It is clear from what has been said above that the theory of "Dhvani" attaches the greatest value in poetry to what is unstated and implied–to all that is beyond the stated. Naturally, Ānanda defines "Dhvanikāvya" in the 13th kārikā of the first "udyota" of *Dhvanyāloka* in the following words:

यत्रार्थः शब्दो वा तमर्थमुपसर्जनीकृतस्वार्थौ
व्यङ्क्तः काव्यविशेषः स ध्वनिरिति सूरिभिः कथितः।।

[Where the literal sense or the literal-sense-denoting word, having subordinated itself or its meaning, suggests, through the power of vyanjanā the extraordinary (and charming) meaning, the poetry is called by the learned "Dhvanikāvya".]

Clearly, "Dhvani" exists in poetry where the literal sense–whether in the form of thought, figure of speech or sentiment–becomes less important and some other thought, figure of speech or sentiment is suggested through the power of "vyanjanā". Thus the prerequisites of "Dhvani" in poetry are: 1. the operation of the verbal power called "vyanjanā"; 2. the suborndination of the literal sense, stated "Rasa" or figure of speech used, to some extraordinarily charming thought, sentiment or figure of speech. It must be placed here on record that in case the suggested sense is less important or less charming than the literal sense, there would be no Dhvani-Kāvya; it would be another category of poetry called "Guṇībhutavyangya" (गुणीभूतव्यंग्य काव्य). For example, let us consider the following famous verse quoted by Anandavardhana in his *Dhvānyālokā;*

अनुरागवती सन्ध्या दिवसस्तत्पुरःसरः ।
अहो दैवगतिः कीदृक् तथापि न समागमः ।।

[The evening is full of redness/love and the day is in front of her. But Ah! what a strange way of Destiny! Despite all this, their union is not taking place!]

In the verse, under consideration, we have a description of the Evening, conceived as a beloved who has her lover in the form of the Day. The Evening, though full of redness [or love for her lover (i.e. the Day)] is not able to get united (in coupulation) with the Day who, in his turn, is favourably inclined to her, though. That is the strange way of Destiny. In point of fact, the description is that of a moment when the sun is quite visible and the night has not set in, allowing the Evening to remain reddened all over and thus averting Twilight (i.e. the union of the Day with the Evening). From the description, given in the verse, we have the suggestion of a couple whose love-making is hampered by the presence of elders. The latter thought (वस्तु) emerges from the description, though it is no where stated in the verse. However, the verse cannot be called an example of "Dhvanikāvya", though there is some "vyangyārtha" present here. This is so because the "vācyārtha" (i.e. the literal sense) of the verse is far more charming than the suggested sense; there are two figures of speech, involved in the "vācyārtha", namely, "Samāsokti" and "Viśeṣokti". That being the case, the verse is an example of "गुणीभूतव्यंग्यकाव्य" rather than of ध्वनिकाव्य. The figure समासोक्ति is there on account of the words

"अनुरागवती" and "पुरःसरः"–both of which bear two meanings. The first word applies to the Evening considered as a natural phenomenon through its literal sense of "full of redness"; it also applies to the Evening considered as a bride through the word's second sense, namely, "full of love". Similarly, the word "पुरःसरः" bears two senses: one literal and the other metaphoric. The literal sense of the word is "standing in front of" and is for the Day, considered as a natural phenomenon. The metaphoric sense of the word is "obedient or favourably inclined" and applies to the Day considered as the suggested lover of the Evening. Clearly, both the words are 'श्लिष्ट' (i.e. have puns) and are used as epithets and that is the essence of the figure called "समासोक्ति". The verse also contains the figure called "विशेषोक्ति" because of the lack of desired action in it inspite of the presence of the conditions required for the fruition of the action. The use of the simultaneous use of the two figures makes the verse quite beautiful and naturally its "Vyangyārtha" remains quite inferior to its "Vācyārtha", making it miss the mark of "Dhvani-Kāvya".

Thus, it follows that there cannot be "Dhvani" in poetry if the "vācyārtha" is far more charming than the "vyangyārtha" (i.e. the suggested sense); the superiority of the "vyangyārtha" to the vacyārtha" is, beyond doubt, the first prerequisite of "Dhvani Kāvya" no matter whether it is of words or of sense: "वाच्यार्थशायिनि व्यंग्ये ध्वनिस्तद् काव्यमुत्तमम्" [That is first rate poetry called "Dhvani" where "Vyangyārtha" overpowers Vācyārtha] as Ācārya Vishvanātha puts it succinctly in साहित्यदर्पण।

Kinds of "Dhvani"

Indian mind usually indulges in hair-splitting and the subject of "Dhvani" is no exception to this. The followers of the school talk about 10455 varieties of "Dhvani". However, the three basic kinds called वस्तुध्वनि, अलंकारध्वनि and रसध्वनि will be discussed here as these are broad and comprehensible, fit for universal application. The first (i.e. Vastudhvani) occurs where some idea or thought is suggested which is far more charming than the "vācyārtha" or plain sense; the suggested sense is determined by reading the poem between the lines in the light of the nature of the speaker, the addressee or the particular situation in which the statement has been made. Let us take up the following verse in Prākṛta which is followed by its Sanskrit version:

कस्स वण होइ रोसो दट्ठूण पिआए सव्वणं अहरम्।
सभमरपउमग्धाइणि! वारिअवामे! सहसु एह्निम्।।

कस्य वा न भवति रोषो दृष्ट्वा प्रियायाः सव्रणमधरम्।
सभ्रमरपद्माघ्रायिणि! वारितवामे! सहस्वेदानीम्।।

[(Some female friend of some lady whose lips have the marks of the tooth-bites, is addressing her friend (i.e. the lady concerned)]: "O smeller of the lotus having bees! O woman who hadst been restrained (by me) from wrong act! now forbear the wrath of thy husband! Which husband (in the world) would not take ill on seeing his wife's injured lips?"]

Apparently, the speaker in the verse is rebuking her friend (i.e. the lady at issue) of wilfully smelling lotuses having bees inside despite her having been restrained repeatedly by her (i.e. the speaker) from her foolish act. But from the reading of the verse between the lines, we come to know that the speaker's intention is not to rebuke the lady but rather to lead the lady's husband (who is clearly within the hearing of the words uttered by the speaker) to believe that the injury-marks on the lady's lips are not the result of her dalliance with her paramour but of the beebites, caused by her foolish act of smelling lotuses, having bees inside. Thus the intention of the speaker is to save her friend from being subjected to punishment by her husband who is very likely to conclude that the injury-marks on the lips of the lady are those of some paramour's tooth-bites. Thus the plain and straight meaning of the verse is the rebuking of the lady by her female friend (i.e. the speaker of the verse) but the suggested sense is her attempt at beguiling the husband of the lady by means of her own concocted story of the bee-bites caused by the lady's habit of smelling lotuses, having bees inside, in total disregard of the speaker's warning to the lady against smelling lotuses with bees inside. The real suggested intention of the speaker is to save her friend from her embarrassing situation rather than the rebuking of the lady, the vācyārtha of the verse. No doubt, the suggested intention is far more charming and fascinating than the plain, apparent meaning of the verse. Clearly, the Prākṛta verse is an example of "Vastu-Dhvani". Yet another example of "Vastu-Dhvani" is the following verse from *Amaruśatakam:*

निःशेषच्युतचन्दनं स्तनतटं निमृष्टरागोऽधरः,
नेत्रे दूरमनञ्जने पुलकिता तन्वी तवेयं तनुः।
मिथ्यावादिनि दूति बान्धवजनस्याज्ञातपीडागमे!
वापीं स्नातुमितो गताऽसि न पुनस्तस्याधमस्यान्तिकम्।।

[Some heroine, expert in the art of love, is addressing her female friend, who had been sent by her to convey her secret message to her lover but who has come to report that the lady's man could not be contacted, he being not at his home): "O lie-telling female messanger! O woman, unaware of the pain descending on thy close associates (owing to thy misconduct)! thou hadst gone hitherfrom to the pond for a bath certainly, and not to the residence of that wicked fellow (for) I can clearly see that the foreground of thy breasts has its sandal-paste completely removed; thy lower lip has its redness wiped out; both of thy eyes have their corners without collyrium or black pigment and thy frail frame is full of horripilation.]

It is clear from the paraphrase of the verse, given above, that the female messanger, who had been sent by the heroine of the piece to bring her lover or to convey her secret message to him, has come back to report to the lady that the lover is not available at his place and, with a view to explaining to the heroine the great delay in coming back from the lover's residence, the messanger narrates that she has taken so long to come back from the residence of the lady's lovcer because she had a long bath in the near-by pond. Her, explanation, is palpably false and concocted; as a matter fact, the female messanger has come back after having spent a nice time with the lover of her friend, the heroine of the piece. But since the heroine, who is well-versed in the art of love, has discerned the marks of dalliance on the person of her female messanger, she states that her statements are all false. She, quite ironically, says that she (i.e. the female messanger) had indeed gone from her house (i.e. the house of the heroine of the piece) to the pond for a bath, and not at all to the place of that scoundrel (i.e. the lover of the heroine of the piece) and that the marks of bath on the person of the female messanger indeed confirm it. The literal reading of the verse leads us to believe that the description of the marks of the bath on the person of the female messanger are indeed those of the actual bath in the pond that the messanger has had. However, when we read the verse between the lines, we get the "vyangyārtha" of the speaker (i.e. the heroine of the piece). Each detail of the bath is actually that of dalliance. If the female messanger had actually bathed herself in the pond, as she is claiming, the sandal-paste, besmeared on her breasts, should have been removed completely by the water of the pond in the course of the bath she says she has had. But it is only the "स्तनतट" (i.e. the forefronts of the breast) that have lost the sandal paste. Clearly, she has had a dalliance with the lover of the heroine at his residence. An experienced partner in love-making that the heroine of the piece is, she knows that in actual love-making the male pays his attention to the forefronts of the breasts and causes them to lose the sandal-paste besmeared on them by embracing them. It is only the lower portion of the female messanger's lip that has lost its redness for the upperportion of the lip has got its redness intact. It is as actually happens in expert love-making in accordance with the rules of the science of love (कामशास्त्र) according to which the lower-lip of ladies is the real source of sexual pleasure (रतिसर्वस्वम्). Similarly, the fact that only the corners of the eyes of the female messanger have lost the black pigment that had been besmeared on the entire eyes, is proof positive of the fact that the heroine's lover, as an expert lover, kissed only the corners of the eyes and not the other portions. Lastly, the physical frame of the messanger, full of horripilation, is speaking of the sexual satisfaction that she had and that is still writ large on each of its parts; the horripilation caued by bath in a cold pond disappears after the bath whereas the horripilation, resulting from a successful and satisfying love-making lasts long. Thus the heroine of the piece implies that she knows the pond in which the messanger has bathed herself–it is the pond in the form of her own lover's bed-room (अन्तिकम्). Evidently, the "vyangyārtha" here is far more charming than its "vācyārtha". It must be recorded here that the "vyangyārtha" of the verse on hand includes (i) the speaker's (i.e. the heroine's expertise in the science of love-making called कामकलावैदग्ध्य, revealed in her knowledge of the special parts of the female physique which are the special attention of the male partner's love-making as provided in the treatises dealing with the science of love-making such as कामसूत्रम् by sage Vātsyāyana and रतिरहस्यम् by Kokaka and (ii) the manliness of the heroine's lover who can make women 'पुलकित' by rendering them sexually fully satisfied through his command over the art of love-making combined with his infidelty, leading to the heroine's use of the word 'अधम' for him–he who has time for the heroine's female messanger (दूती) and not for her, belonging as he does to the category of "शठनायक".

We can now take up one or two examples of "Vastudhvani" from English poetry and drama. As hinted earlier, "vyangyārtha" is the basis of "Dhvani" and it is determined by the following factors: 1. Who is the speaker and who is the addressee? 2. What is the Context? 3. What is the time of the statement? 4. What is the place where the statement has been made? 5. What is the mood of the speaker at the time when the statement is made? Consider the following lines from Shakespeare *Macbeth* I.iv:

There's no art
To find the mind's construction in the face:
He was a gentleman on whom I built
An absolute trust.

The speaker of the lines, cited above, is King Duncan, reacting to the death of the rebel –Thane of Cawdor– who was full of repentence and remorse and had implored His Highness's pardon for his part in the rebellion. The statement of Duncan, taken literally, means that His Highness had been deceived by the apparently innocent face of the Thane of Cawdor, the object of the King's complete trust which, unfortunately, was belied. Indeed, it is impossible to make out from one's face the kind of person he/she is. The "vacyārtha" of the King's speech is no doubt His Highness's confession of his beguilement at the hands of Cawdor but it applies with a greater force to Macbeth whom His Highness praises as his "worthiest cousin" in the next line of his continuing speech. As the plot of the play reveals, this "worthiest cousin" of the King emerges to be his greatest traitor, who murders his own king who is his guest also. The spectator, already acquainted with the outline of the play, will instantly realize the relevance of the thought expressed in the king's speech, under consideration, to the character and conduct of Macbeth, the hero of the play, who proves to be worse than the Thane of Cawdor by means of his disloyalty and treachery, confirming the truth of the king's speech. I think that the relevance to Macbeth, inherent in the speech, is its "vyangyārtha" and that is more important than its "vacyārtha", for Macbeth's conduct gives us a greater shock than that of Cawdor and is thus trgically more significant.

We can also take up the last but one speech of Hamlet in the play of that name by Shakespeare, included by Matthew Arnold in the list of touchstone passages against which we can judge the worth of any given poem (Vide his essay entitled "On the Study of Poetry"):

If thou didst ever hold me in thy heart,
Absent thee from felicity awhile,
And in this harsh world draw thy breath in pain
To tell my story.

(*Hamlet* V.ii. 357-60)

The Prince of Denmark has taken very long to avenge the murder of his father by his uncle and the latter's hasty marriage with his mother

Gertrude. His uncle Claudius, the present king of Denmark, has arranged a duel between the Prince and Laertes, son to Polonius and brother to Ophelia, whom the Prince used to love but who has already committed suicide for which Laertes holds the Prince wholly responsible. In the duel Hamlet and Laertes–both are mortally wounded by a venomed rapier, used first by Laertes and then accidently by Hamlet who kills Claudius, too, with the same weapon. While Hamlet is dying, he asks his close friend Horatio to live on to reveal the real history of the Prince and the enigmatic delay in taking revenge on Claudius of the murder of his father. When Horatio refuses to survive the Prince, the latter makes the immortal speech, cited above. The vācyārtha of the speech is that Horatio, if at all he loved the Prince, must live for a while in the uncongenial world, full of pain and suffering, only to tell the true story of Hamlet to the world at large. The word 'felicity' used in the speech is highly remarkable. Normally, the word means 'happiness' and looks odd. The question is: 'What does Hamlet mean by requesting Horatio to keep himself aloof from 'Felicity' for the time being?' From the context we come to know that Hamlet is restraining Horatio from dying for a while for his own sake. Thus 'Felicity' is to be identified with 'death'. But 'Death' is, in its general sense, something undesirable for people are afraid of it–they prefer 'life' to 'death'. However, Hamlet has felt the futility of 'Life' in the short span of life that he has lived; it means for him treachery, disloyalty, infidelty and all that is sham; the only way to get free from all this is 'Death'–a real source of happiness because 'Death' will put an end to all this and provide freedom to his soul. Thus, 'Death', being a state of liberation from all ills of 'life', is 'Felicity' or 'Happiness'. Horatio has to wait for a while before he gets freedom from the painful existence called 'Life' for the sake of his friend Hamlet: he will be called upon to enlighten the world on the true story of his friend which he alone knows full well and can unravel its secrets. This is the 'vācyārtha' of the passage. But if we choose to read the passage between the lines, we will come to underline a very great idea underlying it. That great or sublime idea is: Man should live and die for 'Honour' which means an existence, free from ignominy or public disagrace. Death can put an end to all your sufferings–mental, physical and spiritual–but not from disrepute. So before you die, you should get rid of all misunderstandings people may have about you. Hamlet wants to be cleared of all charges people may have got against him. He himself cannot do that for he has now no time, he being already in the jaws of 'Death'. But Horatio can remove all public misgivings against Hamlet by letting it know his true story. Thus Horatio is called upon to make a sacrifice in the interest of his friend by postponing the embracing of a state of bliss called 'Death' until he clears his friend of all possible charges to be subjected to by the public. The choice before Horatio is between (a) the acceptance of 'Death' which will provide him a state of true happiness and freedom from all ills of 'Life' and (b) enduring the pains of 'Life' for the time being for the sake of his friend who must be freed from all ignominy attaching to his name. I believe that this is the 'vyangyārtha' of Hamlet's speech and it is far more interesting than its 'vācyārtha', given above. Clearly, the passage is an excellent example of "Vastudhvani".

Alamkāradhvani

The normal 'alamkāras' or figures of speech depend either on the words or on the literal senses of words or on words and senses combined. But "alamkāradhvani" happens when some "alamkāra" suggests another "alamkāra" or some "alamkāra" gets suggested through the "vyangyārtha" of the poem and dominates the scene. Ānandavardhana says:

अर्थशक्तेरलंकारो यथाप्यन्यः प्रतीयते ।
अनुस्वानोपमव्यङ्ग्यः स प्रकारोऽपरो ध्वनेः ।।

(ध्वन्यालोक 2/48)

[Where some "alamkāra" other than what is based on the literal sense of words is suggested by the verbal power called "vyanjanā", which depends on sense, we have another form of "dhvani" (called "alamkāradhvani"]

As an illustration we can cite the following verse from *Śiṣupālavadham* by Māgha:

रम्या इति प्राप्तवतीः पताका रागं विविक्ता इति वर्धयन्तीः
यस्यामसेवन्त नमद्वलीकाः समं वधूभिर्वलभीर्युवानः ।।

[(In which Dwārikāpurī) young men enjoyed roof-rooms along with young women–(roof-rooms) that had flags because they were beautiful; (roof-rooms that) increased passion because they were secluded; and (roof-rooms that) had their jets projected.]

Here 'पताकाः प्राप्तवतीः', 'विविक्ताः' and 'नमद्वलीकाः'–these three epithets have been clearly stated for highlighting the 'roof-rooms' of Dwārikāpurī that were enjoyed by the youngmen of the city. But the poet says that the young-men enjoyed the roof-rooms along with young women. Thus the verse has the "alamkāra" called "Tulyayogitā" which consists in

एकधर्माभिसन्धि (common attributes) of 'upameya' as well as 'upamāna'. Since the subject of the verse is 'वलभीः' (roof-rooms), these should be regarded as the "Upameya" or "Prastuta" and "वधूः" (young women) should be treated as 'उपमान' or 'अप्रस्तुत' in the verse on hand. The two having the common attribute of being enjoyed by the young men of the city, the "alamkāra" used is "Tulyayogitā". However, the three epithets used for "वलभीः" can be applied to "वधूः" also with changed meanings. The epithet "पताकाः प्राप्तवतीः" in reference to "वधूः" will mean "attained fame or gone famous"; the term "विविक्ताः" will mean "spotless or clean" and "नमद्वलीकाः" will mean "possessing the three hair-lines on the belly that are a little bent". Now, these senses of the three epithets used for the "वधूः" are not the directly obtained literal senses of the terms but rather suggested senses, acquired analogically from the description of the "वलभीः". Since, this is what happenes when the alamkāra called "श्लेष" is used, the verse, under consideration, becomes an example of "श्लेषालंकारध्वनि."

We can take up another verse from शिशुपालवध by Magha:

त्रासाकुलः परिपतन्परितो निकेतान्
पुम्भिर्नकैश्चिदपि धन्विभिरन्वबन्धि ।
तस्थौ तथापि न मृगः क्वचिदङ्गनानाम्
आकर्णपूर्णनयनेषु हृतेक्षणश्रीः ।। (5/26)

[(Describing the different scenes of Lord Krishna's camping on Mt Raivataka, the poet calls our attention to one scene concerning a deer and says)
"Terrified by the sight of Krishna's army, the deer, flying around the camps of (the Lord's party), though unpursued by any of the bowwielding persons, did not stop at all anywhere, being deprived of his glow by the arrows of the eyes, hanging from the ears of the beautiful ladies (of Krishna's entourage)."]

Here the cause of the deer's non-stoppage has been described. The non-stoppage of the deer is not due to the pursuit of any of the bow-wielding persons but rather due to the humiliation felt by the deer at being deprived of its glow by the eyes of the beautiful ladies in Krishna's party–eyes that were touching their ears. This is an imagined cause which should have been expressed by the term 'इव'. Had that been the case, there would have been the figure of speech called हेतूत्प्रेक्षा here. But the poet has suggested that हेतु without the employment of that indicator; namely, 'इव'. Clearly, the cause has been suggested and not stated and therefore the verse is an example of हेतूत्प्रेक्षाध्वनि: Now, the question is: 'Has the poet achieved greater poetic effect through the avoidance of the indicator 'इव' or not'? I think the use of the indicator was likely to render the beauty of the eyes of the ladies less effective than they are without the use of the indicator 'इव'. For, heard meldies are sweet, but those unheard are sweeter, as the English romantic poet John Keats had declared in his 'Ode on a Grecian Urn'.

Let us now consider some examples of "Alamkāradhvani" in Western writings. Consider, for example, the following lines from the opening stanza of Keats's 'Ode to a Nightingale':

It's not through envy of thy happy lot,
But being too happy in thine happiness
That thou lightwinged Dryad of the trees
In some melodious plot of beechen green
And shadows numberless,
Singest of summer in full-throated case.

Keats is obviously trying to suggest some 'हेतु' or cause of his death-like experience, described in the opening lines of the stanza, such as aching of the heart and benumbing of the limbs. This strange experience, he asserts, is not due to any envy of the bird's happy lot but rather due to his being excessively happy in the happy fortune of the nightingale, a virtual wood-nymph, singing of summer at the highest pitch of her voice in some plot outgrown with beech-trees and overflowing with the melody of the Dryad (that the nightingale is). The poet has not used any adverbial expression such as 'as though', 'as it were' or 'as if' for venting his 'हेतु'; the 'हेतु' is only suggested and not stated. Had the poet done that, the passage would have been an example of उत्प्रेक्षा or हेतूत्प्रेक्षा, to be precise. But since there is no indicator like 'As though' 'As if' or 'as it were', we take it that the peculiar 'हेतु' is suggested, not stated and thus we have here हेतूत्प्रेक्षाध्वनि' which makes the poet's argument all the more effective, for, the use of the indicator would have taken away some of the shine of the poet's 'हेतु' through its direct assertion. We should not forget the famous aesthetic principle: 'Art lies in concealing art'.

Now consider Shakespeare's sonnet no. LIII (53) which is a long-drawn example of प्रतीपालंकार in which उपमेय or Tenor or Minor Term is poetically shown to be better than उपमान or Vehicle or Major Term-the reversal of what happens in रूपक or Metaphor. But the last line of the sonnet is all the more remarkable:

'But you like none, none you, for constant heart'.

In this line the figure of speech known as अनन्वय is suggested, the classic example of which is : 'रामरावणयोर्युद्धं रामरावणयोरिव' [The battle between Rāma and Rāvaṇa was like that of Rāma and Rāvaṇa]. Since the line clearly implies negatively that Mr W.H., the addressee of the sonnet, is his own pattern, the figure अनन्वय is "vyangya", not "vācya" and thus the line is an example of अनन्वयालंकारध्वनि.

Rasadhvani:–'Vastudhvani' and 'Alamkāradhvan' are the broad divisions of what Ānandavardhana calls संलक्ष्यक्रमध्वनि–'dhvani' in which the steps in arriving at the 'vyangyārtha' can be discerned. And on the contrary, the 'dhvani' in which those steps are not clearly discerned, he designates as असंलक्ष्यक्रमध्वनि, otherwise known as 'Rasadhvani'. All constituents and kinds of "Rasas" and "Bhāvas" are included in this broad head, even "Rasābhāsas", "Bhāvabhāsas", "Bhāvaśānti", "Bhāvodaya" and "Bhāvaśabalatā". Earlier, the theory of "Rasa" was thought to be based on the literal sense of words in poetry but Ānandavardhana, while acknowledgig the supremacy of "Rasa", expressed the view that "Rasa" is suggested and not stated–it is "vyangya" and never "vācya". His position is very close to that of T.S. Eliot who, in his most famous critical essay "Tradition and the Individual Talent", boldly holds that "the poet has, not a "personality" to express, but a particular medium, which is only a medium and not a personality, in which impressions and experiences combine in peculiar and unexpected ways". A romantic poet like Wordsworth tends to express his own personality and has recourse to "vācaka" words instead of "vyanjaka" words that are the favourites of classical poets for whom "medium" is the be-all and end-all of the poetic creation. Indeed, the expression of the "medium" is the essence of "Rasadhvani", the highest form of the expresion of "Pratibhā" or "Imagination". But the question is : 'What do we actually mean by "medium?" Eliot, in my view, explained the "medium" in terms of his famous theory of the "Objective Correlatives", spelled out in his essay entitled "Hamlet and His Problems" in the following words:

> "The only way of expressing emotion in the form of art is by finding an "objective correlative", in other words, a set of objects, a situation, a chain of events which shall be the

> formula of that particular emotion; such that when the external facts, which must terminate in sensory experience, are given, the emotion is immediately invoked.

Eliot is against the practice of describing emotions; he wants the poet to present the external facts about the emotion he seeks to invoke. What Eliot means by the termination of the external facts in sensory experience is the perception of the "vācyārtha" by the reader which is bound to invoke the emotion concerned. This invocation of the emotion is what Ānanda means by the "vyangyatā" of "Rasa" called "Rasadhvani". The means of achieving this result are innumerable–right from the use of "Nipāta", special prefixes and suffixes and verb-forms to the whole structure of the work. Let us see what miracle the 'Nipāta' 'तु' does in the following verse from Kālidāsa's *Abhigyanśākuntalam* Act III. verse 23:

> मुहरङ्गुलिसंवृताधरोष्ठं प्रतिषेधाक्षरविक्लवाभिरामम् ।
> मुखमंसविवर्तिपक्ष्मलाक्ष्याः कथमप्युन्नमितं न चुम्बितं तु ।।

> [(Duṣyanta is regretting the non-fulfiement of his heart's desire even after a secret meeting with his lady-love Śakuntalā:) "Even after having been lifted somehow, the face of that (lady), with eyes looking beautiful owing to plentiful eye-lashes, could not be kissed at all–the face that was being closed with fingeres again and again and (looked) all the more beautiful on account of the restraining words, caused by perturbation, and was being turned towarls her shoulder".]

The dissatisfaction of the lover with the non-fulfilment of his desire (i.e. the kissing of the lips of his lady-love) has been most powerfully conveyed by the "Nipāta" 'तु' which is just an indeclinable particle but highly suggestive. The "Nipāta" 'तु' has increased severalfold the effectiveness of the feeling of the speaker's dissatisfaction caused by the non-fulfilment of his long-cherished desire of kissing Śakuntalā. It is through the deft use of "Nipātas" even that great poets can make their writings "vyangyātmaka" or suggestive. Let us consider the last but one stanza of Tennyson's little lyric "Break, Break, Break":

> And the stately ships go on
> To their haven under the hill;
> But O for the touch of a vanished hand,
> And the sound of a voice that is still!

In the third line of the extract, cited above, we have the letter 'o' serving as what the Sanskrit grammar calls 'निपात'; by means of this "Nipāta" Tennyson has given expression to his inexpressible grief, caused by the untimely death of his friend, philosopher and guide–Arthur Henry Hallam, his sister's fiance and his benefactor. The entire "Vedanā" or pathos of the poet has been concentrated in this letter which invokes that feeling in the most effective manner possible.

The indirect method of referring to the death of Hallam in terms of "vanished hand" and "a voice that is still" has its own miraculous powers which a matter of fact statement can never achieve. The stanza is definitely illustrative of "Rasadhvani".

Repetition of words and phrases is normally avoided in poetry but great poets can use repetition as an effective tool for the invocation of emotions and feelings. Consider the following Sanskrit verse:

> यद्वञ्चनाहितमतिर्बहुचाटुगर्भं कार्योन्मुखः खलजनः कृतकं ब्रवीति
> तत्साधवो न न विदन्ति विदन्ति किन्तु कर्तुं वृथा प्रणयमस्यनपारयंति

> [That an evil person, who is interested in getting his work done and whose mind is ever engaged in deceiving (good people), speaks falsely and flatteringly variously, the good people do not know–that is not the fact–they (rather) know (all that very well). But they are not able to set at naught the (false) love of the evil person concerned.]

In the above verse (vide line no. 2) we have the repetition of the negative word 'न' and of the verb 'विदन्ति' twice each; that reinforces our belief in the extraordinary power of the good men in distingusihing between the true and the false though they do not use that power because of their refinement and gentleness. This two-fold repetition of 'न न' and विदन्ति विदन्ति' is thus the source of great suggestion and has the power to thrill the sensitive readers by means of the "vyangyārth" that it yields.

It has to be borne in mind that for purposes of "Rasadhvani", the "vyangyārtha" is required to be preeminent. If that is not the case, then, according to Ānanda, there will be "Rasavadalamkāra" etc and not "Rasadhvani" etc. If the "Rasa" is subordinate, there will be "Rasavadalamkāra"; if the "bhāva" is subordinate, there will be "Preysalamkāra"; if "Rasābhāsa and Bhāvābhāsa" have the subordinate positions, there will be "Urjasvī alamkāra" and in case "Bhāvaśānti" is having a subordinate position, there wil be "Samāhita Alamkāra". (Vide *Dhvanyāloka* II. 27 & III. 91 and the extended commentary on it.). Let us illustrate this with a few examples. Consider the following Sanskrit verse:

> किं हास्येन न मे प्रयास्यसि पुनः प्राप्तश्चिराद्दर्शनं,
> केयं निष्करुण! प्रवासरुचिता? केनासि दूरीकृतः?
> स्वप्नान्तेष्विति ते वदन् प्रियतमव्यासक्तकण्ठग्रहो
> बुद्ध्वा रोदिति रिक्तबाहुवलयस्तारं रिपुस्त्रीजनः।।

> ["What is the use of thy laughter? Thou, who hast come within the range of my sight, canst not go away from me again? O cruel one! of what kind is this thy interest in living abroad? By whom hast thou been sent away (from me)?" uttering thus the group of the women belonging to thy enemies that had given intense embracings in the necks of the husbands, in the deep sleeps (O king), start weeping bitterly on finding their embraces empty after waking up.]

Apparently we are led to believe that the verse, cited above, is the expression of some lady's pangs of separation, intending to invoke विप्रलम्भ शृंगार. But when we realize that it is, in point of fact, some flatterer's eulogy of some king who has slayed his enemies and has thus compelled the women-folk of his enemies to bewail the absence of their husbands, we feel that the विप्रलम्भशृंगार has lost all its charms for us, which charms have been stolen by the 'flatterer's eulgistic words, addressed to the king concerned. The question is: what is the actual subject of the verse: the praising of the king's bravery or the venting of the miserable plight of the women of the king's enemies, feeling the pangs of separation from their husbands? Clearly, the focus of attention is the king and his suggested bravery rather than the pangs of separation, felt by the womenfolk of the king's enemies. The verse, thus, was *prima facie*, an example of विप्रलम्भशृंगारध्वनि but eventually turned to be an example of वस्तुध्वनि, suggesting the king's extra-ordinary prowess. Ānanda regards it as an example of "Rasavadalamkāra"

An English example of "Rasavadalamkāra" for Ānandavardhanācārya's formulation would be the following extract from the fourth canto of Alexander Pope's mock-epic poem entitled *The Rape of the Lock:*

> "For ever curs'd be this detested Day,
> Which snatch'd my best, my favrite Curl away!
> Happy, ah ten times happy, had I been,
> If Hamton-Court these Eyes had never seen!
> Yet am not I the first mistaken maid,

By Love of Courts to num'rous ills betray'd.
Oh had I rather un-admir'd remain'd
In some lone Isle, or distant Northern Land;
Where the gilt Chariot never marks the way,
Where none learns Ombre, none e'er tastes Bohea!

The extract apparently suggests the speaker's (i.e. Belinda's) "vyabhicāribhāva" called "Glāni". However, the nature of the poem, which is a high burlesque or mock-epic, leads us to believe that the poet is actually satirising here the senseless fashions indulged in by the ladies of the 18th century, represented by Belinda and this suggests the satirical bhāva called "Prabodha" which has got the primacy here, making Belinda's "Glāni" subordinate or "apradhāna". In the technical language of the Sanskrit theorists, the extract is an example of "Preyasalamkāra". The references to "Hamton Court", "gilt Chariot", "Ombre" and "Bohea" are pointers to the poet's actual intention here–all alluding to the recently introduced fashions in the 18th century England, indulged in by the fashionable ladies of the day. In the opinion of the poet, these fashions are irrational and destructive and should therefore be shunned. This moralist stance of the poet is the "vyangyārtha" of the passage conveyed to us through the "Glāni" of Belinda which, to all intents, is the proper subject but which, in point of fact, gives way to her "Prabodha" (i.e. Belinda's realization of the futility and destructiveness of the fashions concerned). Thus the apparently suggested "sancārī" called "Glāni" gives precedence to "Prabodha" and that makes the passage an example of "Preyasalamkāra". Had Belinda's "Glāni" been the prime concern of the poet, the passage would have been illustrative of "Bhāvadhvani" but its primacy is usurped by the poet's "Prabodha" and thus it becomes subsidiary ("Gauṇa") by becoming a kind of "alamkāra". When a "bhāva" loses its primacy, it is designated as "Preyasalamkāra".

Let us consider an example of "Ūrjasvī" which happens when some "Rasābhāsa" or "Bhāvābhāsa" becomes an "anga" (subordinate) to some "Rasa" or "Bhāva". The following verse is illustrative of "Śṛngārarasābhāsa", becoming the handmaid of "Bhaktirasa":

समस्तगुणसम्पदः सभमलंक्रियाणां गुणै र्भवन्ति
यदि भूषणं तव तथाऽपि नो शोभसे।
शिवं हृदयवल्लभं यदि यथा तथा रञ्जयेस्तदेव
वाणि! ते जगति सर्वलोकोत्तरम्।।

[O goddess of speech! even though all the wealth of the figures of speech along with the poetic virtues become thy ornament, thou dost not appear beautiful but if thou somehow pleasest Lord Shiva, the darling of thy heart, that becomes in this world thy best ornament transcending all.]

Here "Bhaktirasa" born out of the poet's devotion to Lord Shiva is suggested and that is the "vyangyārtha" of the verse. But there is "Śṛngārābhāsa" here, too on account of the verb "रञ्जये:," making Shiva the husband of Sarasvatī (whose recognized husband is Brahmā). However, the Śrngārābhāsa is subordinated to the "Bhaktirasa", the centre of attraction, in the verse. Thus the verse, cited above, is an example of "Ūrjasvī". Another example of "Ūrjasvī" is the following Sanskrit verse:

स पातु वो यस्य हतावशेषास्तत्तुल्यवर्णाञ्जनरञ्जितेषु
लावण्ययुक्तेष्वपि वित्रसन्ति दैत्याः स्वकान्तानयनोत्पलेषु

[Let that Lord (Shiva) protect you (i.e. the spectators in the theatre)–the Lord whose remaining enemies in the forms of demons unslayed, fear the red lotuses of the eyes of their ladyloves that are besmeared with the collyrium of the colour of the Lord, though these eyes are full of youthful lustre.]

Here the prowess of the Lord Shiva is suggested by the description of the terror pervading the army of the demons who have survived the destruction of their brethren by the Lord–who are so terrified that they see the Lord in the eyes of their womenfolk–the eyes that are having two colours–red and blue or black–the colours of the Lord called "Neil-lohita", not withstanding the fact that these are full of youthful lustre and are expected to arouse passion, and not fear, in their husbands. Clearly, the "sancārībhāva" called "Trāsa" which is, to all intents, the subject-matter of the verse, is improper and thus here is a case of "bhāvabhāsa" which becomes subsidiary to the suggested depiction of the extraordinary prowess of Lord Shiva. In this way the verse, under discussion, is illustrative of "Ūrjasvī" in which the "bhāvabhāsa" becomes "apradhāna" and the suggested prowess of Lord Shiva becomes "Pradhāna" by assuming the focus of attention.

As an English example of "Ūrjasvī", we can cite the following passage from Lamb's famous essay "Christ's Hospital Five and Thirty years Ago":

> There was now and then the formality of saying a lesson, but if you had not learned it, a brush across the shoulders (just enough to disturb a fly) was the sole remonstrance. Field never used the rod; and in truth he wielded the cane with no

> great good will–holding it 'like a dancer'. It looked in his hands rather like an emblem than an instrument of authority; and an emblem, too, he was ashamed of.

To all intents, the extract suggests the speaker's (i.e. Lamb's) tribute to his old teacher at Christ's Hospital, Matthew Field by name, and thus his "Guruviṣayakarati" is the "vācyārtha" of the passage. But since the tone is a little light-hearted and not reverential, it is "Guruviṣayakaratyābhāsa' and not 'Guruviṣayakarati' pure and simple. However, in the context of the essay as a whole, a "sancāribhāva" called "Asuyā" (denigration) against the speaker's institution, namely, "Christ's Hospital", is suggested here and that bhāva gets precedence over the "sthāyibhāva" called "Guruvisayaka-Rati' for the former is the central theme of the essay in which Lamb, assuming the personality of Coleridge, seeks to point out the various shortcomings and weaknesses of "Christ's Hospital" which Lamb had praised sky-high in his earlier essay entitled "Recollections of Christ's Hospital", rather undeservedly. Thus in a very subtle manner, Lamb corrects his earlier view of his *alma mater* by means of the dhvani-based alamkāra called "Ūrjasvī" and poohpoohs the institutions like "Christ's Hospital" where teachers like Matthew Field have practically no time for teaching, their primary and basic business, and spend most of their time in socialization instead.

Other dhvani-based figures are: "Bhāvodaya", "Bhāvaśanti" "Bhāvasandhi" and "Bhāvaśabalatā". All these are different forms of "Aparāngavyangya" or Gunībhuta-vyangya". Where some "Bhāva" or feeling suggestively arises but remains a handmaid to some other "Bhāva", we have "Bhāvodaya". Consider the following Sanskrit verse:

> मधुपानप्रवृत्तास्ते सुहृद्भिः सह वैरिणः।
> श्रुत्वा कुतोऽपि त्वन्नाम लेभिरे विषमां गतिम्।।

> [(O king!) hearing from someone thy name, thy enemies, engaged in drinking wine in the compandy of their friends, achieved an odd state.]

Here the "vyabhicāribhāva" called "Trāsa" is suggested as arising in the hearts of the enemies of the king, addressed by the speaker. But this "Bhāva" artistically helps the expression of the speaker's feeling of love for the king, his "Rājaviśayakarati" which is the central theme of the verse, its chief "Bhāva". Thus the aroused feeling of "Trāsa" is helpful in the speaker's love for the king. The passage is, therefore, an example of "Bhāvodaya". An English example of "Bhāvodaya" is to be found in the following extract from the second scene of the fifth Act of Shakespeare's *Othello*:

Emilia : My husband!

Othello : What needs this utterance, woman? I say thy husband.

Emilia : O mistress! villany hath made mocks with love. My husband say that she was false!

The second speech of Emilia, in the extract cited above, suggests the birth of the "vyabhicāribhāva" called "Vitarka" for she is not convinced that her husband Iago could have poisoned the ears of Othello against Desdemona's alleged infidelity. But this "vitarka" in a very charming way helps the expression of Emilia's "swāminīviśayakarati" (love for her mistress Desdemona). The speech of Emilia is indeed an excellent example of "Bhāvodaya", her "vitarka" simply heightening the intensity of her loving regard for Desdemona whom she takes to be the embodiment of true love.

"Bhāvaśanti" exists when some bhāva which has already been aroused suddenly subsides and helps some other "bhāva" by being subordinited to it. A Sanskrit example of "Bhāvaśānti", also known as "Samāhita" is the following verse:

अविरलकरवालकम्पनैः भृकुटीतर्जनगर्जनैर्मुहुः।
ददृशे तव वैरिणां मदः, सगतः क्वापि तवेक्षणे क्षणात्।

[O king!) the exultancy of thy enemies, perceived in the continual crossing of swords and casting of angry glances as also in their hectorings, disappeared instantly somewhere at thy sight.]

The "vyabhicārī bhāva" called "Mada" (mad rejoicing) which had already been aroused in the hearts of the enemies of the king concerned instantly subsides at the very sight of the king. Clearly, the subsiding of the "Mada" of the king's enemies at his very sight helps the speaker's expression of "Rajaviṣayakarati" which is the central "bhāva", sought to be invoked by the speaker. This is, evidently, a fine example of "Bhāvaśānti". A very interesting illustration of "Bhāvaśānti" in English literature is to be found in the following passage from Charles Lamb's essay entitled "Christ's Hospital Five & Thirty Years Ago":

Extinct are these smiles, with that beautiful countenance, with which (for thou wert the *Nireus formosus* of the school,),

> in the days of thy maturer waggery, thou didst disarm the wrath of infuriated town-damsel, who, incensed by provoking pinch, turning tigress-like round suddenly converted by the angel-look, exchanged the half-formed terrible "bl-" for a gentler greeting-"bless thy handsome face".

In the extract, cited above, Lamb is actually paying his tribute to one of his classmates at Christ's Hospital, Allen by name, who was noted for his pranks as also for his beautiful face: in fact, he was nick-named 'Nireus formosus, Nireus, the fair' after the king of Samos, who was next to Achilles in the Trojan war. Allen had once played a practical joke with some town-girl by pinching her from behind. Naturally, she was on the point of pronouncing 'blasted be thou' but hardly had she uttered the particle 'bl' when she caught the sight of the charming Allen and being overwhelmed by Allen's beauty, she changed her mind and pronounced 'bless thy handsome face' in stead of her earlier decision of saying 'blasted be thou'. No doubt, her earlier "vyabhicāribhāva" called "Amarṣa" instantly subsides at the mere sight of the beautiful face of Allen. But the disappearance of the town-damsel's "Amarṣa" only helps the writer's expression of his "Mitraviṣayakarati" (love for his friend Allen) which is the chief theme of the above extract.

"Bhāvasandhi" occurs where two equally powerful "bhāvas" (vyabhicāribhāvas) are aroused in the same subject but both remain auxilary to some other "bhāva" which is the real centre of attraction. Consider the folloing verse:

> जन्मान्तरीणरमणस्याङ्गसमुत्सुका
> सलज्जा चान्तिके सख्याः पातु नः पार्वती सदा।।

> [(Some devotee of goddess Pārvatī is blessing his disciples): "Let Pārvatī protect us always who is ardently desiring the conjugal union with her husband of the previous births and who is full of bashfulness in the company of her female friend!"]

The speaker of the above verse is clearly projecting goddess Pārvatī having the conflicting feelings of "Autasukya" (ardent desire for conjugal union with Shiva) and "Vrīdā" or "Lajjā" (bashfulness). However, the mixture of "Autsukya" and "Vrīda"-the two "vyabhicāribhāvas"--skilfully and charmingly helps the "Devatāviṣayakarati" of the speaker by magnifying the glamour of the subject of his devotion through her association with Lord Shiva as also through her sobriety reflected in her bashfulness. It is the speaker's devotion to Pārvatī which is the central idea of the verse; the reference to the two "vyabhicāribhāvas" of "Vrīdā" and "Autsukya" are here just to enhance the effect of the speaker's "devatāviṣayakarati", his devotion to goddess Pārvatī.

A very good example of "Bhāvasandhi" in English literature is to be found in the following passage from the essay entitled "My Relations" by Charles Lamb:

> He is courageous as charles of Sweden, upon instinct; chary of person, upon principle, as a travelling Quaker.

Here Lamb is describing his elder brother John Lamb under the garb of a cousin J.E. or James Elia who was a bundle of contradictions. In the extract, cited above, we have two opposite bhāvas, namely, "Utsāha" and "Dhṛti", described as co-existing in the heart of John but both the "bhāvas" help Lamb's expression of his "Bhrātṛviṣayakarati" (brotherly love) which is the central bhāva in the passage, beautifully suggested. Thus the passage is illustrative of "Bhāvasandhi".

"Bhāvaśabalata" consists in several "bhāvas" arising in the heart or mind of a person one by one, serving as the handmaids of some other bhāva in a charming manner, that other "Bhāva" being the "Pradhāna Bhāva" of the composition. Consider the following verse:

> क्वाकार्यं शशलक्ष्मणः क्व च कुलं, भूयोऽपि दृश्येत् सा
> दोषाणां प्रशमाय नः श्रुतमहो कोपेऽपि कान्तं मुखम्।
> किं वक्ष्यन्त्यपकल्मषाः कृतधियः स्वप्नेऽपि सा दुर्लभा,
> चेतः स्वास्थ्यमुपैहि कः खलु युवा धन्योऽधरंपास्यति।।

> [(The king of Pratisthānapurī–Pururavā–is reflecting on Urvāśī whom he has lately seen): "How ignoble is (indulgence in a sage's daughter) and how great is the lunar dynasty? Will she be visible again? My Vedic studies were for subduing psychic evil tendencies. Her countenance was so lovely even in anger. What will the sinless virtuous people say (on my conduct)? She is even beyond my dream. O my heart! be at rest. Who will be that lucky young man who is destined to drink of her lips!"]

The poet has suggested 8 "vyabhicāribhāvas" in the above verse. The first sentence suggests "Tarka"; the second "autsukya"; the third "mati"; the fourth "Smṛti"; the fifth "Śamkā"; the sixth "Dainya"; the seventh "Dhṛti" and the eighth "Cintā". Since 8 "vyabhicāribhāvas" exist in one subject simultaneovsly, the verse, under review, is an example of "Bhāvaśabalatā" (a collection of variegated "bhāvas)". However, these "vyabhicāribhāvas" are only subsidiary to the "sthāyibhāva" called "Rati" born in the heart of Purūravā for Urvaśī, and that is the chief (Pradhāna) "bhāva" that the passage suggests. For the main interest of the verse lies in invoking "Śrngāra" in our minds. Clearly, the eight "vyabhicāribhāvas" are illustrative of "Guṇībhūtavyangya". An English example of "Bhāvasabalatā" is to be found in the following passage from Lamb's essay entitled "Christ's Hospital Five and Thirty Years Ago":

> There was love for the bringer; shame for the thing brought, and the manner of its bringing; sympathy for those who were too many to share in it; and, at top of all, hunger (eldest, strongest of all the passions!) predominant, breaking down the stony fences of shame, and awkwardness, and a troubling over-consciousness.

The above extract mentions several "bhāvas" like "Gurujanaviṣayakarati", "Vrīda", "Dainya", "Vitarka" in the form of "a troubling overconsciousness" and "Kṣudhā" but all these are in the mind or heart of Lamb, the school boy at Christ's Hospital. Thus the passage has "Bhāvaśabalatā". However; all these "bhāvas" are subsidiary to the controlling motive of the essay as a whole which we can define as the condemnation (Asūyā) of Christ's Hospital which is the "pradhāna bhāva" of the essay. The 4 "bhāvas" help the controlling motive of the essay by highlighting through suggestion the utter discrimination that was rampant in Lamb's *alma mater* which he had unduly admired in his earlier essay "Recollections of Christ's Hospital". Thus the "bhāva" called "Asūya" is the "Angībhāva" here and the explicit four "bhāvas" of "Vrīda", "Dainya", "Vitarka" and "Kṣudhā" are "Anga" or "Gunībhuta" bhāvas.

The Difference Between "Rasa" and "Rasadhvani"

Theoretically speaking "Rasa" belongs to the category of "dhvani" called "Asanlakṣyakrama-dhvani" or the "dhvani" in which the different stages of arriving at the "vyangyārtha" from the "vacyārtha" are not discerned just as the steps remain unmarked when a pile of lotus-petals is pierced with a needle. "Rasa" is, in the normal parlance of aesthetics, recognized. as "vyangya" (suggested) and not stated. And yet there can be cited numerous instances where "Rasa" has been and can be invoked in a direct way. Consider the following Hindī verse, for example:

बोले कर सिंहनाद गर्जन, जो कहो तो सिन्धु को पी जाऊँ।
या कहो तो लंक को गिरि समेत सागर के बीच डुबा आऊँ।।

[(The monkey hero Hanumān declares roaringly in the open court of Rāvaṇa:) "If you ask (O Rāvana!) I can drink the entire ocean or if you ask, I can drown your country Lankā in the sea along with its mountain (on which it is situated)"]

The "sthāyibhāva" called "Utsāha" in the heart of Hanumān has found a beautiful expression here. Is not the brave Sentiment (Vīrarasa) clearly invoked here? Instances like this can be called examples of "Rasa" but they cannot be called, in my view, "Rasadhvani". Had there been no difference between "Rasa" and "Rasadhvani", Ānandavardhana would not have invented the term "Rasadhvani", for "Rasa" would have served his purpose fairly well. I think by the term "Rasadhvani" he wanted to stress the point that it exists wherever some "Rasa", "Rasābhāsa", "Bhāva" or "Bhāvabhāsa" is invoked pointedly by means of "vyanjaka-words" rather than by means of plainsense words. He had in his mind verses such as "निःशेषच्युतचन्दनं स्तनतटं etc. that we considered earlier as an example of "Vastudhvani". In other words, "Rasa" plus "Vastudhvani" taken together make what is called "Rasadhvani". Let us take up the following passage from *Hanumānnātakam:*

न्यक्कारो ह्ययमेव मे यदरयो तत्राऽप्यसौ तापसः
सोऽप्यत्रैव निहन्ति राक्षसकुलं जीवत्यहो रावणः।।
धिक् धिक् शक्रजितं प्रबोधितवता किं कुम्भकर्णेन वा
स्वर्गग्रामटिकाविलुण्ठनवृथोच्छूनैः किमेभिर्भुजैः।।

[(Rāvaṇa is reacting to the news of Rāma's army devastating Lankā): "It is itself a shame for me that I have enemies and that, too, a penitent. And he is slaying the demon-horde here itself and oh! Rāvaṇa lives. Shame, Shame to Śakrajit or what of Kumbhakarṇa awakened? Of what avail are these arms that are unnecessarily feeling fat owing to their having looted a hamlet like the paradise?"]

The above verse is expressive of the speaker's anger, full of utter helplessness and sense of defeat. "Raudrarasa" is clearly suggested here whose "sthāyibhāva" is anger ("krodha"). Rāma and his army of monkeys constitute the "ālambanavibhāva"; the slyaing of the demons and devastation of Lankā by Rāma's army are the "uddīpanavibhāva". "Glāni",

"Dainya" and "Cintā" are the "Vyabhicāribhāvas". Rāvana's self-accusation is the "anubhāva" here. The beautiful organization of the different constituents of "Raudrarasa" lead the "sthāyibhāva" "Krodha" to assume the form of that "Rasa". However, what makes the entire passage an example of "Rasadhvani" is the profuse use of "vyanjaka" (emotionally charged) words. The word "अरयः" (literally, enemies) is highly emotive indeed. Even a single enemy of Rāvana would be enough to give him a shock but in the form of Rāma, Lakṣamana, Hanuman etc. he has innumerable enemies to make his sense of shock intenser several folds. The word "तापस" (literally, someone undergoing penance) brings home to us the utter contempt that Rāvaṇa has for Rāma who is not even a तपस्वी but a तापस, slaying the demon-army mercilessly. The expression "अत्रैव" (right here in Lankā) increases Rāvaṇa's shock for Rāma is slaying his people in his very home.

That indeed is the greatest possible shame for a ruler of the eminence of Rāvaṇa. The expression "जीवत्यहो रावणः" suggests the speaker's surprise at his survival, notwithstanding his intolerable tight corner, fraught with insults of all description. Is not death better for him in the given circumstances? That is what Rāvaṇa wants to convey through that expression. The reference to Śakrajit or Meghanāda highlights Rāvaṇa's dependence on his son who has proved to be of no avail–the son "Śakrajit" (literally the winner of the mightiest god "Śakra" or "Indra", noted for his victory over demons like Vṛtrāsura and Ahi–that is the suggested sense of the synonym of Indra, namely, "Śakra", derived from the root √"शक्" pointing to the immense possibilities of Indra's prowess. But the winner of that mighty god has been of no avail and that is why Rāvaṇa feels ashamed of himself for his having rated Meghnāda rather too highly. Similarly, the mention of "Kumbhakarṇa" is intended to heighten the effect of shock, felt by Rāvaṇa, by bringing home to the readers the helplessness of Kumbhakarṇa in counteracting the attack on Lankā launched by Rāma–"Kumbhakarṇa" whose very name meaning 'one who has ears as big as pitchers' should have deterred the army of Rāma for he was reputed to swallow thousands of people in one gulp. The adjective 'प्रबोधितवता' (one who has been awakened) refers to the arrangement made by Brahmā in regard to Kumbhakarṇa to the effect that he would remain asleep for six months for in one day he would eat up lacs of people and was thus a great danger to His (i.e. Brahma's) Creation. Thus Rāvaṇa is utterly shocked by the futility of his effort to awaken Kumbhakarṇa so that he could eat up the entire army of Rāma but all to no purpose. The verse from *Hanumānnātakam* is thus an example of "Rasadhvani" and not just of "Rasa" by virtue of a large number of "vyanjaka" words and expressions in it which are highly charged and suggestive and pregnant with deeper meanings–deeper than the senses they have in normal contexts. For example, the word 'शक्र' normally means 'Indra', the leader of the gods but in the present context we are called upon to take account of its 'etymological meaning', suggested by the root शक् from which it has been formed. Clearly, "Rasadhvani" occurs where in invoking a particular "rasa", vyanjaka words play a major role as opposed to plain words, capable of arousing that rasa in a direct way as they do in the case of the Hindi verse beginning with the words "बोले कर सिंह नाद गर्जन etc." that I have discussed earlier.

A Brief History of the Sanskrit Criticism Based on the "Dhvani" Doctrine

The critical school in Sanskrit that holds "Dhvani" to be the most significant aspect of poetry begins with the text entitled ध्वन्यालोक, attributed to the poet Ānandavardhana who flourished in the reign of the king of Kashmira–Avantivarmā of the latter half of the ninth century. The text consists of two forms of statements called "kārikā" and "vṛtti". The first kind comprises aphoristic verses and the second prose commentaries on the 'kārikas'. There is a view in scholarly circles led by Abhinavagupta that the 'kārikā' portion of the text was by some critic Sahṛdaya and Ānandavardhana had written the "vṛttis" on the kārikās of Sahṛdaya. This view gets some support from the fact that in certain texts *Dhvanyāloka* has been called *Sahṛdayāloka.* If that were a fact, then *Dhvanyāloka* would lose the status of an original work; it would instead be identified with the "vṛtti" portions and would remain just a commentary on the kārikas of Sahṛdaya. However, the most popular and prevalent view on the matter is that Ānandavardhanācārya is the author of both portions of the text-"kārikā" as well as the "vṛtti". The greatest opponent of Ānandavardhana, namely, Mahimabhatta, author of *Vyaktiviveka,* regards Ānanda as the sole author of the "kārikas" as well as "vṛttis" of *Dhvanyāloka.* And Mahimbhatta was in the latter half of the 11th century. Since he was an avowed enemy of Ānanda, his attribution of the authorship of the entire text of *Dhvanyaloka* to him, can be easily trusted. For, being Ānanda's enemy, he would be the last man to conede to his enemy the exalted position of the original and sole authorship of *Dhvanyāloka.* Moreover, Rājaśekhara, Jalhaṇa, Jayaratha, Viśvanātha, Kṣemendrā, all regard Ānanda as the common author of the "kārikā' and "vṛitti" portions of the treatise.

The "Dhvani" doctrine had to face a lot of opposition from several quarters. It was opposed tooth and nail by critics like Bhattanāyaka, Mukulbhatta, Pratihārendurāja, Dhananjaya, Kuntaka, and several others. But Abhinavagupta, Bhojarāja, Mammata, Viśvanātha and Panditarāja Jagannatha were the great upholders of the doctrine and it was thanks to their painstaking efforts that the doctrine of "Dhvani" emerged as the greatest poetic theory propounded in India and slowly and gradually the West has started recognizing its worth and power. Many dictionaries of critical terms have entires on "Dhvani" and "Rasa".

The Doctrine of "Dhvani": Its Universal Applicability.

The doctrine of "Dhvani" can be a valid doctrine only when it is shown to be of help in the critical evaluation of all imaginative writings in any language of the civilized world. So far as imaginative literature in verse is concerned, the applicability of "Dhvani" to the various branches of it, including Epic, is unquestioned. In the IVth Chapter of *Dvanyāloka,* Ānanda considers the "Rasadhvani" of the two epics of India, namely, the *Rāmāyaṇa* and the *Mahābhārata* in terms of the "Angī Rasas" of the works concerned. We can consider any epic or longer poem in terms of the work's "Angī Rasa". Now, the modern age is noted for novels and any critical theory, claiming to be of universal applicability, has to prove its usefulness in the study of Fiction–Novel, Novella, Novelette, Short story etc. Ānanda has cited passages from works of fiction like *Kādambarī, Harṣacarita* and *Nalacampū* and thus has provided hints that "Dhvani" can be applied to prose fiction also. If the critic has tact and is well-versed in the different tenets of the doctrine of "Dhvani", he/she can produce first rate critical studies of novels and epics alike. Critics like late Professor Krishna Rayan have successfully applied the doctrine of "Dhvani" to all forms of imaginative literature, written in various languages of India in *The Burning Bush* (B.R. Publishing Corporation, Delhi, 1988) and thus has established beyond doubt the universal applicability, of "Dhvani".

How to Apply the Theory of Dhvani in The Evaluation of a Literary Text?

It is not difficult to apply the theory of "Dhvani" to shorter pieces such as Ben Jonson's famous lyric "To Celia". But when it comes to applying it to longer poems or full-length novels, the critic is likely to be bewildered. I think that the task is indeed difficult but in no way unsurmountable. The critic is required to master the text in its entirety and then use his imaginative faculty in finding out the "vyangyārtha" suggested by each literary device employed by the author of the text to convey his intended meaning. The justification of the title and of the chapter-division along with that of the length of the work as a whole has to be discerned. The choices in respect of words and sentences, exercised by the author at all levels of his creation have to be accounted for. Even if the work, under review, happens to be a novel, it will have to be subjected to the rigours of the same evaluation as any lyric is from the point of view of "Dhvani" whether we are discussing "Vastudhvani" "Alamkāradhvani" or "Rasadhvani". If the work concerned is found satisfactory in respect of all the points listed above, it should be declared to be an "uttamakāvya"–first-rate literary piece. I think this wise the "Dhvani" theory could be put to a fruitful critical use.

Regarding the viability of the "Dhvani" doctrine, especially of "Rasadhvani", I would like to cite the finding of an expert committee that had surveyed the papers presented at the Literary Criterion Centre, Dhvanyāloka, in Mysore in a seminar on 'The Formulation of a common poetic for Indian Literatures Today', held in January 1984. The committee's considered view was spelt out in no ambiguous terms in the following words:

> ....in constructing a new poetic, it is advisable to make use of an existing frame work of a poetic which will suit the genius of India and (i) preserve our link with tradition and foster a sense of continuity: (ii) assimilate the best elements in Western criticism... The Rasa-Dhvani theory is more widely known in Indian literatures than any other critical system, and its concepts are in vogue in our arts and literatures....It is therefore more capable than any other existing theory of serving as the basis of a common poetic for Indian literatures. The Rasa-Dhvani theory needs, however, to be enlarged to incorporate the insights of subsequent aesthetic theories...

The committee was indeed diffident about the applicablity of the "Dhvani" theory to the literary master-pieces of the West. I believe that the theory can be applied with fruitful results to literatures produced in any part of the world because literary sensibility is, more or less, the same in all parts of the world, whether we are talking of India or England or any other country of the planet called the earth.

Vakrokti–Sampradāya

Just as the "Dhvani" Sampradāya held "Dhvani" or Suggestion to be the soul of poetry, a school of critics led by one Kuntala or Kuntaka came forward with the view that the poetriness of poetry resides in its being an out-of-the-way speech. It is the off-beat speech that is the essence of the office of the poet. Kuntaka called it "vakrokti" or oblique statement and erected on it a whole edifice of his poetics in a treatise entitled *Vakrokti-Jīvitam,* containing 4 "unmeṣas" or chapters–each having "kārikās" (versified aphoristic statements) and critical commentaries thereon. By the term "Vakrokti" Kuntaka means some word or meaning which makes the poet's statement striking, charming, skilful and wonderful, rendering the reader ecstatic and exultant. Kuntaka declares:

उभावेतावलंकार्यौ तयोः पुनरलंकृतिः ।
वक्रोक्तिरेव वैदग्ध्यभंगीभणितिरुच्यते ।।

(वक्रोक्तिजीवितम् 1/10)

[These two–word and sense–both are worthy of being decorated and their decorator is called "Vakrokti" which is nothing but a statement having the charm of poetic skilfulness.]

Clearly, according to Kuntaka, a statement becomes poetry only when it contains something that is extraordinarily charming and he locates that something in what he calls "vakrokti" which he defines as "वैदग्ध्यभंगी भणितिः" (a statement marked by turns of expressions. revealing aesthetic artfulness). This quality called वैदग्ध्यभंगी is all-pervading in poetry; it can reside in the arrangement of words, choice of special words out of numerous options available, in the sentence-structure, in the episodes conceived of by the poet's imaginative faculty and in the work, considered as a whole. Thus वर्णविन्यासवक्रता, पदपूर्वार्द्धवक्रता, प्रत्यय-वक्रता, वाक्यवक्रता, प्रकरणवक्रता and प्रबन्धवक्रता are the major categories of "Vakrokti" and these may have their numerous sub-categories. Evidently, the doctrine of "Vakrokti" is a formalist approach to imaginative writing and lays utmost emphasis on the Skilful Craftsmanship displayed in the work under discussion. However, it lays down criteria of poetic excellence that are thoroughly objective and attaches no great importance to subjectivity in art.

I believe that the doctrine of "Vakrokti" is by far the most practical and pragmatic approach to the understanding and appreciation of poetic greatness. It can make a greater appeal to the west than the doctrine of "Rasa" or the doctrine of "Dhvani". Let us consider each of the six major categories that Kuntaka has dealt with in his treatise, one by one.

The first category or form of "Vakrokti" that Kuntaka mentions is called "Varṇavinyāsavakratā" which creates a joyous impact by means of a special arrangement of letters. Perhaps, what the "alamkāravādī" thinkers had designated as the figure of speech called "Anuprāsa", Kuntaka chooses to call "Varṇavinyāsavakratā". However, this category of "Vakratā" subsumes not only "Anuprāsa" but also figures like "Yamaka" and "yamakābhāsa", all the three "guṇas" like "Oja", "Prasāda" and "Mādhurya", all the "Vrttis" such as "Paruṣā" "Komala" and "Upanāgarikā" and all the "Rītis"-Vaidarbhī", "Pāncālī" and "Gaudī". Kuntaka's concept of "Varṇa-vinyāsavakratā" is very broad indeed. But he wisely rules out the existence of it where the arrangement of "varṇas" (letters of the alphabet of the language) is for its own sake. In other words, it exists only where some aesthetic miracle is wrought by the poet by means of a skilful arrangement of "varṇas". He consistently stresses the point that the clever arrangement of letters should, in no way, hinder the sense of the verse concerned and that the rule of propriety should not be violated at any cost. Consider the following Sanskrit verse:

> उन्निद्रकोकनदरेणुपिशङ्गिताङ्गा
> गुञ्जन्ति मञ्जु मधुपाः कमलाकरेषु।
> एतच्चकास्ति च रवेर्नवबन्धुजीव-
> पुष्पच्छदाभमुदयाचलचुम्बि बिम्बम्।।
>
> [(Describing the beauty of nature at day-break, some observer of natural phenomena says:) "Bees (literally honey-drinkers), whose limbs have become yellowish on account of the pollen grains of red lotuses, are producing murmerous sounds in the ponds (literally, dwelling places of lotuses). And the disc of the sun, kissing the top of Udaya-hill and resembling the cluster of fresh Bandhujīva or Javākusuma flowers in its lustre, is shining forth rather brilliantly".]

Here, the poet has wrought an art-miracle by the sheer power of his skilful manipulation of combined letters in expressions like 'पिशङ्गिताङ्गा' and 'गुञ्जन्ति मञ्जु' and 'चुम्बि बिम्ब' which simply thrill us by means of the music produced by the sounds of the letters involved. The clever arrangement of the letters infuses in us a sense of wonder, full of admiration for the poet's craftsmanship. An English example of "varṇavinyāsavakratā" is the following extract from the first Chorus of *Atlanta in Calydon* by the Victorian poet Algernon Charles Swinburne:

When the hounds of spring are on winter's traces,
The mother of months in meadow or plain
Fills the shadows and windy places
With lisp of leaves and ripple of rain;
And the brown bright nightingale amorous
Is half assuaged for Itylus
For the Thracian ships and the foreign faces,
The tongueless vigil, and all the pain.

The passage is full of alliterations and assonances and naturally their skilful arrangement renders the passage charming beyond measure, filling the minds of readers with a sense of amazement at the poet's artistry. It must be placed on record that the Sanskrit poet Jayadeva, the Hindi poet "Padmakara" and the English poet Swinburne are to be recognized as the poets who create poetic marvels by resorting to "Varṇavinyāsavākratā".

The second category of Vakratā is called "Padapurvārdhavakratā" which creates poetic charm by means of making a very skilful use of words; it has eight subdivisions: रूढिवैचिज्य वक्रता, पर्यायवक्रता, उपचारवक्रता, विशेषणवक्रता, संवृतिवक्रता, वृत्तिवक्रता, लिंगवैचित्र्यवक्रता and क्रियावैचित्र्यवक्रता.

"Rūdhivaicitryavakratā" consists in using words in such a manner that they take on a meaning other than their normal, conventional sense. For example, the normal, conventional meaning of the word "Rāma" is the son of Dāśaratha, king of Ayodhyā. But see how the same word can be transformed into the source of an extraordinary and marvellous sense, capable of giving a thrill to the sensitive readers:

स्निग्धश्यामलकान्तिलिप्तवियतो वेल्लद्‌वूलाका घनाः,
वाता शीकरिणः पयोदसुहृदामानन्दकेकाः कलाः ।
कामं सन्तु दृढं कठोरहदयो रामोऽस्मि सर्वं सहे
वैदेही तु कथं भविष्यति हहा हा देवि! धीरा भव।।

[(Rāma is talking to himself of his own and his wife's (who has been kidnapped by Rāvaṇa) supposed reactions to the rainy season while he has been separated from his ladylove:] "The clouds in which cranes are frolicking gaily and in which sky has become covered with a shine of deep blue colour; breezes that are laden with droplets of rain; the happy and pleasant cries of the friends of the clouds (i.e. of peacocks)– let all these be as intoxicating and inciting as these might choose to be, the hard-hearted Rāma will bear all. But I do not know how Vaidehī might be at this moment. Oh, madam, be patient and forbearing".]

In the penultimate line the word "Rāma" does not just mean "the son of Dasharatha" but"a man who can undergo any hardship however difficult it might be". And this meaning is highly effective in the context of the verse for it suggests all unbearable situations that Rāma has passed through without any complaint–the renouncing of his coronation, forest-going, bereavement of the father and separation from his ladylove and numerous others of like nature. This is indeed an excellent example of रूढिवैचित्र्यवक्रता variety of पदपूर्वार्द्धवक्रता in which something miraculous has been infused in the normal conventional sense of the word "Rāma". A western example of "Rūdhi-vaicitryavakratā" variety of "Padapūrvārdhavakratā" is to be found in the opening speech of Oedipus in the *Oedipus Tyrannus* by Sophocles:

Children,
I would not have you speak through messengers,
And therefore I have come myself to hear you–
I, Oedipus, who bear the famous name.

In this extract, the name 'Oedipus' does not mean the son of Laius and Jocasta nor does it carry its etymological sense of the swollenfooted one'. Here the name carries the sense of 'the great one' who had solved the riddle of the Sphinx and thus saved the city of Thebes, known for its line of glorious kings like Cadmus, Labdacus etc. This new sense of the name highlights the 'Hubris' of the speaker and prepares the audience for his most tragic end, 'Hubris' being the root-cause of the tragedies of all such people-'Hubris' which the gods do not tolerate. And it very subtly and artistically provides the antecedents of Oedipus who became the king of Thebes in consequence of his having solved the riddle of the Sphinx who had appeared as a scourge of Thebes. Thus the use of the word 'Oedipus' in the passage is very subtle and indirect and full of what Kuntaka calls 'vakrokti'–विचित्रभंगीभणिति.

"Paryāyavakratā" is another variety of 'Padapūrvārdhavakratā'. It occurs when the poet chooses a word from a list of its synonyms with some special purpose. And when a sensitive reader perceives that special purpose, he/she dances with joy and undergoes ecstasy. Consider the following Sanskrit verse by Kālidāsa:

द्वयं गतं सम्प्रति शोचनीयतां समागमप्रार्थनया कपालिनः।
कला च सा कान्तिमती कलावतः त्वमस्य लोकस्य च नेत्रकौमुदी।।
(कुमारसम्भव 5/71)

[(Lord Shiva himself in the guise of a Brahmin/student is dissuading Pārvatī from her rigorous penance, intended to get Shiva as her husband:) "Two things have become miserable on account of their prayer for obtaining the union with Kapālī (literally, the holder of the garland of skulls): that lustrous digit of the moon and thou, the moon light for the eyes of the whole world".]

Here Shiva, in the guise of a student, is testing the genuineness of the love in the heart of Pārvatī for Himself by provoking her through a censure of Shiva left and right. He wants to convey to Pārvatī a hateful site of the Lord by calling her attention to the fact that Shiva wears the garland of skulls from the burning ghat. Naturally, the purpose of the test is served best by calling Shiva 'कपाली' and not 'पिनाकी' or any other name of the Lord. Thus the word 'कपाली' has 'विचित्रभंगीभणिति'–a sharply charming turn of expression. It is indeed an excellent example of "Paryāyavakratā" of which Kālidāsa is a grand master. An English example of "Paryāyavakratā" is to be found in Milton's invocation to the Heavenly Muse Urania in the first verse-paragraph of the *Paradise Lost:*

...I thence
Invoke thy aid to my adventurous song,
That with no middle flight intends to soar
Above the Aonian mount, while it pursues
Things unattempted yet in prose-or rhyme.

The expression "Aonian mount" has "Paryāya-Vakratā" because what Milton wants to convey through that expression cannot be conveyed by its synonym Mt. Helicon, the dwelling place of the Muses. Milton purports to state that his proposed epic is going to be nothing short of the highest, even much higher than anything attempted in Greek antiquity. Had he used just "Mt. Helicon", the range of the Greek achievements that he intends surpassing would have been limited to poetry–whereas the word "Aonian" or "Ionian" calls our attention to the fact that in the Greek region called "Ionia" twelve rich cities had arisen in the 11th century B.C. and Ionian schools of philosophy, art, poetry and literature flourished as a consequence of their rise and these proved to be the source of Greek excellence in all fields in subsequent ages. Thus the expression "Aonian mount" which is a synonym of "Mt. Helicon" is far richer and of far larger significance than "Mt. Helicon" and conveys Milton's message much more powerfully than "Mt. Helicon" could ever have done. Evidently, its "Vakratā" cannot be questioned on any count whatsoever; it is bound to exhilerate a sensitive reader of English poetry.

"Upacāravakratā" exists where inanimate things are treated as if these were living beings; it also exists where something abstract and formless is treated as if it were concrete and embodied. The examples of "Gauṇī Laksanā" and "Rupakālamkāra" are covered by this form of vakratā which creates a wonderful impression on the reader. Consider, for example, the following Sanskrit verse from *Meghadūtam:*

> गच्छन्तीनां रमणवसतिं योषितां तत्र नक्तं
> रुद्धालोके नरपतिपथे सूचिभेद्यैस्तमोभिः ।
> सौदामिन्या कनकनिकषस्निग्धया दर्शयोर्वी
> तोयोत्सर्गस्तनितमुखरो मा स्म भूर्विक्लवास्ताः
>
> (पूर्वमेघ–41)

> [(The Yakṣa is directing his messenger–the Cloud, taking his message to his Yakṣiṇī in Alakā:) "There (in Ujjayinī) thou shouldst show the path by (thy) shining lightning, as sharp as the line drawn by gold on a touchstone, for the young women, going during the night, to the residences of their lovers, the thoroughfares having been rendered dark by the darkness worthy of being pierced by needles."]

The adjectival expression "सूचिभेद्यैः" used to qualify "तमोभिः" has "upacārabakratā" because darkness, which is formless, has been presented here as a thing such as a bedsheet that could be pierced through by a needle. This account of the darkness lends an extraordinary charm to the entire description of the thoroughfares of Ujjayinī at night. Keats's expression "embalmbed darkness" in the sixth stanza of 'Ode to a Nightingale' is an English example of "Upacāravakratā" because darkness has been pictured here as human bodies that used to be embalmed in ancient times in countries like Egypt by means of spices of different varieties that prevented them from decaying. In Keats's poem the world of the nightingale is that of darkness which knows no decaying because it has been enbalmed by the fragrances and smells of all kinds of flowers. The expression 'embalmed darkness' captivates the hearts of sensitive-readers by means of the "Upacāravakratā" that underlies it. It must be noted that all examples of 'transferred epithets' fall within the purview of "upacāravakratā". The best example of this, of course, is the expression "weary way" in the opening stanza of Gray's 'Elegy Written in a Country Church-Yard' where the way has been treated as a tired man, though, in point of fact, the adjective fits the 'ploughman'.

The next variety of "Padapūrvārdhavakratā" is what Kuntaka calls 'Viṣeṣaṇavakrata'. This variety of "Vakratā" consists in an extraordinary beauty created by means of an imaginatively rich epithet. Consider the following Sanskrit verse:

> करान्तरालीनकपोलभित्ति वांष्पोच्छलत्कूणितपत्रलेखा।
> श्रोत्रान्तरे पिण्डितचित्रवृत्तिः शृणोति गीतध्वनिमत्र तन्वी।।

> [(An onlooker is describing a lady listening to a song during her separation from her lover;) "The frail-bodied one is listening to the melody of a song here. Her cheeks' wall is lost between her palms and the figures of leaves and flowers drawn on her (cheeks) have been spoiled by her over flowing tears and her entire mind is centred on the function of her ears".]

In the above verse, the word 'तन्वी' is most striking and remarkable for it heightens the effect of the miserable plight of the lady concerned much more powerfully than any other qualifying expression used in the verse–the intensity of the lady's anguish and pangs of separation. The entire miracle of the verse has been wrought by this very epithet–the lady's तनुता or frailness speaks volumes about her adverse situation. An English example of "Viśeṣaṇavakratā" is the following passage from Wordsworth's "Tintern Abbey":

....that serene and blessed mood,
In which the affections gently lead us on,-
Until, the breath of this corporeal frame
And even the motion of our human blood
Almost suspended, we are laid asleep
In body, and become a living soul.

The penultimate word which is an adjective of the noun 'soul', is, I believe, the most arresting word in the extract. It is so striking because it is a travesty of the age-old notion regarding 'soul' considered as something that is immortal and imperishable. Is 'soul' sometimes dead? Can it ever die? Negative invariably will be the answers to these questions.

If the soul is immortal, the qualifying word 'living', used just before it, is redundant. Otherwise, we shall have to interpret that word differently. To my mind, the expression 'living soul' here means 'spirituality embodied'. Wordsworth, in the extract, under discussion, is describing man's state during 'Samādhi'–a mental state in which all physical activities cease and spirituality pervades the entire being of the person as the person concerned is in communion with Brahm or God. Thus the adjective 'living' emerges as the most significant word in the extract whose beauty centres around it. Clearly, it is an excellent example of "Viśeṣaṇavakratā".

The next variety of "Padapūrvārdhavakratā" is "Samvṛtivakratā". This consists in the use of some pronoun which creates a wonderful effect, making the entire description charming and beautiful. The essence of this "vakratā" lies in hiding the details of the description and pointing to them through some suggestive word which leaves a lot unsaid. Consider the following Sanskrit verse from Kālidāsa's *Kumārasambham* (8/11):

> दर्पणे च परिभोगदर्शिनी पृष्ठतः प्रणयिनो निषेदुषः ।
> वीक्ष्य बिम्बमनुबिम्बमात्मनः कानि कानि न चकार लज्जया ।।

> [(The poet is describing the love-making of the newly wedded couple (Shiva and Pārvatī:) "Which which acts did not (Pārvatī) do out of sheer bashfulness when she, while viewing the signs of love-making left on the different parts of her body in a mirror, found the reflection of her lover cast on her own reflection--her lover who had (silently) arrived on the seene from behind?"]

Here the pronoun phrase "कानि कानि" is the source of the entire beauty of the passage because it leaves all the details of Pārvati's acts to the imagination of the reader and thus assumes great charm for, art lies in concealing art. An English example of "Samvṛtīvakratā" is the following passage from Browning's dramatic monologue "My Last Duchess":

> She had
> A heart...how shall I say?...too soon made glad,
> Too easily impressed; she liked whate'er
> She looked on, and her looks went everywhere.

The entire beauty of the passage lies in the parenthetical clause 'how shall I say?' which suggests a lot that remains unstated but at the same time gives the reader a thrill by stirring his/her imagination regarding the feeling of the speaker who expresses his inability to describe the true nature of his first wife's 'heart' by opening vistas of interpretation in the mind of the reader. Clearly, it is an excellent example of "Samvṛtīvakratā". The following passage from the same poet is also illustrative of the 'vakratā' under discussion:

> She thanked me,-good; but thanked
> Somehow....I know not how....as if she ranked
> My gift of a nine-hundred-years-old name with anybody's gift.

The "Samvṛtīvakratā" of the passage lies again in the parenthetical clause 'I know not how' which gives expression to the speaker's feeling of shame and humiliation without mentioning either, leaving a lot unstated.

Another king of "Padapūrvārdhavakratā" is what Kuntaka designates as "Vṛttivakratā". Here by the term "Vṛtti" Kuntaka means grammatical items like "Taddhita, Samāsa" etc. I think Kuntaka intends covering all sources of pleasure ācārya Vāmana had called Rīti under the rubrick of Vṛttivakratā. For example, in the following Sanskrit verse "vakratā" or poetic charm has been created simply by means of a special arrangement of compounds (Samāsas):

> एतत्तालतमालसालसरलव्यालोलवल्लीलता-
> च्छन्नंसूर्यकरप्रतापरहितं शंखेन्दुकुन्दोज्वलम् ।
> गन्धर्वामरसिद्धकिन्नरवधूतुंगस्तनास्फालितं
> स्नानाय प्रतिवासरं भवतु मे गाङ्गं जलं निर्मलम् ।।

> [May the water of the Ganges be free from dust for my daily bath–the water that remains covered by these trees of Tāla, Tamāla, Sāla, and Sarala as also by creepers and bushes flourishing on all sides, is far removed from the heat of the rays of the sun and is as white as conch-shell, the moon and the 'Kundaflower' and has been torn asunder by the lofty breasts of the brides of Gandharvas, the gods, the Siddhas and the Kinnaras!]

The modern English romantic poet, Dylan Thomas, too, creates a marvellous poetic effect (vakratā) by means of compound expressions in his famous elegy 'A Refusal to Mourn the Death by Fire of a Child in London':

> Never until the mankind making
> Bird-Beast-and flower.
> Fathering and all-humbling darkness

Tells with silence the last light breaking
And the still hour
Is come of the sea tumbling in harness
And I must enter again the round
Zion of the water bead
And the synagogue of the ear of corn
Shall I let pray the shadow of a sound
Or sow my salt seed
In the least valley of sackcloth to mourn
The majesty and burning of the child's death.

Similarly, Shakespeare creates a wonderful poetic effect by means of the compounds of epithets in the following speech of *Macbeth:*

Will all great Neptune's ocean wash this blood
Clean from my hand? No: this my hand will rather
The multitudinous seas incanradine
Making the green one red. *(Macbeth II.i.)*

Consider the compounds 'multitudinous' and 'incarnadine' and the magic wrought by them.

Both passages, cited above, from the works of Dylan Thomas and William Shakespeare are excellent examples of "Vṛttivakratā" as Kuntaka used and expounded the term.

"Vakratā" can also be produced by referring to an object skilfully through a gender where the same object could have been alluded to by another possible gender. This kind of "vakratā" is known as "Lingavaicitryavakratā" and feminine gender is normally the instrument by means of which this kind of "vakratā" is produced. Consider the following lines by the Hindī poet Sumitrānandana "Panta":

सिखा दो ना हे मधुप-कुमारि!
मुझे भी अपने मीठे गान।

[Teach me also O bee-maiden!
How thou singest thy sweet songs.]

Here the poet is addressing the black bee, a species of wasp. The Hindi word for the black bee that the poet has chosen is 'मधुप' (i.e. the drinker of honey). In Hindī the word is in masculine gender. However, the context being that of singing, the poet has chosen to address the black bee as 'मधुप-कुमारि' (i.e. O daughter of the blackbee) rather than 'मधुप

कुमार' (i.e. O son of the blackbee). This creates a very special kind of charm for the lovers of poetry because they know that in point of sweetness the female voice is regarded as superior to male voice all over the world. Thus the use of the feminine gender in the given context has created a wonderful poetic effect. It is a really wonderful example of 'Lingavaicitryavakratā'. An English example of this is to be found in Wordsworth's famous sonnet entitled "The World is Too Much With us" 1 5:

'This sea that bares her bosom to the moon'

The subject of the line is the high tide that occurs when there is full-moon in the sky. This phenomenon has been presented here by the poet as the advances made by the sea towards her male lover 'the moon'. Now, the sea in English can be used as a male or a female, depending on the choice of user and his need. In the context of the line, the presentation of the sea as the female partner, making advances to her male, is very charming indeed. Had the poet used the word 'his' in place of the word 'her' of the line cited, the effect would not have been even half of what has been produced by the word 'her'. We remember the same poet having presented the sea as a male in the sonnet entitled 'It is a Beauteous Evening':

Listen! the mighty Being is awake,
And doth with his eternal motion make
A Sound like thunder-everlastingly.

But there it was in the fitness of things that the poet presented the sea as a male, performing some very hard task, unfit for women. But making gestures of love befits the female partner better than the male and hence the presentation of the sea as a female in "The world Is Too Much With Us". No doubt the line is an excellent example of "Lingavaicitryavakratā".

Capable poets can create wonders even by skilful employment of 'verbs'. This Kuntaka calls "Kriyāvaicitryavakratā". Consider the following Sanskrit verse:

'स दहतु दुरितं शाम्भवो वः शराग्निः'

[May that special fiery arrow of Śambhu (Lord Shiva) burn your sin!]

An arrow, by its nature, is destructive but even destruction has a positive side and it is this positive side of Śhiva's arrow that has been highlighted by the poet in the above citation; it would destroy the sin of the audience and the sin's destruction is highly desirable. Thus the act of Shiva's arrow has assumed some kind of charm about it. The charm is a little strange in that an arrow normally destroys only concrete and solid things. But sin is something abstract and not concrete and thus the act of the arrow is charmingly strange.

An excellent English example of "Kriyāvaicitryavakratā" is to be found in the last half line of D.G. Rossetti's famous poem "The Blessed Damozel":

"I heard her tears."

The cited half-line is a lover's reaction to what is happening to his beloved long dead, thought by the lover to be residing at the momet in the heaven, millions of miles away from the earth, up in the sky. The lover is trying to express the utter helplessness of his beloved in the heaven whose entire effort to embrace her lover on the earth is in vain and as a result of this the lady lays "her face between her hands/and" weeps. The lover on the earth comments: "I heard her tears". A human being can hear the sound of something at some distance from him or her. But can one hear from the earth the sound produced in the heaven? And do tears produce sounds: supposing, they can be heard when they fall in the form of droplets on a solid ground, the droplets from the eyes of the Blessed Damozel, if they fell at all, could not have fallen on any heavenly ground because she was leaning out from the gold bar of heaven–they must have evaporated in the air. However, the lover is being very emphatic on his having heard his lady's tears. There is no denying that there is a great charm about the line and that charm centres on the strangeness of the verb 'heard'. Even if the lover's act is a mere psychological effusion, it has a tenderness of feeling about it and fascinates us deeply. It is undoubtedly an excellent example of "kriyāvaicitryavakratā;" its "kriyā" or verb has a compelling power to arrest our attention to it by means of the apparent impossiblity of its accomplishment as also by means of its inherent power of suggestion regarding the lover's supposed spiritual bond with his beloved who had died long ago.

Pratyaya-Vakratā:–Just as there are "Pada-Purvārdha vakratās", Kuntaka contemplates "Pada-Parārdha-Vakratas", otherwise known as "Pratyaya-Vakratās" also. Its first variety is known as "Samkhyāvaicitrya-Vakratā". This exists where a great poetic charm is created by means of the skilful and clever use of numbers–singular or plural. Consider the following Sanskrit verse:

"फुल्लेन्दीवरकानननानि नयने पाणी सरोजाकराः"

> [(Some bystander is commenting on the beauty of a beautiful maiden): "The two eyes (of the maiden) are the jungles of blue lotuses and her two hands those of red."]

Here the number two has been projected as equal to numberless things: the two eyes are worth numberless blue-lotuses and the two hands of the maiden are worth numberless red-lotuses. The use of the numbers (2 for minor terms–eyes and hands–and numberless for major terms–blue and red lotuses respectively) bring home to us the extraordinariness of the maiden's eyes and hands. The English poet John Donne wrights a miracle by equating 'two' with 'one' in "A Valediction Forbidding Mourning":

> Our two soules therefore, which are one,
> Though I must goe, endure not yet
> A breach, but an expansion,
> Like gold to ayery thinnesse beate.

The reader, perceiving the logic of the poet behind equating the number 'two' with the number 'one' in regard to the soul of his wife and of himself, gets a thrill and his aesthetic enjoyment of the lines increases manyfold. This is entirely due to what Kuntaka chooses to call "Samkhyā-Vaicitrya Vakratā".

A kindred "vakratā" is "Kāla Vaicitryavakratā" which occurs when the suffix, added to a verb, signifying a particular tense, performs a poetic miracle. Consider the following Hindī "Dohā":

> नासा मोरि नचाय हग करी कका की सौंह।
> काँटे सी कसकति हियें गड़ी कटीली भौंह।।

> [(Someone, who had gone to a beautiful maiden to enquire whether she knew the whereabouts of some object that he had lost, is meditating on the lady's reaction and reporting to his friend "Twisting her nostril and rolling her eyelids, she swore by her uncle and her sharply dense eye-lashes pierced my heart and thorn-like are causing pain in my heart"]

The word 'कसकति', having the Hindi suffix 'ति', indicates continuity of the action that had taken place sometimes ago and thus makes the description all the more poignant: the lady's sharp dense eye-lash had pierced his heart long ago but its impact on his mind and heart is still the same: it is paining him even today and will go on paining him even in times to go. Thus the simple suffix 'ति' in the verb 'कसकति' has rendered the line extraordinarily beautiful by suggesting the extraordinaniness of the eyelash of the lady concerned. An English example of this "Vakratā" is to be found in Wordsworth's sonnet entitled "Composed upon Westminster Bridge' l. 12:

'The river glideth at his own sweet will'.

The suffix 'th' added to the verb 'glide' stresses the assured continuity of the flow of Thames; it is suggestive of the poet's unflinching faith that the river will never cease to glide at his own sweet will. Note that this shade of the verb was beyond the form 'glides'. The suffix 'th' added to the verb 'glide' enables the verb to express the free smooth and ceaseless movement of Thames. No doubt it has "Kāla-Vaicitrya-Vakratā" of Kuntaka's formulation.

Then there is what Kuntaka designates as "Kāraka-Vaicitrya vakratā" which resides in the clever use of Tenses such as normally instrumental inanaimate things serving as doers in stead of the normal doers in the form of some person or persons. This device lends a unique charm to the entire description and makes the verse really beautiful. The following Sanskrit verse illustrates it very well:

पाणिः सम्प्रति मे हठात् किमपरं स्प्रष्टुं धनुर्धावति ।

> [(Rāma, who had been requesting the ocean to make way for his army but all in vain, says in utter desperation:) "My hand now rushes per force to touch the bow."]

The hand is the normal instrument in wielding a bow but it has become here the actual doer (wielder). This makes the line far more effective and beautiful than the normal statement "पाणिना धनुगृहीतुभिच्छामि" (I wish to take the bow in my hand") can ever hope to be. For an English example of "Kāraka-Vaicitrya-Vakratā" we can cite the following passage from the "Dagger Scene" of Shakespeare's *Macbeth:*

–Now o'er the one-half world
Nature seems dead, and wicked dreams abuse
The curtain'd sleep; now witchcraft celebrates
Pale Hecate's offerings; and wither'd murder,
Alarum'd by his sentinel, the wolf,
Whose howl's his watch, thus with his stealthy pace
With Tarquin's ravishing strides, towards his design
Moves like a ghost.

Here we have several cases of "Kāraka-Vaicitrya-Vakratā" piled up together: 'wicked dreams abuse/The curtain'd sleep', 'now witchcraft celebrates/ Pale Hecate's offernings' and 'wither'd murder...moves like a ghost'. It is the sleeping man's sleep, closed in his eyes, that gets abused or disturbed by wicked dreams. But wicked dreams themselves have become the nominative case here rather than the instrumental case. Similarly, witchcraft is normally the means by which witches perform their rituals to placate the goddess of the underworld–Hecate. But in the present passage "witcheraft" itself is the nominative case of celebrating offerings to Hecate. In like manner, the abstract idea of murder rather than the murderer (i.e. Macbeth) is moving towards the victim (i.e. Duncan). Thus the transfers of cases create a marvellously poetic effect here which is beyond the powers of the normal arrangements of cases.

"Vakratā" can also be created by the transfer of grammatical category called Puruṣa or Person in a very skilful manner. For example, in place of the second person, the poet can render his speech quite charming by using the third person. Consider the following Sanskrit verse:

वक्तुं नोत्सहते मनः परमतो जानातु देवी स्वयम्

> [(Some minister is reporting his king's mismanagement of the state-affairs to the Chief Queen:) "Beyond this my mind does not dare say anything; your ladyship herself ought to know (that)".]

Here in the expression 'जानातु देवी स्वयम्' the speaker has used the third person in stead of the second person. But the use of the third person is far more effective than the use of the second person could have been. This is a very good example of "Puruṣa-Vakratā". An equally good English example is available in the following speech of Malvolio, addressed to Olivia in Shakespeare's *Twelfth Night I.V.*: "I marvel your ladyship takes delight in such a barren rascal; I saw him put down the other day with an ordinary fool that has no more brain than stone."

Here, too, the use of the third person in place of the second person, has made the statement very effective. Malvolio's intention is to pooh-pooh the liberty granted to Feste, the Fool, by Olivia. The purpose of Malvolio is served best by stating the fact through the use of the third person as if Olivia were a person of no great significance–a person inviting public censure of the highest kind.

Vākya-Vakratā: According to Kuntaka, Vakratā is not confined to a word-particle or a word; it can exist even in a whole sentence or statement.

"Vastu-Vakratā", "Vācyārtha-Vakratā" and "Vakya-Vakratā" are, according to him, interchangeable terms, conveying the same idea. Any statement which is charming and thrilling on account of the skilful craftsmanship of the poet can be called the possessor of "Vākya-Vakratā". This can be natural ("Sahaja") or studied (Āhārya). The first kind covers what is normally known as "Svabhāvokti" (the description of something as it actually is in its natural form). Consider the following Sanskrit verse:

> हंसानां निनदेषु यैः कवलितैरासज्यते कूजताम्
> अन्यः कोऽपि कषायकण्ठलुठनादाघर्घरो विभ्रमः ।
> ते सम्प्रत्यकठोरवारणवधूदन्तांकुरस्पर्धिनो
> निर्याताः कमलाकरेषु विसिनीकन्दाग्रिमग्रन्थयः ।।
>
> [(Some observer of natural phenomena is describing the growth of stalks on the lotuses at the commencement of the rainy season:) "The knots of fresh stalks that compete with the newly grown smooth toothlets of the she-cubs of elephants, have appeared on the lotuses–the stalks after eating which some extraordinary grace is lent to the melodious murmurous voice of the she-swans".]

It is indeed a matter-of-fact description of a natural phenomenon but the description is expressive of the inimitable genius of the poet who is full of tender feelings displayed in each detail of the description, under review.

It is clear that "Vākya-Vakratā in its 'svabhāvokti' form exists in a realistic description that reveals the poet's imaginative faculty, full of tenderness and graciousness. An excellent English example of "Vākya-Vakratā" of Kuntaka's above formulation is to be found in the following description by king Duncan and Banquo of Macbeth's Castle in Inverness;

> Dun. This castle hath a pleasant seat: the air nimbly and sweetly recommends itself unto our gentle senses.
>
> Ban.– This guest of summer,
> The temple-haunting martlet, does approve,
> By his lov'd mansionry, that the heaven's breath
> Smells wooingly here: no jutty frieze, buttress,
> Nor coigne of vantage, but this bird hath made
> His pendant bed and procreant cradle:
> Where they most breed and haunt, I have obser'd
> The air is delicate.

Forget for the time being the tragic irony, lurking in the description of the castle in Inverness going to become the sluaghter-house of Duncan and concentrate on the description of the apparently serene and peaceful atmosphere of Macboth's castle and realize Shakespeare's extraordinary tenderness which has transformed and transmuted something quite ordinary into an object of imperishable joy and beauty, though the facts described are true to life.

"Āhārya Vākya-Vakratā" covers all the figures of sense called "Arthālamkāras". Kuntaka acknowledges only 20 figures of sense: रूपक, अप्रस्तुतप्रशंसा, पर्यायोक्त, व्याजस्तुति, उत्प्रेक्षा, अतिशयोक्ति, उपमा, श्लेष, व्यतिरेक, दृष्टान्त, अर्थान्तरन्यास, आक्षेप, विभावना, ससन्देह, अपह्नुति, संसृष्टि and संकर plus रसवद्, दीपक and सहोक्ति. "Sabdālamkāras" or figures of words, it must be noted, fall within the category of "vakratā" called "Padapūrvārdha-Vakratā", more precisely, within its sub-division called "Varṇa-Vinyāsa-Vakratā". English poetry can provide examples of all the figures listed here. For example, the figure called "Paryāyokta" or "Paryāyokti" consists in saying something in an indirect and suggestive way. Its Sanskrit example is the following verse:

> यं प्रेक्ष्य चिररूढाऽपि निवासप्रीतिरुज्झिता
> मदेनैरावतमुखे मानेन हृदये हरेः।।

(From "हयग्रीववध" by Maintha)

> [(The poet is describing the hero of his poem, namely, Hayagrīva:) "After witnessing whom, ecstasy abandoned her grown love for residing in the countenance of Airāvata and self-pride that of residing in the heart of Hari (Indra)"]

The poet wanted to say that Hayagrīva's personality was very colourful, marked by ecstatic exultation in his youth and self-pride. Now, the abode of the first is the heavenly horse Airāvata and that of the latter is the king of the gods–Indra alias Hari. The poet's intention is to prove that at the very sight of Hayagrīva Airāvata forgot his intoxicating youthfulness and Indra his self-pride. This very thought he expresses indirectly by stating that the abstract idea of "Mada" or ecstatic exultation in one's youthfulness, which had stayed in the mouth of Airāvata for a very long time, left the same and took its position on the face of Hayagrīva. Likewise, the idea of self-pride left its habitation in the heart of Indra and took refuge in the heart of Hayagrīva. This is "Paryāyokta", pure and simple. An English example of the figure is the following stanza from

Gray's famous "Elegy":

> The struggling pangs of conscious truth to hide,
> To quench the blushes of ingenuous shame,
> Or heap the shrine of Luxury and Pride
> With incense kindled at the Muse's flame.

The context of the stanza is a comparison between the humble peasants of the hamlet of the poem on the one hand and the so-called highly civilized rich people of the cities, proud of their refined taste and material achievements which are, really speaking, devoid of essential purity and spirituality. The poet wants to congratulate the countrymen on their good luck which has saved them from a life of sins and corruptions of all description, though it has placed them in adversity. The country-people might be living a simple and plain life but unlike the city-people, they are not required to suffer the pricking of the conscience in the wake of some wrong-doing whose truth the so-called civilized people of the city seek to suppress by all means at their command. The city people commit all kinds of shameful acts through their ingenuity and craftiness and try to escape the results of those acts through bribery or compensation to the victims of their shameful acts but the poor villagers have no chance of such acts and are thus saved from situations of that nature. The city people have the knack of placating their political and administrative bosses, leading a life of luxury and pride, with their writings of flattery and panageric, which should have properly been addressed to the goddess of poetry. But the countrymen are fortunately free from the tricks adopted by the city-people for their self-promotion. All these ideas have been expressed by the poet through a very oblique sentence and their lies the entire charm of the piece. The figure of speech is evidently "Paryāyokta" and that is a form of "Vakya-Vakratā". We need not deal with all other figures of the sense, recognized by Kuntaka; "Paryāyokta" gives a sufficient idea of the "Vakya-Vakratā" of Kuntaka's formulation.

Prakaraṇa-Vakratā:–The scope of "Vakratā" is not confined to word-particles, words and sentences; Kuntaka has extended it to the various episodes that poets introduce in their compositions–be they narrative or dramatic. The poets invent, by means of their inventive and imaginative powers, episodes that are quite clever and enthral the reader and audience whose delights increase severalfold when they realize the beauty of the episode concerned. For example, in Vālmīki's *Rāmāyaṇa*, it is Rāma who goes for the hide of the golden deer and hearing the exclamations "Oh Lakṣmaṇa!" "O Sītā!" produced by the illusory deer (actually the demon Mārīca), Sīta thinks that the exclamations are made by Rāma in some great distress and sends Lakṣamaṇa for the rescue-operation. This episode in the "Araṇyakānda" seems to be quite improper because Lakṣamaṇa the assistant of Rāma, should have gone in search of the deer concerned and not the chief of the team–Rāma himself. Moreover, Rāma, the superman that he is, hardly needed Laṣamaṇa's help in His distress. Sitā's logic is flawed indeed. Guided by this line of thought, the writer of the play *Udāttarāghava* reconstructs the same episode in such a way that Lakṣamaṇa is first sent in search of the deer and later hearing the exclamations "Oh Rāma!" "Oh Sīta!", Rāma rushes to rescue Laksamana, leaving Sītā all alone in the cottage. This change in the episode is proof positive of the charming artistry of the author of *Udāttarāghava* who has wrought an aesthetic miracle by introducing the aforesaid change in the "Māricavadha Prakaraṇa" of his work. An English example of "Prakaraṇa-Vakratā" is to be found in the seventh stanza of Keats's 'Ode to a Nightingale' in the allusion to the Biblical character Ruth. In the "Book of Ruth" in the 'Old Testament' of the *Holy Bible* there is no mention of the nightingale. But in his 'ode' Keats invents the fact that when the widow Ruth felt homesick while working in "an alien corn" (i.e. in the field of Boaz), the voice of the nightingale of the poem itself had brought solace to her in her distress. In the context of the poem, through the introduction of a slight change in the story of Ruth, an art miracle has been wrought and the reader is enthralled by it. This is an excellent example of "Prakaraṇa-Vakratā" in English poetry.

There are several forms of "Prakaraṇavakratā" that Kuntaka discusses in the fourth "Unmeṣa" of his treatise but the kind discussed above is the most significant.

According to Kuntaka, "Vakratā" can be created not only by certain "Prakaraṇas,–"Vākyas", "Padas" or "Padānśas"–but also by the work considered as a whole. The "Vakratā" that the entire work, taken as whole, creates, is called "Prabandha-Vakratā" in the sense of what western criticism chooses to call 'moral' or "message" of the work which gives a new and extraordinary direction to the reader for making his or her life better and meaningful. This explains why works on the same subject dealing with the same story differ from one another There are so many works dealing with the story of Rāma–*Rāmābhyudaya, Udāttarāghava, Vīracarita, Bāla Rāmāyaṇa, Kṛtyārāwaṇa, Māyāpuṣpaka* etc. and yet each has its own point of view to impress on the mind and heart of the audience. There lies the "Prabandha Vakratā" of each of them. So far as Western literature is concerned, the story of sorceress Maedia has been treated of by the Greek dramatist Euripides as well as the Roman dramatist Seneca but each play has its own character and its own elan. And precisely in that individual elan lies the Prabandha-Vakratā of that work.

Thus since 'vakratā' is what pervades the entire being of a given work of poetry, from its letters and word-particles to its entire body, 'vakratā' deserves to be called the be-all and end-all of poetry, its very soul and that justifies the title of Kuntaka's work–वक्रोक्तिजीवितम्–whose literal translation is "(On Poetry) whose life is वक्रोक्ति (Vakrokti)". I think the doctrine of "Vakrokti" propounded by Kuntaka is the most sensible, practical and pragmatic account of the poetriness of poetry which provides us critical tools, fit for universal application.

How to Apply the Doctrine of "Vakrokti" to a Given work?

Any text, claiming to be an expression of poetry–in verse or prose–can be very easily subjected to Kuntaka's "doctrine". First of all, we should find out the various forms of "vakratā" available in the body of the text under discourse–पदपूर्वार्द्ध as well as पदपरार्द्ध–with the sub-divisions of these. Then we should look for the प्रकरणवक्रता's that we are able to discern in its various episodes. Lastly, we should try to pinpoint the प्रबन्धवक्रता of the work as a whole. We should, then, try to place the work in the मार्ग–सुकुमार, विचित्र or मध्यम–to which it belongs. This will, no doubt, be a very rewarding and satisfying approach–liberal, democratic and critical.

Aucitya-Sampradāya

"Aucitya" or "Propriety" has been regarded all over the world as the most essential quality of human conduct and even in the field of poetry that statement holds good. What is right, what is apt to a particular situation, what should not be uttered in certain circumstances; what is timely, what is out of tune–all these considerations are covered in the critical concept called "Aucitya". Bharata, Aristotle, Horace, Dandī, Bhāmaha, Ānandavardhana, Sydney, Dryden, Samuel Jonson, Coleridge, T.S. Eliot, F.R. Leavis–all first-rate critics have recognized the importance of "aucitya" in imaginative writings. But to the Kasmīrī poet and critic–Kṣemendra–goes the credit of having erected the facade of "Aucityavāda" according to which the most significant element of poetry, its very soul, is "Aucitya" which is to be the deciding factor of all of its aspects, beginning with the choice of words to the entire composition, character-portrayal, structuring of its events and the depicting of the atmosphere of its various parts. There is hardly an element of poetry which can afford to neglect "aucitya" at all. If "Rasa" is the ultimate end of all imaginative writings, there is no greater obstacle in the way of the production of "Rasa" than the violation of the principle of "Aucitya" or "Decorum". Ānandavardhana has boldly declared.

अनौचित्यादृते नान्यद्रसभंगस्य कारणम्।
प्रसिद्धौचित्यबन्धस्तु रसस्योपनिषत् परा।।

(ध्वन्यालोक 3/70 के पश्चात्)

[There is no other cause of damage to the cause of Rasa than impropriety. The organisation of propriety in regard to the stories of well-known (heroes and heroines) is the Upaniṣad of Rasa.]

Since the observance of the principle of "Aucitya" is essential at all levels and in each component of poetry-making, Kṣemendra declared it to be soul of poetry. He affirms unequivocally:

अलंकारास्त्वलंकारा गुणा एव गुणाः सदा।
औचित्यं रससिद्धस्य स्थिरं काव्यस्यजीवितम्।।

(औचित्यविचारचर्चा 5/4)

[Figures (in poetry) are just figures or external beautifiers and guṇas are just guṇas (certain features of the personality of poetry). But it is (fully) established that the life of Rasa-realized poetry is Aucitya.]

He also declares rather boldly:

काव्यस्यालमलंकारैः किं मिथ्याजनितैर्गुणैः।
यस्य जीवितमौचित्यं विचिन्त्यापि न दृश्यते।।

(औचित्यविचारचर्चा 5/5)

[If in a poem its life (called) "Aucitya" is not to be found even after a thorough search, of what avail are its figures and to waht purpose are the guṇas that have been generated in vain?]

Kṣemendra has brought home to us the significance of "Aucitya" in poetry by means of a practical analogy:

कण्ठे मेखलया नितम्बफलके तारेण हारेण वा,
पाणौ नूपुरबन्धनेन चरणे केयूरपाशेन वा।

शौर्येण प्रणते रिपौ करुणया नायान्ति के हास्यताम्,
औचित्येन विना रुचिं प्रतनुते नालंकृतिर्नो गुणः ।।
(औचित्यविचारचर्चा 6 वृत्ति)

[By wearing the girdle in the neck and the brilliant garland (of pearls) on the buttocks or by tying anklets to the arms and armlet to the foot, by displaying valour of the foe who has surrendered and showing compassion towards the fierce enemy, who will not be the butt of laughter? Indeed in the absence of "Aucitya" neither figures nor "guṇas" can create the (reader's) interest in the poem.]

Evidently, "alamkāras" and "guṇas" are of secondary importance in poetry; of paramount importance is "Aucitya" or propriety, by all means and by all standards.

Kṣemendra recognizes 27 types of "Aucitya" which pertain to the following elements:

1. पद 2. वाक्य 3. प्रबन्धार्थ 4. गुण 5. अलंकार 6. रस 7. क्रिया 8. कारक 9. लिङ्ग 10. वचन 11. विशेषण 12. उपसर्ग 13. निपात 14. काल 15. देश 16. कुल 17. व्रत 18. तत्त्व 19. सत्त्व 20. अभिप्राय 21. स्वभाव 22. सारसंग्रह 23. प्रतिभा 24. अवस्था 25. विचार 26. नाम and 27. आशीर्वाद

The above items are only suggestive; in point of fact, there is no limit to the extent of the authority that the principle of "aucityha" wields. A Hindi scholar–Candrahāsa Pāthaka–has contemplated 34 "aucityās" other than what Kṣemendra has mentioned.

We can illustrate the concept of "aucitya" by discussing a few varieties mentioned by Kṣemendra. Let us first take up पदौचित्य or propriety pertaining to individual words. In poetry, worth its name, any and every word cannot and will not serve the purpose of the poet. We remember Coleridge's considered view that poetry means "best words in their best order". The really poetic piece is one in which the individual words are significant and apt and thus justify their significance. Consider the following Sanskrit verse:

तस्मिन्नद्रौ कतिचिदवलाविप्रयुक्तः स कामी,
नीत्वा मासान् कनकवलयभ्रंशरिक्तप्रकोष्ठः ।
आषाढस्य प्रथमदिवसे मेघमाश्लिष्टसानुं,
वप्रक्रीडापरिणतगजप्रेक्षणीयं ददर्श ।।

(मेघदूत, पूर्वमेघ 2)

> [Separated from his beloved, that lover (i.e. the Yakṣa of the poem), having spent a few months on that mountain (i.e. Rāmagiri), (and) having his arms bereft of the unconsciously fallen golden armlets, beheld a cloud, clustering around a peak, looking as fascinating as an elephant engaged in the (elephantine) sport of felling a hill, on the very first day of the month of Āṣārha.]

Is the word 'कामी' used in the first line of the verse appropriate or not? Certain puritanical-minded critics might find fault with the word, interpreting it in the sense of 'lustful', but when we bear in mind the fact that the word 'काम' also means 'love' (and pure love at that) and that Kālidāsa regards it as highly desirable since it is the very basis of creation, its use in the verse becomes fully justified and appropriate. Kālidāsa has presented his 'Yakṣa' as an ideal lover for whom separation from his wife was unbearable. This is clear from the expression 'कनकवलयभ्रंशरिक्तप्रकोष्ठः' which depicts the "yakṣa" as a man whose arms had become empty owing to the unconscious fall from them of the golden armlets. Had the Yakṣa been a merely 'lustful' person, he would have found out ways and means to satisfy his carnal desires; but since he was a true lover of his "Yakṣinī", he remained lost in her thoughts and in the process became so emaciated that his armlets fell from his arms unnoticed. Thus the use of the word 'कामी' is very apt and appropriate and means "full of the कामना or desire for the company of Yakṣinī." An English example of "पदौचित्य" is to be found in the use of the word "viewless" for the "wings of poesy" in Keats's 'Ode to a Nightingale':

> Away!, Away!, for I shall fly to thee
> Not charioted by Bacchus and his pards,
> But on the viewless wings of poesy, though the dull brain
> Perplexes and retards.

Here the question is : "What is the justification of the use of the word "viewless" for the "wings of poesy" or poetic imagination considered as a "bird!". There is a structural justification. The nightinagale has been described in the first stanza of the "Ode" as a "light-winged Dryad", suggesting the over-sensitivity of the nightingale which is sure to be disturbed by the heavy wheels of the chariot of "Bacchus and his pards" and therefore it is imperative for the poet to resort to some delicate means of transport for reaching the world of the nightingale. And hence his decision to fly to the nightingale on the "viewless wings of poesy". The oversensitivity of the Dryad called the nightingale, suggested by the expression "light-winged" is properly balanced and matched by the viewlessness of the wings of poesy called the imagination. Thus the poet was fully justified in his use of the word "viewless" in his description of the "wings of poesy" whose help he finally seeks for reaching the world of the nightingale.

Like individual words, the sentences in a poem should be so constructed that their strucutre becomes functional. When that happens, we have वाक्यौचित्य. An example is the following Sanskrit verse:

> सम्बन्धी पुरुभूभुजां मनसिजव्यापारदीक्षागुरु-
> गौरांगीवदनोपमापरिचितस्तारावधूलवल्लभः ।
> सद्यो मार्जितदाक्षिणात्यतरुणीदन्तावदातद्युतिः
> चन्द्रः सुन्दरि! दृश्यतामयमितश्चन्द्रीशचूडामणिः ।।

> [(Some lover is calling the attention of his sweet heart to the moon:) "O beautiful one! look at this moon: it is a relative of the kings of the Puru dynasty; it is the teacher of the lesson connected with the act of love; it is famous as a simile for the counteneances of beautiful ladies and it is the lover of the stars and it has the white sheen like that of the newly washed teeth of the women of southern India and (above all) it is the jewel in the crown of the lord of Candīdevī.)"]

The sentence, in which the above verse has been couched, contains six parts or clauses and each part or clause highlights the aphrodisiac properties attributed to the moon and thus serves as a great excitant or "uddīpanavibhāva" and is suitable for the occasion. The reference to the kings of the Puru-dynasty, believed to be descended from the moon, calls the attention of the readers to the romantic stories connected with the kings of that dynasty, including those of Pururavā, Duṣyanta and Śāntanu. The reference reinforces the thought that the moon is the fountainhead of all erotic desires. This is evidenced by the fact that the progeney of the moon was highly romantic, be it Pururavā or Śāntanu. The second clause openly states that the moon teaches all beings the art of love. The third clause highlights the fact that the moon is the highest form of beauty for we use it as the "upamāna" when we want to depict the face of a fair lady and beauty is the immediate source of passion. The fourth clause highlights the sexual power of the moon by asserting that it is the lover of all the stars of the sky which are numberless. The fifth clause brings home to us the idea that the moon is a highly shining object–its brilliance can match that of the newly washed teeth of the ladies of the Southern India, known for their skill in love-making. And the last clause strengthens the thesis that the moon can never be ignored by any lover–male or female–because it is the jewel of the head of Shiva, Pārvatī's husband, Śṛngārarasa incarnate. Thus the whole sentence becomes a unified and well-knit structure for the expression of the lover's persuasion for love-making, directed to his ladylove and is wholly apt and appropriate in its context. An English example of वाक्यौचित्य can be cited from the first Book of Milton's *Paradise Lost*, namely, the first verse paragraph, containing the poet's invocation to the Muse Urania:

Of Man's first disobedience and the fruit
Of that forbidden tree whose mortal taste
Brought death into the world and all our woe.
With loss of Eden till one greater man
Restore us and regain the blissful seat
Sing heavenly Muse that at the secret top of Oreb
Or of Sinai did inspire that shepherd
Who first taught the chosen seed
In the beginning how the heavens and earth rose out of chaos
Or if Zion hill delight thee more
Or Silava's brook that flowed fast
By the oracle of god, I thence invoke
Thy celestial aid to my adventurous song
That with no middle flight intends to soar
Above the 'Aonian' height while it pursues
Things unattempted yet in prose or rhyme.

The above is a periodic sentence in which the finite verb remains suspended and the listener becomes curious as to what the poet is going to communicate. Thus there is a sense of mystery lurking from the very beginning. Now, Miltion has chosen to deal with the story of the birth of the human civilization and of the loss of heaven by Man–all shrouded in mystery. So the statement about that mystery deserves to be couched in a sentence, smacking of mystery. Thus the periodic sentence structure is in place and the sentence emerges as an illustration of what Kṣemendra calls "Vākyaucitya"

Kṣemendra talks about a variety of "aucitya" called "alamkāraucitya" which occurs where the subject of the verse gets vividly expressed owing to some figure of speech. For example, consider the following Sanskrit verse:

अपसारय घनसारं कुरु हारं दूर एव, किं कमलैः?
अलमलमालि मृणालैरिति वदति दिवानिशं बाला।।

[(Some lady messenger is reporting the condition of her love-lorn mistress, spending her days in separation from her lover (i.e. the listener of the verse:) "Friend, leave aside the camphor and take the necklace of pearls away. What is the use of the lotuses? Desist, desist, O friend dear! (from bringing) the stalks of lilies", so keeps uttering day and night the young lady".]

The verse, under consideration, is of 'Vipralambhaśṛngāra', evoked primarily through words of the lady in distress. Her thoughts and sentiments are very delicate indeed and the skilful use of the figure 'anuprāsa', manifested in the repetitions of 'r' sounds in the first line and of 'l' sounds in the second, adds to the intensity of the feelings of the heroine. Evidently, the figure used here is well-deserved and appropriate. What is true of the Sanskrit verse, cited above, is equally true of the following extract from Shakespeare's sonnet no. XXX which expresses the poet's melancholy mood:

When to the sessions of sweet silent thought
I summon up remembrance of things past,
I sigh the lack of many a thing I sought
And with old woes new wail my dear time's waste;
Then can I drown an eye, unused to flow.
For precious friends hid in death's dateless night,
And weep afresh love's long since cancelled woe,
And moan the expense of many a vanished sight:

Here too, we find a fine use of alliteration or anuprāsa, available in the repetitions of 's' sounds in the first, of 'w' sounds in the fourth, of 'd' sounds in the sixth, of 'l' sounds in the seventh and of 'n' sounds in the eighth line. The use of these alliterations augments the note of sadness sought to be communicated by the poet and thus illustrates "alamkāraucitya". A fine poet always uses figures in keeping with the spirit of the context.

It is not impossible to cite examples of all kinds of "aucitya" contemplated by Kṣemendra from both traditions–eastern as well as western and that fact makes the doctrine of "aucitya" a thing of universal significance.

A Brief History of the Growth of the Concept of 'Aucitya'

Kṣemendra, it is true, is the founder of what came to be known as "Aucitya Sampradāya" but that does not mean that the concept of "aucitya" was not in existence before him. In point of fact, the concept is as old as the Vedic period. For example, the following vedic injunction presumes and presupposes the concept of "Aucitya":

एकः शब्दः सम्यक् ज्ञातः सुप्रयुक्तश्च स्वर्गे लोके च
कामधुक् भवति।

[A single word, well-understood and well-employed, fulfils (man's) wishes in the heaven and on the earth.]

In the above injunction, the theory of "aucitya" has been indicated by means of the prefix 'सु' and the adverb 'सम्यक्'. It is true that the statement cited is from Patanjali's *Mahābhāṣya* but the thought is undoubtedly Vedic as is clear from the fact that Patanjali quotes in the same place an aphoristic verse from शतपथब्राह्मण which is also available in पाणनीयशिक्षा, forming verse no. 52:

दुष्टः शब्दः स्वरतो वर्णतो वा मिथ्याप्रयुक्तो न तदर्थमाह।
स वाग्वज्रो यजमानं हिनस्ति यथेन्द्रशत्रुः स्वरतोऽपराधात्।।

[A word rendered bad from the view-point of pronunciation of the vowel or any letter in it used incorrectly does not convey its meaning. The verbal bolt (rather) kills the sacrificer as the wrong pronunciation of the expression 'इन्द्रशत्रु' did, involving as it did the criminally wrong pronunciation of a vowel (which should have been accented in the beginning and not at the end as was the case).]

It must be mentioned here very clearly that the doctrine of "aucitya" is presumed in the concept of "kāvyadoṣas" and that concept is as old as the art of poetry-making. The very first text, dealing with the art of poetry, available today, namely, *Nātyśāstra,* has a long discourse regarding what should be done and what should be avoided in drama in deference to the public opinion. For example, in the following verse, Bharata, the author of *Nātyaśāstra*, clearly uses the concept of "aucitya" under the garb of "Anurupatā":

वयोऽनुरूपः प्रथमस्तु वेषः, वेषानुरूपश्च गतिप्रचारः
गतिप्रचारानुगतं च पाठ्यं, पाठ्यानुरूपोऽभिनयश्च कार्यः।।

(नाट्यशास्त्र, 14/68)

[(While staging a play, care should be taken that) first of all the dress of the (actor) is in keeping with (his) age; his (i.e. of the actor) movement and gait etc. are in keeping with his dress; (his) speech is in keeping with his movement and his acting is done in consonance with his speech.]

Thus Bharata is fully aware of the doctrine of "aucitya" and if we could trust his claim that he had written the first play of the world entitled *Samudramanthana* in the Tretāyuga, the antiquity of the concept of "aucitya" gets established automatically. The post-Bharata theorists of poetry–Bhāmaha, Dandī, Vāmana etc–all discuss the concept directly or indirectly. Bhāmaha discusses "aucitya" in the guise of terms like "न्याय्य", "युक्तता" and "अनुरूपता". But Ānandavardhana, the author of *Dhvanyāloka* discusses "aucitya" directly; in his view the aesthetic experience called "Rasa" can be guaranteed only by the avoidance of all that is against the rule of "aucitya". He asserts in very clear terms:

अनौचित्यात् ऋते नान्यत् रसभङ्गस्य कारणम्

(ध्वन्यालोक 3/15)

[There is no other cause of the hurt to the aesthetic experience than impropriety.]

Clearly, Ānanda, the apostle of "Dhvani", is equally devoted to the doctrines of "Rasa" as well as "Aucitya" alike. If "Rasadhvani", in his system, emerges as the highest form of poetry, "aucitya" is the greatest controlling force behind that form. However, the credit of having established "aucitya" as the be-all and end-all of poetry goes to ācārya Kṣemendra, the author of *Aucitya-Vicāra-carcā,* who declared at the highest pitch of his voice that "aucitya" is the very life-blood of the poetry while "Rasa" is its ultimate end:

"औचित्यं रससिद्धस्य स्थिरं काव्यस्य जीवितम् ।"

We know that the Roman critic–Horace–the author of *Ars Poetica* was an ardent admirer of "Decorum" or "Aucitya" for whom poetry realizes its two-fold function of "delight and instruction" only by observing the principle of "Decorum" at all levels of creation. Thus, notwithstanding the fact that "aucitya" is the surest guarantee of the end of poetry, "it" cannot be regarded as the soul of poetry; at best, it can be accepted as a means of the supreme importance in the poetic creation. Ānanda's view, I think, clinches the matter.

How to Apply the Doctrine of "Aucitya" to a Given Text?

We have argued above that the doctrine of "Aucitya" is essential to the success of poetry and all forms of imaginative writing. But the question is how to apply the doctrine to a given text. I think the answer lies in the kind of analysis to which we intend subjecting the text, under review. If our analysis involves genre criticism, for example, we will be required, first of all, to know what that particular genre should ideally avoid. Once we have decided that, we can take up the text concerned and see whether it has been able to avoid those items or not. Allied to this is the question of the essential features of the genre within whose range our given text falls; we must pinpoint those essential features of the genre concerned in the given piece. Thus can our genre criticism of the text concerned reach a precise and almost decisive conclusion. For example, let us take up the case of *Abhigyānaśākuntalam* by Kālidāsa and evaluate it in the light of genre criticism. To all intents and purposes, it is a play because it is in the form of dialogues and has been divided into seven Acts. Now, the greatest dramaturgist of India, ācārya Bharata, has discussed ten forms of Drama. In the view of the majority of the experts of the subject, the play is a नाटक (Nātaka), one of the aforesaid forms of Nātya or Drama. Whether the present play is really a 'Nātaka' or not can be decided only if we subject the work to the yardstics fixed by Bharata in his monumental work called the *Nātyaśāstra* chapter 20, verses 10 to 43. There may be scholars in favour of characterzing this play as "Prakaraṇa" on the basis of its expansion into seven Acts. However, the plot of a "Prakaraṇa" is entirely invented by the poet, according to Bharata, whereas that of a "Nātaka" is based on some historical record. Since the plot of *Abhigyānaśākuntalam* is based on the *Mahābhārata* and *Padmapurāṇa* both of which are regarded by the Hindus as their historical records, the play falls within the category of the "Rūpaka" or "Nātya" called "Nātaka", its hero Duṣyanta having been the father of king Bharata of the lunar dynasty after whom our country came to be known as Bhārata. Bharata defines the dramatic form called "Nātaka" in the following words:

प्रख्यातवस्तुविषयं प्रख्यातोदात्तनायकञ्चैव।
राजर्षिवंश्यचरितं तथैव दिव्याश्रयोपेतम्।।
नानाविभूतियुक्तं ऋद्धिविलासादिभिर्गुणैश्चैव।
अङ्कप्रवेशकाढ्यं भवति हि तन्नाटकं नाम।।

(नाट्यशास्त्र 20/10-11)

> [(The dramatic form, in which) the plot-story is famous and historical; the hero is well-known and performs noble deeds, belonging to some royal family; the presence of divine beings is felt; glorious properties are present; prosperties and graces are displayed and Acts and introductry episodes in proper numbers have been arranged, is called "Nātaka".]

Viewed in the light of the above definition of "Nātaka", furnished by the sage Bharata, Kālidāsa's work is found to be a perfect example of the genre known as "Nātaka", corresponding to the dramatic form of the West called "Tragedy", developed primarily by the Greeks, especially Aeschylus, Sophocles and Euripides. The story of the play deals with how king Bharata, after whom India came to be called Bhārata, was born of the union of Śakuntalā, the daughter of the celestical damsel Menakā, with king Duṣyanta, the ruler of Hastināpura, who had by chance visited the hermitage of the sage Kaṇva who had adopted Śakuntalā out of sheer compassion on finding her as an abandoned child, being nurtured by the birds in some forest. The play demonstrates how Śakuntalā and Duṣyanta fall in love with each other and how Duṣyanta leaves the pregnant Śakuntalā in the hermitage on account of an urgent call from the court of Hastināpura, with the promise that he will come back soon and make her his chief queen and how Śakuntalā is not recognized by the king when she visits his court in the company of a team from the sage Kaṇva's hermitage, on account of a curse from Durvāsā, the sage, who had taken exception to Śakuntalā who had paid no heed to his call, being lost in the thought of Duṣyanta during her separation from her husband. The sage (i.e. Durvāsā) relents a little at the request of Priyamvadā, Śakuntalā's female friend in Kaṇva's hermitage, by saying that Śakuntalā's husband will recognize her instantly on witnessing any memento given to her by himself. The play concentrates on how Duṣyanta, under the influence of the sage's curse, fails to recognize his ladylove in spite of several pleas and arguments of Śakuntalā herself and her entourage from Kaṇva's hermitage–Śārangarava, Śāradvat and Gautamī and declares her a fallen woman and how in desperation the sage's party leaves her on the street to fend for herself and how heavenly damsel Menaka takes her to the hermitage of sage Kāśyapa on Mt. Hemakūta where king Duṣyanta stops to have the blessings of that sage on his ethereal return journey after a war between Indra and the demons in which the king had taken part in favour of Indra and had won the war. Here on Mt. Hemakūta Śakuntalā along with her son Sarvadamana has taken refuge. The meeting of Duṣyanta, Śakuntalā and Bharata (Sarvadamana) takes place in a natural but moving manner and the play ends on a happy note after a long ordeal. Since the true recognition of Śakuntalā by Duṣyanta and the clarification of the king's failure to recognize who Śakuntalā is, form the real focus of attention, the title of the play, namely, *Abhigyānāśākuntalam,* stands fully justified and is most suitable and proper for conveying to the general reader the main theme of the play. Thus the play exemplifies what can be called शीर्षकौचित्य or Propriety of the title. Now we can consider the propriety behind the division of the play into seven Acts. The theme or controlling idea behind the composition of the play is the union of Duṣyanta with his lady-love Śakuntalā whom once he had failed to recognize under the influence of Durvāsā's curse. Now, a typical Hindu marriage passes through a ritual called सप्तपदी in which the pair of would-be husband and wife take seven rounds of the fire. Clearly, Kālidaāsa seeks to demonstrate the process through which Duṣyanta regains the company of his sweet-heart in Seven Acts, each Act corresponding to a step in the "Saptapadī" of the Hindu marriage. Each Act has its own significance and thus justifies its existence in the play. No doubt the judicious division of the play into seven Acts is proper and just and seems to have been dictated by the nature of the subject, treated of by Kālidāsa in the play.

Now, let us see as to how far the play fulfils the requirements of a Nātaka.

The hero of the play is Duṣyanta, king of Hastināpura. He belongs to the lunar dynasty and his story of love with Śakuntalā, the product of a union between the sage Viśvāmitra (who had initially been a ksatriya king and had achieved the position of 'Rājarṣi' by means of his austere penances in the wake of his defeat at the hands of sage Vaśiṣta, and the celestical damsel Menakā, is a historical one, at least to the Hindu mind, believing in the historicity of the episodes narrated in the *Mahābhārata* and the Purāṇas, especially *Padmapurāṇa.* The historicity of the story concerned is self-evident from the fact that the country known as India was called "Bhāratavarṣa" after Bharata, the son of Duṣyanta and Śakuntalā. The character of Duṣyanta is indeed very noble and exalted. He is the king of Hastināpura who is very concerned about the well-being of his subjects, including the sages in the forests. The sage Vaikhānasa, in the very first Act of the play, highlights the king's excellent and benign administration:

रम्यास्तपोधनानां प्रतिहतविघ्नाः क्रियाः समवलोक्य।
ज्ञास्यसि कियद्भुजो मे रक्षति मौर्वीकिणाङ्क इति।।

[O king! after witnessing the delightful and unimpeded activities of the penance-makers (in the hermitage of sage Kaṇva) thou wilt know how and to what extent thy arm, having the scars on its laps, caused through friction, protects (thy subjects).]

The nobility of the king is further revealed when the king protects the hermitage of Kaṇva from the demons who were likely to disturb the the "yagna" ceremony being performed there in the absence of the sage who had gone to Somatīrtha for the well-being of Śakuntalā. However, the king's greatness is best revealed when he is summoned by Indra, the leader of the gods, to help him in his war against the demons called "Durjaya", descended from the demon Kālanemi. The following verse of Indra's chariot-driver Mātali highlights the true glory of Duṣyanta:

सुखपरस्य हरेरुभयैः कृतं त्रिदिवमुद्धतदानवकण्टकम्
तव शरैरधुना नतपर्वभिः पुरुषकेसरिणश्च पुरा नखैः ।।

(Act VII. 3)

[For the sake of the pleasure-loving Indra, only by two things has the heaven been rid of the demonic thorns: in the past by tha nails of god Nṛsimgha (i.e. literally the lion-shaped man) (who had killed Hiraṇyakaśipu. the snatcher of the heavenly kingdom from Indra) and now by the bent-knotted arrows of thy lordship.]

Thus by elevating Duṣyanta to the level of god Nṛsimgha, the poet, through the speech of Mātali reveals the true nobility of Duṣyanta, the hero of the play, under consideration, as ought to be the case with the hero of a true 'नाटक' of Bharata's formulation. The heroine of the play also has royal connections, she being the daughter of sage Viśvāmitra (who had been a king in his youth) from the womb of the celestial damsel Menakā.

So far as the requirement suggested in Bharata's phrase 'दिव्याश्रयोपेतम्' is concerned, we can refer to the scene of Duṣyanta's journey through the milky way (Ākāśagangā), flowing on the winds called 'Parivāha' and his sojourn on the Mt. Hemakūta in the hermitage of Kaśyapa, the son of Marīci and one of the "Prajāpati's"–the progenitor of all gods, demons, men, birds, animals and insects. The transcendental elements of the play are vividly described in the following verse, uttered by the king himself:

प्राणानामनिलेन वृत्तिरुचिता सत्कल्पवृक्षे वने
तोये काञ्चनपद्मरेणुकपिशे धर्माभिषेकक्रिया।
ध्यानं रत्नशिलातलेषु विबुधस्त्रीसन्निधौ संयमो
यत्कांक्षन्ति तपोभिरन्यमुनयस्तस्मिंस्तपस्यन्त्यमी।।

[These penance-makers here are performing penances in the midst of things after which other sages aspire: living by the drinking of winds in the forest of true trees called "kalpavṛkṣa", religious bathing and the observing of religious rities with the help of water that has been rendered yellow in colour by the pollen grains of golden lotuses, meditation on the rocks of gems and self-control in the presence of the heavenly damsels.]

The elements of the नाटक form, suggested by Bharata's phrase "नानाविभूतियुक्तम्" can be found in the descriptions of the pursuit of the antelope by the king, sitting in his chariot with his bow, fully stretched (Act I, verse 7, beginning with the words ग्रीवाभंगाभिरामम् etc.), that of the hermitage of sage Kaṇva in two verses (verse 14 & 15 of Act I), beginning with words "नीवाराः शुकगर्भकोटरमुखभ्रष्टास्तरूणामधः" and "कुल्याम्भोभिः प्रकृतिचपलैः शाखिनो धौतभूलाः" etc; the account of the gifts from different agents of Nature for bidding Śakuntalā adieu as reported by one of the disciples of Kaṇva in Act IV, beginning with the words "क्षौमं केनचिदिन्दुपाण्डुतरुणा मांङ्गल्यमाविष्कृतम्" etc; the description by the two royal maids of mango-flowers in Act VI, beginning with the प्राकृत words "तुमं सि मए चूदंकुर" etc; the description of the frail king, provided by the कंचुकी, beginning with the words "प्रत्यादिष्टविशेषमण्डनविधि वामप्रकोष्ठार्पितम्" etc; the description of the portrait of an art-work that Duṣyanta had planned but remained unfinished, beginning with the words कार्या सैकतलीनहंसमिथुना स्रोतोवहा मालिनी" etc; the account of the adulation and recognition accorded to Duṣyanta by Indra as reported by Mātali in the second verse of Act VII, beginning with the words "अन्तर्गतप्रार्थनमन्तिमस्थं"; the description of the divine chariot with Duṣyanta, flying across the clouds, beginning with the words "अयमरविवरेभ्यः चातकैः निष्पतद्भिः हरिभिरचिरमासां तेजसा चानुलिप्तैः" etc. and शैलानाभवरोहतीव शिखरादुन्मज्जतां मेदिनी; the description of the pranks of the babies, prompted by the behaviour of Bharata, beginning with the words "आलक्ष्यदन्तमुकुलाननिमित्तहासैरव्यक्तवर्णरमणीयवचःप्रवृत्तीन्" and above all the blessings showered on Bharata by Mārīca, beginning with the words

"रथेनानुद्धातस्तिगतिना तीर्णजलधिः" etc bear testimony to the various glories the play abounds in; these make the present play of Kālidāsa one of the most glorious achievements in the history of world drama.

What is true of नानाविभूतियुक्तम् is equally true of Bharata's requirement suggested by the expression "ऋद्धिविलासादिभर्गुणैश्चैव (युक्तम्)". The expression clearly refers to the delineation of the various erotically appealing acts of women characters that make a play aesthetically charming; this is indeed a very significant formal requirement of the dramatic form called नाटक. That Kālidāsa's play, under review, excels in this area also will be clear if we just mention the fact that Kālidāsa has been regarded in India as the greatest poet of शृंगाररस in both of its varieties: संयोग as well as वियोग. So far as अभिज्ञानशाकुन्तलम् is concerned, it is the best piece from the pen of Kālidāsa, depicting शृंगार–both संयोग and वियोग–in the most sensuous but suggestive manner. The following verse (Act I 18) recording Duṣyanta's reaction to the naturally beautiful form of Śakuntalā is indeed a masterpiece of poetic expression:

इदं किलाव्याजमनोहरं वपुः तपःक्षमं साधयितुं य इच्छति
ध्रुवं स नीलोत्पलपत्रधारया शमीलतां छेत्तुभृषिर्व्यवस्यति।।

[The sage, who wishes to prepare this naturally beautiful form (i.e. the physique of Śakuntalā) to be capable of performing penances, should be trying to cut the (hard) Śamī creeper with the edge of the petal of blue lotus.]

Duṣyanta purports to state that beautiful ladies like Śakuntalā are meant for the embraces of people like him rather than for harsh peances to be performed by austere persons. The king describes the physical appearance of Śakuntalā in the 20th verse of the first Act of the play:

अधरः किसलयरागः कोमलविटपानुकारिणौ बाहू।
कुसुममिव लोभनीयं यौवनमङ्गेषु सन्नद्धम्।।

[Her lips have the redness of newly appeared leaves (on the plants) and her two arms imitate delicate trees (and) youthfulness is permeating her limbs like some inviting flower.]

The king later depicts the virginal purity of Śakuntalā in a verse matchless in its suggestivity and sensuousness all at once:

अनाघ्रातं पुष्पं किसलयमलूनं कररुहै–
रनाविद्धं रत्नं मधु नवमनास्वादितरसम्।
अखण्डं पुण्यानां फलमिव च तद्रूपमनघं
न जाने भोक्तारं कमिह समुपस्थास्यति विधिः।।

(Act II 10)

[Her sinless form is virtually a flower that has remained unsmelt; it is a newly appeared leaf (on a plant) that has not been scratched by nails; (it is) a gem that has remained unpierced; a fresh wine that has not been tasted (by any one); the fruit of good deeds that has remained unenjoyed. I do not know whom the Creator has destined to be its enjoyer!]

Śakuntalā does not lack the seductive charms, naturally to be found in ladies of taste. Duṣyanta recalls her erotically provocative glances and other acts:

स्निग्धं वीक्षितमन्यतोऽपि नयने यत्प्रेरयन्त्या तया
यातं यच्च नितम्बयोर्गुरुतया मन्दं विलासादिव।
मा गा इत्युपरुद्धया यदपि सा सासूयमुक्ता सखी
सर्वं तत्किल मत्परायणमहो कामी स्वतां पश्यति।।

[The casting of the two eyes by her in some other direction was interpreted by me in terms of my having been softly glanced through. Her slow gait caused by the heaviness of her buttocks was taken by me as if she were trying to bewitch me by means of her seductive charms (vilāsa's). 'Do not go' prevented thus by her female friend (i.e. Priyamvadā) she scolded her angrily and I think she did all this with me in mind. Indeed a lustful lover sees everything from the viewpoint of his self.]

The different aspects of "Viyoga-Śṛngāra" have also been depicted in the play most skilfully. Duṣyanta's distressful condition in separation has been portrayed in an inimitable manner by Kālidāsa in the following verse, put in the mouth of the Kancukī:

प्रत्यादिष्टविशेषमण्डनविधि र्वामप्रकोष्ठार्पितं
विभ्रत्काञ्चनमेकमेव वलयं श्वासोपरक्ताधरः।
चिन्ताजागरणप्रतान्तनयनस्तेजोगुणादात्मनः
संस्कारोल्लिखितो महामणिरिव क्षीणोऽपि नालक्ष्यते।।

[Except for the shining golden armlet, put on the left hand, (the king) has abandoned special decoration techniques. His lower lips have been reddened by his heavy breathings; his eyes are tight on account of his sleeplessness caused by anxieties and yet he does not appear to have been emaciated owing to his inner glow like the great jewel (i.e. diamond) that does not look in any way smaller, even after being cut on the sharpening machine, on account of its natural effulgence.]

And Śakuntalā's condition during her separation has been expressed in a very moving passage, put in the mouth of Duṣyanta himself:

वसने परिधूसरे वसाना नियमक्षाममुखी धृतैकवेणी।
अतिनिष्करुणस्य शुद्धशीला मम दीर्घं विरहव्रतं विभर्ति।।

[Wearing dusty garment and having only one lock of hair, with her mouth rendered dry owing to the observance of several rules of austerity, this virtuous lady (Śakuntalā) is undergoing harsh pledge of separation from me, the most cruel person that I am.]

But ऋद्धि and विलास as required by Bharata for a successful नाटक are not confined to शृंगाररस; they have a very wide range and have their impact on other contexts as well, such as भयानक, वीभत्स, वीर and आश्चर्य. And *Abhijnānāśākuntalam* is rich in all these areas. Both ऋद्धि and विलास pertaining to भयानक रस stand exemplified in the following verse of the first Act of the play:

ग्रीवामङ्गाभिरामं मुहुरनुपतति स्यन्दने बद्धदृष्टिः
पश्चार्धेन प्रविष्टः शरपतनभयाद्भूयसा पूर्वकायम्।
दर्भैरर्धावलीढैः श्रमविवृतमुखभ्रंशिभिः कीर्णवर्त्मा
पश्योदग्रप्लुतत्वाद्वियति बहुतरं स्तोकमुर्व्यां प्रयाति।।

[Riveting its eye-sight on my chariot and diverting repeatedly its neck (in the direction of my pursuit), this antelope looks very beautiful; it is penetrating its upper part in its heavy back-portion on account of the fear of my arrow befalling it. It is sprinkling its way with the half-eaten wild grass called 'Darbha' that is falling from its mouth, blown wide on account of the labour it is undergoing and see (O driver!)

how it appears to remain mostly in the sky and only partly on the earth owing to its stupendous flight!]

The "Vilāsa" of the "Āścarya Rasa" is available in the following verse, depicting how the arrangement of the farewell ceremony has been made by the Dryads and trees of Kaṇva's hermitage through their various gifts:

क्षौमं केनचिदिन्दुपाण्डुतरुणा माङ्गल्यमाविष्कृतम्
निष्ठ्यूतश्चरणोपभोगसुलभो लाक्षारसः केनचित् ।
अन्येभ्यो वनदेवताकरतलैरापर्वभागोत्थितैः
दत्तान्याभरणानि तत्किसलयोद्भेदप्रतिद्वन्दिभिः ।।

[Some student is reporting to the matron of the hermitage, namely, Gautamī:) "An auspicious silken "sāri" has been invented by some young tree, as yellowish as the moon, and to decorate the feet of (Śakuntalā) the dye called 'lac' has been produced by some (other) tree. And ornaments have been gifted by the Dryads through the palms of their hands, projected upto the joint portion, rivalling in their tenderness the newly grown leaves on the trees."]

Similarly, the "vilāsa" of Śānta Rasa" is writ large on the following two verses, the first describing the landscape of Kaṇva's hermitage and the second bringing forth before our eyes the picture of a true yogī in samādhi. Let us cite the first verse first:

नीवाराः शुकगर्भकोटरमुखभ्रष्टास्तरूणामधः
प्रस्निग्धाः क्वचिदिङ्गुदीफलभिदः सूच्यन्त एवोपलाः ।
विश्वासोपगमादभिन्नगतयः शब्दं सहन्ते मृगाः
तोयाधारपथाश्च वल्कलशिखानिष्यन्दरेखाङ्किताः ।।

(Act I. 14)

[Here are fallen scattered the grains of Nīvāra (a crude paddy called "Tinnī") from the mouths of the nests of parrorts, beneath the trees and there are spread sharp stones that tell of the fruits of "Ingudī" that were broken with them (from their trees). There are antelopes, listening to the sound (produced by my chariot) and standing still fearlessly under the belief that these cannot be molested (in the hermitage) and here on the paths leading to reservoirs of water are lines made by the water oozing from the tops of the garments of the sages, called (valkala's).]

The verse, just cited above, contains the excitants of "Śāntarasa"–Uddīpanas of that "Rasa". And now see how the play depicts the "Āsraya" of the same "Rasa" along with the "Uddipanas" through the portrayal of a yogī in "Samādhi", lost in meditation:

वल्मीकार्धनिमग्नभूर्तिरुरसा सन्दष्टसर्पत्वचा
कण्ठे जीर्णलताप्रतानवलयेनात्यर्थसम्पीडितः ।
अंसव्यापि शकुन्तनीडनिचितं बिभ्रज्जटामण्डलं
यत्र स्थाणुरिवाचलो मुनिरसावभ्यर्कबिम्बं स्थितः ।।

[See, O Mātali, how the frame of (Sage Kaśyapa, the son of sage Marīci) stands riveted there to the disk of the sun like a pollard. Half of his body is covered with white ant-hills and his breast is dovetailed with the sloughs of snakes. His neck is badly entangled with the chain of dry creepers. The coil of his matted locks, hanging over his shoulders, abounds in the nests of birds.]

In point of fact, the entire play is full of such graphic and picturesque descriptions which contribute to the dramatic effect of the play, taken as a whole. These are, in no way, purple patches but significant for characterization and the unfolding of the plot.

Apart from what has been said so far about the features of the dramatic form called नाटक, we must note that Bharata mentions yet another feature in the phrase 'अङ्कप्रवेशकाढ्यम्' (i.e. rich in Acts and Introductories through inferior characters). So far as अभिज्ञानशाकुन्तलम् is concerned, the play has seven Acts and we have clarified above why Kālidāsa used seven Acts for the present play. But we have not discussed the प्रवेशका's in it, used to enlighten the audience on what has happened during the interval between the Act/Scene that precedes it and the Act/Scene that is going to follow. For example, Kālidāsa uses a प्रवेशक in the Sixth Act of अभिज्ञानशाकुन्तलम् soon after the scene of the Fisherman and the recovery of the lost royal ring. We must bear in mind the fact that after the king's dismissal of Śakuntalā in the Fifth Act, the lady was mysteriously taken to Mt. Hemakūt by her mother (i.e. the heavenly damsel Menakā). The audience must naturally be curious as to what has happened to Śakuntalā after her arrival on Mt. Hemakūta and how Duṣyanta is faring after the recovery from the Fisherman of the royal ring that he had given to Śakuntalā who had mysteriously lost it in the course of her journey from Kaṇva's hermitage to the court of Duṣyanta. Through a प्रवेशक, Kālidāsa quenches the above curiosity of the audience through the soliloquy of सानुमती, the female friend of Menakā and the dialogue between the two gardner-maids who have come to collect mango-flowers for the rituals sacred to the god of love Kāmadeva, when they are restrained by the कंचुकी from their act of plucking the mango-buds and flowers. The प्रवेशक is clearly meant to allay the fears of the audience regarding the plight of Śakuntalā by letting it know that she is being properly looked after by her mother and that the king, after the recovery of the lost ring, realizes that he had unwittingly caused a grave hurt to Śakuntalā whom he had actually married in the fashion of the Gandharvas. There cannot be any doubt whatsoever that the present "Praveśaka" is very essential to the unfolding of the plot and thus stands fully justified and fulfils the laws of औचित्य. And what is true of this "Praveśaka" is equally true of the "Viṣkambhaka", another kind of introductory episode, introduced in the fourth Act, to inform the audience that a long time has elapsed since the departure of the king for his court and that there has been no news from him since then–all necessitating the bidding of fare well to Śkuntalā by the inmates of the hermitage with the blessings of Kaṇva who has returned from Somatīrtha where he had gone to assuage certain evil planets in the horoscope of his foster-daughter Śakuntalā, as informed in the very first Act by the sage Vaikhānasa. Thus every part of the play is in place and contributes to its well-formed and well-developed body and to its being well-knit; no part is without its function, significance or utility. No doubt, our play is an ideal "Nātaka", fulfilling as it does all the requisite requirements of its genre. Even the names of characters chosen by Kālidāsa are meaningful and pinpoint their true nature. For example, a female friend of the heroine of the play, is प्रियंवदा and the name highlights her light-heartedness and pleasantries that she exchanges with the heroine. On the other hand, another female friend of the heroine is अनसूया and the name is true to her character–her friendliness, concern for all, seriousness and decorum that she maintains throughout. The matron of the hermitage is Gautamī (गौतमी) and her name suggests the ethical code she embodies and represents the lady as the descendent of sage गौतम who had founded the Nyāya-school of philosophy. The name of the hero of the play, namely, दुष्यन्त, calls our attention to how first he impregnates Śakuntalā and later abandons her by refusing to recognize her, presumably under the influence of the curse of Durvasā and also to how he redeems himself by denying himself the normal pleasures of life and losing himself in the thought of his jilted wife and ultimately owning her and her son by him before sage Marīci. Both aspects of the hero are subsumed in his name Duṣyanta. The significance of the heroine's name has already been brought out. Clearly, नामौचित्य is to be discerned in the names of the characters and in the title of the play.

"Aucitya" is again to be seen in the innovations made by Kālidāsa in the story as it is available in the *Mahābhārata* and *Padmapurāṇa*, the two chief sources that had provided our play-wright the story for the present play. The main innovation is the introduction of the character of Durvāsā and his curse to the heroine of the play. But for Durvāsā, Duṣyanta would have remained a lustful sensualist without any scope of self-purification. Duṣyanta achieves gratness of the soul in the eyes of the righteous audience only when he realizes that his desertion of Śakuntalā is due to the curse of Durvasā who had felt humiliated by this utter disregard shown to himself by Śakuntā (who was lost in the thought of Duṣyanta and thus failed to pay any heed to his calls). The audience forgives Duṣyanta when the latter charges Śakuntalā with unchastity and craftiness because he/she thinks that all this is due to the curse of the sage and that the king is helpless and therefore not to blame in the matter. Clearly, the innovation concerned absolves the king of his irresponsible and immoral behaviour towards Śakuntalā, clearing the way for the audience's sympathy and identification with the hero. This is an example of "Prakaraṇaucitya"

Regarding the "aucitya" of the language employed in the play, we can say that this is in accordance with the dramatic convention set by the theorist Bharata himself (नाट्यशास्त्र 18). presumably under the belief that drama, being realistic and imitative of the social reality (लोकानुवर्तन), should demonstrate that in the society depicted on the stage, too, women and low characters use प्राकृत and high-caste men and sages and gods speak संस्कृत. However, the jester (विदूषक), Madhavya by name, also speaks प्राकृत and not संस्कृत, though he is a brahmin by birth. We can justify this by the argument that though a brahmin by birth, his behaviour and conduct are ignoble, i.e. those of low-born people and thus Kālidāsa is fully justified in making him speak प्राकृत instead of संस्कृत, the language of noble people, though the chariot-driver called सूत in the first Act and Mātali, the chariot-driver of Indra in the sixth Act speak Sanskrit, to all intents and purposes, because both seem to be well-informed gentlemen.

Thus *Abhijnānāśākuntalam* emerges as a very good example of नाटक, that is, upto the mark of the raquirements of that genre as laid down by ācārya Bharata in the *Nātya-Śāstra.* The work also provides excellent examples of the various other kinds of "aucitya" as formulated by Kṣemendra in his *Aucitya-Vicāra-Carcā.*

Strengths and Weaknesses of Sanskrit Poetics

We have surveyed above the rise, growth and development of the 6 schools of Sanskrit criticism–we have ignored the seventh school called camatkāravadī school founded by Viśvesvara Pandita of the fourteenth century, author of *Camatkāra-Candrikā,* not to be confused with his namesake of Almoda of the 18th century, author of *Alamkāra-Kaustubha* because it is hardly an independent school; it can be subsumed alike by 'Alamkāra', 'Dhvani' and 'Vakrokti'-schools. What is noteworthy in Sanskrit schools, taken as a whole, is the cryptic style in which very profound critical ideas have been hinted at, which can be grasped only with the help of expert commentaries. The greatest example of this is no doubt the "Rasa-Sūtra" of Bharata whose profundity becomes clear when we read its explication in the commentary of Abhinavagupta called *Abhinavabhāratī.* This observation holds good in the case of the aphorisms of Vāmana, Ānandavardhana and Kuntaka, who express very great critical ideas in the briefest possible words.

Another strength of the Sanskrit critics or ācāryaṣ lies in the examples that they cite to illustrate the critical concept on hand. In majority of cases these examples are from the great classics (which are seldom precisely mentioned) but they can also be the works of the theorists themselves. Ānanda, for example, by and large, gives examples from the classics but sometimes from his own works such as *Viṣama-Bāṇa.-Līlā.* Visvanātha, too, sometimes cites examples from his own works whereas Bhānudatta's examples are invariably his own compositions. Alamkāravādī theorists normally illustrate their points with examples of their own invention. Bhāmaha, Dandī and Jayadeva–all follow this very practice. But the Rītivādī, Dhvanivādī, Rasavādī (with the exception of Panditarāya Jagannātha) and Vakroktivādī as also Aucityavādī theorists mostly cite examples from classics. Vāmana, Ānanda, Abhinavagupta, Mammatha and Kuntaka are examples of this. I believe that a good theorist is one who illustrates his points with examples from the established and well-known texts.

Sanskrit critics specialize in classifications, leading them sometimes to most absurd lengths. Dandī's classification of "Yamaka" into 315 kinds and Ānandavardhana's conception of 10455 "Dhvani's" are no doubt mind-boggling, impractical and even absurd. But, then, we cannot help admiring the painstaking and patient counting in which even the most intelligent of the Sanskrit critics sometiems indulge and tease us out of thought.

Sanskrit poetics is full of theorization but lacks extended discussion of any given text. This is indeed a great blemish and leads people sometimes to doubt the critical calibre of Sanskrit critics. But that is true not only of Sanskrit criticism in Ancient times but also of Greek criticism, including that of Aristotle. Extended critical discussion of a given text begins with John Dryden who has a very long analysis of Ben Jonson's comedy *The Silent Woman* in his famous work of criticism called "An Essay of Dramatic Poesie" (published in 1668 but written three years earlier). So it would not be very fair to attack only Sanskrit poetics on this count. If Aristotle, Horace and Longinus are free from this charge, why should we criticize Bharata, Bhāmaha, Dandī, Ānanda, Vāmana and Kuntaka for their not having left any extended critique of a given text?

Some superficial readers of Sanskrit poetics feel that Sanskrit critics do not resort for help to disciplines other than literary as do critics in the West. But this impression is not true to facts. Religion, philosophy and grammar are the disciplines which are invoked by Sanskrit critics to strengthen their points of view. To clarify the position of 'Dhvani', for example, Ācārya Mammatha, seeks the help from 'Mīmānsā' school of philosophy and in case a reader of *Kāvya-Prakāsa* is not acquainted with the different schools and tenets of Mīmānsā, he is likely to miss the full import of Mammatha's theory. Similarly, if you do not know the Vedāntic theory of knowledge, you cannot grasp the finer points of the theory of 'Rasa' as put forward by Panditarāja Jagannatha and if you do not know the main tenets of 'Pratyabhijnādarśana', you will find it hard to appreciate the 'Rasa' or 'Dhvani' theories as explained by Abhinavagupta.

Reference Section

V

अङ्क (Anka)

The word 'अङ्क' bears two different senses in the field of drama. The first sense of the word is well-known and widely accepted whereas the second sense is quite uncommon, known only to the specialists. In the former sense, the word denotes the parts in which a dramatic composition is divided, corresponding to the words 'काण्ड' and 'सर्ग' that imply the parts in which an epic poem is divided. In this sense the Sanskrit word's English equivalent is the word 'Act', denoting one of the main divisions of a play, other divisions being 'Scenes' which are the sub-divisions of an 'Act. The latter sense of the word denotes 'a special form of drama called उत्सृष्टिकाङ्क'. It must be made very clear that 'रूपक' is the generic term that Sanskrit dramaturgists employ for what the West calls 'Drama' or 'Play', although for the layman in India 'नाटक' is the generic term for all literary compositions called 'Drama' (though that term denotes for the Sanskrit dramaturgists what they call नाट्य or रूपक).

अङ्क in the First Sense

To the question 'What is an 'Anka'?' the father of Indian poetics, namely, sage Bharata, observes: "The Act (Anka) is a conventional term ('Rūdhiśabda'). As by means of a display of Emotions and Sentiments it helps the theme to grow through certain rules and techniques, it is called 'Anka':"

अङ्क इति रूढिशब्दो भावैश्च रसैश्च रोहयत्यर्थान्।
नानाविधानयुक्तो यस्मात्तस्माद्भवेदङ्कः।।

(नाट्यशास्त्र 20/14)

It must be noted that Bharata discusses the concept of अङ्क between verses 14 and 31 of the 20th chapter of his *magnum opus.* In his long descriptive account the sage clarifies all the points relating to the 'Acts' of a given play–their nature, function, composition and their duration. The sum and substance of his argument is that an 'Act' is a characteristic section of a play where a particular phase of the action of the play–its vision of life–terminates; an 'Act' should present the incidents of a single day, connected with the subject-matter of the play. The dramatist, Bharata stresses, should see to it that all the characters, connected with the incident of an 'Act' leave the stage at the end of the 'Act' concerned and all 'Acts' should revolve round the बीजार्थ of the 'Vastu' (i.e. subject-matter) and thus remain united. The image of the garland can make this point clearer. Just as the flowers of a garland may vary in their colour and odours so may the 'Acts' of a given play. But there must be some likeness or internal unity among all the flowers to make them appear as a garland and that uniting factor running invisible through the flowers is the thread. Similarly, in the case of the dramatic plot, the uniting factor of the 'Acts' of the play is the बीजार्थ or the main action which should be felt in all the 'Acts', making them look like a composite whole; without this interconnectedness, the play would be like a collection of different 'Acts' and not a play at all.

Certain activities should not be directly shown on the stage, according to Bharata, and the classical Sanskrit drama followed this injunction of the sage rather ritualistically. The non-presentable are: fits of anger, fever, and grief; pronouncing a curse; running away; marriage; demonstrating a miracle; a battle; loss of kingdom; death; the seizure of a city; pell mell in public places, so on and so forth. In like fashion, Bharata does not favour a horde of characters in an 'Act'; the sage is not precise on that point. However, a later dramatargist, Dhananjaya, restricts the number to 'four'.

Regarding the question as to how many 'Acts' a play can have, the answer could be that it all depends on the kind or variety of drama or the play, under discussion, is; there are forms of drama like 'Bhaṇa', 'Prahasana', 'Vyāyoga', 'Vīthī' and 'Anka' that have just one 'Act', whereas there are forms like 'Nātaka' and 'Prakaraṇa' that have upto ten 'Acts', giving birth to the form called 'Mahānātaka'. *Hanumannātaka* by the dramatist Hanumat is the example of 'Mahānātaka'; it has 'ten' Acts. However, an average 'Nātaka' or a 'Prakaraṇa' has 5 to 7 'Acts'. Kālidāsa's 'Nataka' *Mālavikāgnimitram* has 5 'Acts' whereas *Abhijnānaśākuntalam* by the same dramatist has 7 'Acts'. Thus there is no fixed rule regarding the exact number of 'Acts' that a play should have–that is to be determined by the nature of the subject-matter of the play concerned.

अङ्क in the Second Sense of the Word

The word "Anka" in its second sense refers to a form of drama called by that very word. The dramatic form 'अङ्क' is also known as 'उत्सृष्टिकाङ्क'. It is a one-act play, so called because of a great lamentation by women characters in it–the word 'उत्सृष्टिका', precisely, means 'lamentation on death'. It is naturally a form of drama characterized by 'Karuṇarasa'. 'ऊरुभङ्ग' by Bhāsa is the only extant example of 'Utśṛṣtikānka' in which the death of Duryodhana at the hands of Bhīma is demonstrated, reminding us of the effects produced by Greek tragedies.

अङ्कमुख (Ankamukha):–It is one of the explanatory devices, used by the Sanskrit dramatists to inform the audience in a subtle artistic way as to what is going to happen in the succeeding Scene or Act. It is, as a matter of fact, what western dramaturgists call 'Anticipatory Scene'. Ācārya Bharata defines it in the following words:

विश्लिष्टमुखमङ्कस्य स्त्रिया वा पुरुषेण वा
यदुपक्षिप्यते पूर्वं तदङ्कमुखमिष्यते।।

(नाट्यशास्त्र 21/114)

> ['Ankamukha' is that ('Arthopakṣepaka' or introductory episode in a play) in which at the end of an 'Act' the events to be depicted in the coning 'Act' are summarised by a female or male character.]

It must be mentioned here that the dramatic tradition of Sanskrit has 5 introductory or clarificatory devices called अर्थोपक्षेपक ('Arthopakṣepaka'). These are: प्रवेशक, विष्कुम्भक, चूलिका, अङ्कमुख and अङ्कावतार. Since it is not possible to depict all incidents in the life of the hero, the dramatist is bound to resort to certain devices which clarify for the spectators vitally important facts connected with the story on hand; these devices are collectively called अर्थोपक्षेपक (Arthopakṣepaka's), Clearly, 'Ankamukha' is an 'arthopakṣepaka' or introductory device which prepares the spectator for the events of the coming 'Act'. It is also called 'अङ्कास्य'. We can regard it as a kind of 'prologue' and we have to take it in the form of a soliloquy. A good Sanskrit example of 'Ankamukha' or 'Ankāsya' is the following soliloguy of Hanumāna at the end of the second 'Act' of the 'nātaka' entitled *Abhiṣekanātakam*:

> परभृतगणजुष्टं पद्मषण्डाभिरामं
> सुरुचिरतरुषण्डं तोयदाभं त्रिकूटम् ।
> करचरणविभर्दैः काननं चूर्णयित्वा
> विगतविषयदर्पं राक्षसेशं करोमि ।।
>
> [Let me make the demon-king (i.e. Rāvaṇa) bereft of self-pride and crest-fallen by cutting his garden, Trikūta by name, by means of the assault of my hands and legs–Trikūta which is full of cuckoo-birds, which is looking beautiful on account of lotus-crowds, is possessed of fascinating trees and has the shine of the clouds.]

Here in his soliloquy Hanumāna summarises what he plans to do to Rāvaṇa's garden Trikūta and the coming Act (i.e. Act III) of the play deals with what has been foretold in Hanumāna's short speech. Indeed, the speech can be called an 'Ankamukha' or 'Ankāsya'.

The device called अङ्कमुख can be discerned even in Western drama. For example, the last speech, a brief soliloquy of Helena in Act I. i in *A Midsummer Night's Dream* can be regarded as an 'Ankamukha' as it summarises the pursuit of Lysander by Hermia in Act II. ii by revealing which to Demetrius she hopes to win him back. This is in accordance with Bharata's definition of अङ्कमुख which in the view of a later dramaturgist Śāradātanaya is precisely what the western dramatists and dramaturgists call 'Prologue'. Sāradātanaya defines the device in the following words:

'अङ्कमुखः सूत्रणं सकलाङ्कानां ज्ञेयमङ्कमुखं बुधैः' (नाटकलक्षणकोश p. 17) [अङ्कमुख is what is called by the experts a summary of all 'Acts' of a play.] and he cites as an example the dialogue between Kāmandakī and Avalokitā in Bhabhuti's *Malatīmādhava* Act I which furnishes all the information about the hero and his designs in a nutshell and about the parts to be played by Bhuravasu and others and about the arrangement of the plot of the play as a whole. Evidently, अङ्कमुख in this sense, put forward by Śāradātanaya, is the eastern counterpart of the 'Prologue' of the western tradition of drama used profusely by dramatists like Ben Jonson, Marlowe and Dryden. The first speeches in *Hippolytus* and *Iphigenia in Tauris*–both by the Greek tragedian Euripides (480?-406? B.C.) delivered by

Aphrodite and Iphigenia respectively, can be called "Ankamukha" because they reveal the gists of the plots of the two plays. However, 'Ankamukha', being indirect, is more artistic than the 'Prologue' which is plain and direct.

अङ्कावतार (Ankāvatāra)

The term denotes a technical device meant to acquaint the audience with the continuity of the action of the previous Act. It happens when the characters at the end of a particular Act are also present at the beginning of the next Act as if the preceding 'Act' were in operation without a break. Thus 'Ankāvatāra' is an 'Arthopakṣepaka'. Ācārya Viśvanātha defines 'Ankāvatāra' in very clear terms:

अङ्कान्ते सूचितः पात्रैस्तदङ्कस्याविभागतः ।
यत्राङ्कऽवतरत्येषोऽङ्कावतार इति स्मृतः ।।

(साहित्यदर्पणम् 6/58)

[The development of the action, indicated by certain characters of a particular 'Act', continuing in the next Act, is remembered as Ankāvatāra.]

An example of this अर्थोपक्षेपक is to be found in the Seventh Act of *Abhijnānaśākuntalam* of Kālidāsa. The development of the Action of the play, indicated at the end of the Sixth Act by Mātali, the chariot-driver of Indra, and king Duṣyanta, namely, Duṣyanta's participation in Indra's war against the descentents of the demon-king Kālanemi, appears in the succeeding Act (i.e. at the beginning of the Seventh Act of the play) as indicated by the speeches of Mātali and Duṣyanta and is thus an example of 'Ankāvatāra'.

अङ्कुरितयौवना (Ankuritayauvanā)

This is a term of that section of Sanskrit poetics which deals with heroines and is designated as 'Nāyikābheda'. It denotes the category of heroines who are on the verge of womanhood and have started exuding their youthfulness from each of their limbs. Ladies of this category are in the intermediate stage of development called adolescence or वयःसन्धि; (they have reached puberty but not maturity). Another term for such heroines is 'प्रथमावतीर्णयौवना' (Prathamāvatīrṇayauvanā). The prose-poet Bāna's account of Mahāśvetā in the following extract is that of an

'Ankuritayauvanā' or 'Prathamāvatīrṇayauvanā':

क्रमेण च कृतं मे वपुषि वसन्त इव मधुमासेन,
मधुमास इव नवपल्लवेन, नवपल्लव इव कुसुमेन,
कुसुम इव मधुकरेण, मधुरकर इव मदेन नवयौवनेन पदम्।
(कादम्बरी-महाश्वेताजन्मोदन्तवर्णना)

[And gradually foot was set in my body by fresh youthfulness just as in the Spring season (foot is set) by the month of Chaitra, in the month of Chaitra (foot is set) by fresh leaves, in the fresh leaves (foot is set) by the blossom, in the blossom (foot is set) by the bee, in the bee (foot is set) by intoxication.]

Another example of the 'Ankuritayauvanā heroine' is the following verse by Dhanika, the commentator on *Dāśarūpaka* by his brother Dhananjaya:

उच्छ्वसन्मण्डलप्रान्तरेखमाबद्धकुड्मलम्।
अपर्याप्तमुरो वृद्धेः शंसत्स्याः स्तनद्वयम्।।

[The pair of this lady's teats, that are marked by boundary-lines upto their rounds and are bound firmly like buds in their covers, through their upward rise, is behaving as if the (breast) were not sufficient for its growth.]

Here the advent of fresh youth has been beautifully indicated by the grown teats on the lady's breasts. The Victorian novelist–Thomas Hardy–supplies an English example of the 'Ankuritayavvanā' when he describes the advent of youth in the life of Elizabeth-Jane, the heroine of *The Mayor of Casterbridge:*

> *Elizabeth-Jane* developed early into womanliness...Her face, though somewhat wan and incomplete, *possessed the raw materials of beauty in a promising degree.* There was an under-handsomeness in it, struggling to reveal itself through the provisional curves of immaturity and the casual disfigurements that resulted from the straitened circumstances of their lives. *She was handsome in the bone, hardly yet handsome in the flesh. (emphasis ours)*

(the 7th paragraph of chapter IV of *The Mayor of Casterbridge*)

The underlined portions of the extract, cited above, reveal in very clear terms, that Elizabeth-Jane is an 'ankuritayauvanā'. Shakespeare, too, has portrayed a heroine of the variety, under discussion, in a rather humorous vein in the person of Viola (in the guise of the page-boy Cesario) through the following speech of Malvolio in *Twelfth Night or What you Will* IV:

> Not yet old enough for a man, nor young enough for a boy; as a squash is before 'tis a peascod, or a codling, when 'tis almost an apple: 'tis with him e'en standing water, between boy and man.

The Shakespeare passage, it must be noted, is on a par with the passage from Bāṇa, cited a little earlier.

अङ्गज अलङ्कार (Angaja Alamkāra)

Certain bodily activities of young ladies, revealing their natural sexuality, are called अंगजालंकार's (bodily ornaments). The term pertains to a special section of Sanskrit poetics called नायिकाभेद or the discourse on the classification of the heroines, including the features of each in a scientific fashion. Ācārya Bharata has divided these bodily ornaments under 3 heads: हाव, भाव, and हेला. By 'Hāva' is meant coquettish gestures whereas 'Bhāva' refers to all motions, natural to ladies of taste that reveal their sexual drive and 'Hela' is the intensified form of 'Hāva'. In order to appreciate the full implication of these bodily ornaments of women, we must know what Bharata calls 'Sattva'. 'Sattva' can be defined as the state of innocence when there is hardly any sex-consciousness in the hearts of ladies. However, with the advent of youth there starts growing in the hearts of the ladies sex-consciousness which Bharata chooses to call 'Bhāva' (literally-that which is born in the heart) and this gets manifested in the gait and speech of the ladies. The 'Bhāva' leads to 'Hāva' which is an advanced stage of sex-consciousness when eyes, eye-lashes and the cheek–all become more attractive and express the sexual urge clearly. We can call it the natural "coquettish gesture", expressed through eyes, eyelashes and the cheek. And 'Hāva', when it becomes the most intense, grows into what is called 'Helā' which manifests itself through various physical actions such as seeing oneself repeatedly in the glass and hairdoing again and again and expressing love for the male partner in total disregard of the public. All these three bodily ornaments of ladies are illustrated below through 3 Sanskrit verses. 'Bhāva' has been very beautifully expressed in the following verse:

> दृष्टिः सालसतां विभर्ति न शिशुक्रीडासु बद्धादरा
> श्रोत्रे प्रेषयति प्रवर्तितसखीसम्भोगवार्तास्वपि ।

पुंसामङ्कमपेतशङ्कमधुना नारोहति प्राग्यथा
बाला नूतनयौवनव्यतिकरावष्टभ्यमाना शनैः ।।

[(Somebody is reflecting on a growing young lady:] "See, the girl is gradually being possessed of by new youthfulness: her eyes are now a little languid; she no longer takes interest in the games of children. She lends her ears to the talks of sex, started by her (elderly) friends. Unlike in the past, she does not go in the lap of elderly people fearlessly."]

No doubt the girl of the verse is gradually growing sex-conscious as is revealed in the changes that have overtaken her in the wake of the advent of youth in her. It is this growing sex-consciousness that Sanskrit ācāryas have called "Bhāva"

An example of 'Hāva' is to be found in the following Sanskrit verse:

विवृण्वती शैलसुताऽपि भावमङ्गैः स्फुरद्बालकदम्बकल्पैः ।
साचीकृता चारुतरेण तस्थौ मुखेन पर्यस्तविलोचनेन ।।

(कुमारसम्भवम् 3/68)

[(The poet is describing what happened to Pārvatī when she saw Shiva's eyes riveted to her face:) "In her turn, Pārvatī, too, remained motionless with her face rendered slanted and having her eyes centred on Shiva–Pārvati who was revealing her love (for Shiva) through her different limbs that had horripilation like the blooming buds of the Kadamba-flowers.]

Here Pārvatī has been shown as a lady who is fairly sex-conscious and feels attracted to her male counterpart and reveals the same by casting an oblique glance at him. This is her 'Hāva'.

An example of 'Helā' is to be found in the following Sanskrit verse:

स्निग्धं वीक्षितमन्यतोऽपिनयने यत्प्रेरयन्त्या तया
यातं यच्च नितम्बयोर्गुरुतया मन्दं विलासादिव ।
मा गा इत्युपरुद्धया यदपि सा सासूयमुक्ता सखी
सर्वं तत्किल मत्परायणमहो कामी स्वतां पश्यति ।।

(अभिज्ञानशाकुन्तलम् II.2)

[(King Duṣyanta is reflecting on Śakuntalā's response to him after his having met her in the presence of her female friends:) "The casting of the two eyes by her in some other direction

> was interpreted by me in terms of my having been softly glanced through. Her slow gait caused by the heaviness of buttocks was taken by me as if she were trying to bewitch me by means of her seductive charms. 'Do't go' thus prevented by her female friend (i.e. Priyamvadā) she scolded her angrily and I think she did all this with me in mind. Indeed a lover sees everything from the viewpoint of the self."]

The heroine portrayed in the above verse is clearly quite sex-conscious and she expresses her attraction to the opposite sex through various deliberate ways–casting of slanted glance, slow and soft gait caused by the heavy buttocks etc.. The beauty thus produced is the lady's 'Helā'. which has been artfully indicated in the verse of Kālidāsa.

It would be very interesting to note that just as the East has the concept of 3 bodily ornaments in young ladies, the West, too has the 3 goddesses called Graces, attendents on Aphrodite or Venus. These are: Aglaia, Thalia and Euphrosyne. These goddesses are nothing but certain abstractions that Sanskrit ācāryas have called: 'Bhāva', 'Hāva' and 'Helā'. Thus the concept of the 'Angaja-Alamkāras' is not Sanskrit-specific; it is, in point of fact, universal. This is so because the concept is based on psychological and physical facts, common to all young ladies the world over. Examples of 'Bhāva', 'Hāva' and 'Helā' can be found in English literature itself. Thus 'Bhava' of Elizabeth Boyle, the heroine of Spenser's 'Epithalamion' is fully revealed in the following lines.

> Her modest eyes, abashed to behold
> So many gazers as on her do stare,
> Upon the lowly ground affixed are;
> Ne dare lift up her countenance too bold,
> But blush to heare her prayses sung so loud,
> So farr from being proud

("Epithalamion" ll. 160-165)

The coyness of the lady, experienced by her at her own praises sung, bears witness to her sex-consciousness for the opposite sex. Clearly, it is her bodily ornament called 'Bhāva' which is revealed in her reaction to her gazers.

A very beautiful depiction of 'Hāva' is to be found in the following extract from the speech of Duke Orsino, addressed to the page-boy Cesario (but actually to Viola in disguise):

> Dear lad, believe it,
> For they shall yet belie thy happy years

That say thou art a man: Diana's lip
Is not more smooth and rubious; thy small pipe
Is as the maiden's organ, shrill and sound,
And all is semblative a woman's part.

(*Twelfth Night* I. IV)

The extract, cited above, brings home to us the grown and clearly marked sex-consciousness in Viola, revealed through her lips and throat (shrill pipe). The last line of the extract stresses her grown sex-consciousness, expressed euphemistically. This is indeed her 'Hāva' that has found expression here.

The bodily ornament called 'Helā' is fully exemplified in the following stanza of "La Dame Sans Merci" by John Keats:

I set her on my pacing steed
And nothing else saw all day long
For sidelong would she bend and sing
A faery's song-

The lady of the piece is boldly giving expression to her love for the Knight through her sidelong bending and singing. The 'Helā' of the lady is writ large on each line of the stanza, depicting her physical actions. Wordsworth has also depicted the 'helā' of Mary Hutchinson in his lyric entitled 'She Was a Phantom of Delight':

She was a phantom of delight
When first she gleamed upon my sight.
A dancing shape, an image gay,
To haunt, to startle and waylay.

अङ्ग-अङ्गी रस (Anga-Angī Rasa)

According to the exponents of the 'Rasa' Theory, a work of art is free to delineate any number of 'Rasas' but the work as a whole has to be dominated by one single 'Rasa'. The dominant 'Rasa' is called "Angī Rasa" and the other 'Rasas', helping it, are called 'Anga Rasas'. But regarding the question as to how to determine whether in a given work a particular 'Rasa' is the 'Angīrasa', our ācāryas are silent. Ānanda-Vardhana discusses the "Angīrasa" of both the 'mahākāvyas' of India, namely, the *Mahābhārata* and the *Rāmāyaṇa* in the fourth 'udyota' of his poetics *Dhvanyāloka* after the 109th 'kārika'. According to him, the 'angīrasa' of the *Rāmayaṇa* is 'karuṇā' and that of the *Mahābhārata* is 'śānta' and he bases his judgment on the subject on the moral that the work concerned suggests on the whole and on the largest frequency of the occurrences of that 'Rasa'. Clearly, the 'Angīrasa' of a work can be decided by a statistical analysis of the 'Rasas' in it, the title of 'Anīgirasa' going in favour of the 'Rasa' that has the largest frequency and the title of 'Angarasas' going to the remaining 'Rasas'. I think this is the most judicious and reasonable solution of the problem. But the moot-question is: 'How to do it?' I think the most sensible and reasonable approach would be to make a chart of the classification of all the 'Rasas' canto-wise, Act-wise or chapter-were, as the case may be, of the given work and then to count their frequency. Whichever 'Rasa' has the largest frequency, will be, and should be, declared as the 'Angīrasa' of the work and the remaining 'Rasas' would naturally be declared as 'Angarasas'.

अक्रम (Akrama)

This is a defect of sentence-construction, consisting in the misplacement of words or word-particles, syntactically speaking, and thus creating some problem in the interpretation of the sentence. For example, the following verse from Kālidāsa's कुमारसम्भवम् suffers from the defect 'Akrama' or 'Akramatā':

> द्वयं गतं सम्प्रति शोचनीयतां समागमप्रार्थनया कपालिनः
> कला च सा कान्तिमती कलावतः त्वमस्य लोकस्य च नेत्रकौमुदी।
>
> [(Testing the geuineness of love for Himself in the heart of Pārvatī, the Lord, in the garb of a student, tells Pārvatī:) "Owing to the request for the company of कपाली or the possessor of skulls (i.e. Śiva) two things have now gone miserable: the shining disc of the 'kalāvat' (i.e. the moon) and your ladyship, the moonlight for the eyes of this world".]

In the above verse, the defect lies in the wrong placement of the word-particle 'च', used after the word 'लोकस्य'; it should have been used just after the word 'त्वम्'. Since this is not the normal use of the particle 'च', the verse, as a whole, suffers from अक्रम or अक्रमता. An English example of this defect is to be found in the opening verse-paragraph of Milton's *Paradise Lost:*

> Of Man's first disobedicnce and the fruit
> Of that forbidden tree whose mortal taste
> Brought death into the world and all our woe

With loss of Eden till one greater man
Restore us and regain the blissful seat
Singh heavenly Muse that at the secret top
Of Sinai didst inspire...

In accordance with the established tradition, the first 5 lines of the extract should have been used after the term of injunction 'Sing' and failing that there has occurred अक्रमता here, making the whole verse-paragraph flawed and all this is due to Milton's violation of the English syntax.

अक्रमातिशयोक्ति (Akramātiśayokti)

The term denotes a form or kind of the figure of speech called अतिशयोक्ति, known in the West as 'Hyperbole'. 'Akramātiśayokti' occurs where cause and effect are shown as happening all at once, defying their order or sequence–cause coming first, followed by effect. An example is the following Sanskrit verse:

आलिङ्गन्ति समं देव! ज्यां शराश्च पराश्च ते

[(Some bard is praising his king:) "Your highness! both your arrows and your enemies embrace the string of your bow simultaneously".]

Normally, the arrows should touch the ground first and then will the ground be touched by their victims. But here the poet has created a miracle by stating the fall of the arrows of the king and that of his enemies together. Clearly, there is 'Akramātiśayokti' here. The Hindī poet Tulasīdāsa, too, has made a very beautiful use of this figure in the following 'dohā' of *Rāmacaritamānasa:*

सुर बानर देखे विकल, हँस्यो कोसलाधीश।
सजि सारंग एक सर, हते सकल दस शीश।।
(लंकाकाण्ड, दोहा 96)

[The king of Kośala (i.e. Rāma) laughed on finding the gods and the monkeyhorde perturbed. Tightening his bow Śāranga he slayed all the (ten) heads of Daśānana (i.e. Rāvaṇa) with just one arrow]

Here, too, there is no order or sequence in the felling of the ten heads of Rāvaṇa–normally the ten heads would be felled only one after another and not simultaneously just by one arrow. Since there is violation of sequence in the felling of the heads, the verse has the figure 'Akramātiśayokti'.

An English example of this figure is found in the following lines from Wordsworth's lyric entitled "I Wandered Lonely as a Cloud", popularly known as "Daffodils":

> Ten thousand saw I at a glance,
> Tossing their heads in sprightly dance.
>
> (ll. 11-12)

One can see a host of daffodils one by one but to see ten thousand at a glance is incredible indeed -there in complete loss of order or sequence in the act of seeing ten thousand daffodils all at once and hence the figure here is 'Akramātiśayokti'.

It is clear that 'Akramātiśayokti' happens in two cases: 1. cause and effect taking place simultaneously and 2. effect of some act being described in total disregard of order or sequence.

अगूढ व्यंग्य (Agūdhavyangya)

This is a term pertaining to the 'dhvani' doctrine. It implies a statement in which the suggested sense (vyangyārtha) is not difficult to grasp at all; it is rather as plain as the literal sense (Abhidheyārtha) itself. Let us consider the following verse from the "Ayodhyākānda" of the *Rāmacaritamānasa* by Tulasīdāsa:

> पुत्रवती युवती जग सोई। रामभगत जाकर सुत होई।।
>
> [Only that woman (युवती) is the possessor of a son (पुत्रवती) whose offspring (सुत) is Rāma's devotee.]

The verse at first no doubt creates some problem when the reader realizes that there are without doubt several women in possession of sons who are not devotees of Rāma and yet are called possessors of sons in any case. Then the question for him is: What does the statement mean if it is a sensible one? At a second thought the reader comes to realize that the speaker intends the word 'पुत्रवती' to mean 'praisaworthy' and the suggested sense of the whole statement is that only those women are really praiseworthy whose sons are devotees of Rāma; in case their sons are not the devotees of Rāma, their being possessors of sons is meaningless. The prerequisite condition of being पुत्रवती in the true sense of the word, in the eyes of the speaker (i.e. Sumitrā), is the sons being Rama's devotees. However, this suggested sense of the statement is as plain as the literal sense. Clearly, the suggested sense here is not difficult to grasp (अगूढ!) and we can easily grant it the status of अगूढव्यंग्य, otherwise known as गुणीभूतव्यग्य (Guṇībhūtavyangya).

We can find English examples of अगूढव्यंग्य in the Augustan poetry plentifully. Consider the following lines from the first canto of *The Rape of the Lock:*

Sol thro' white certains shot a tim'rous Ray,
And op'd those Eyes that must eclipse the Day.

(pp. 12-13)

Here the second line of the couplet causes some problem: 'How can eyes eclipse the Day?'. But when the reader bears in mind the fact that the word 'Day' connotes "the sun", he takes the line poetically to mean that the eyes concerned (i.e. the eyes of Belinda) are far more brilliant than the sun for they can eclipse or overpower it. That sense is clear from the epithet of 'Ray', namely, 'Timorous', meaning 'timid'. The sun was rather hesitant in sending its timid ray to open the eyes which could eclipse itself. Thus the suggested sense of the line is that Belinda's eyes are far more brilliant than the sun. However, this suggested sense of the line is as plain as the literal sense of the the whole statement. Thus the passage is an example of अगूढव्यंग्य.

अगूढव्यंग्या (Agūdhavyangyā):–This is a variety of 'Laksanā' or connotation; it occurs where the connotated meaning is very clear and causes no problem to the grasping of the true import of the words. The following Sanskrit verse supplies a very good example:

श्रीपरिचयाज्जडा अपि भवन्त्यभिज्ञा विदग्धचरितानाम्।
उपदिशति कामिनीनां यौवनमद एव ललितानि।।

[Even the blockheads become the knowers of the deeds of men of taste or connoesseurs through their introduction to wealth (श्री or लक्ष्मी). (Likewise) the ardour of youth alone teaches (even the most innocent maidens) the artful tricks of the passionate women.]

Here the word 'उपदिशति' (teaches) causes some problem to its normal dictionary meaning–its denoted sense (अभिधेयार्थ). But when we give some thought to it, the word conveys the sense of 'expresses, brings into limelight or displays'. This is the connotated sense of the word. But this has occurred instantly; even the laymen can infer it. Thus we feel justified in calling it an example of अगूढव्यंग्या लक्षणा. I believe that all examples of the figures of speech such as 'synecdoche' and 'metonymy' are also the examples of 'अगूढव्यंग्या लक्षणा'. Consider, for example, the following line from Gray's 'Elegy Written in a Country churchyard':

And drowsy tinklings lull the distant folds.

Here the folds are being described as being lulled to sleep by the sleep-inducing tinklings. The reader first finds the expression difficult to grasp. How can the inanimate things like the folds be lulled to sleep?' he might question to himself. But instantly he infers that 'folds' mean 'the sheep' that are kept within them. This connotated sense comes from the association of the 'folds' with the 'sheep'. This is true of the expression 'drowsy tinklings'. How can the senseless inanimate 'tinklings' or sounds produced by small bells be 'drowsy' or 'sleepy'? Here too, through the law of assocation, the expression becomes justified when we bear in mind the fact that the 'tinklings' are drowsy because their bearers (i.e. the sheep themselves) are drowsy. Since the connotated senses are inferred here without much of pains on the part of the reader, both expressions–'tinklings' and 'folds'–are examples of अगूढव्यंग्या लक्षणा.

अचिन्त्यनिमित्ता (Acintyanimittā)

The term denotes a variety of the figure of speech called 'Viśeṣokti'. 'Acintyanimittā Viśeṣokti' occurs where effect does not result in spite of the presence of enough cause, defying all logic. Since no reason for this strange phenomenon could be given in this figure, it is called अचिन्त्यनिमित्ता (i.e. that for which no reason comes to mind). The following Sanskrit verse is an example of this:

स एकस्त्रीणि जयति जगन्ति कुसुमायुधः ।
हरताऽपि तनुं यस्य शम्भुना न बलं हृतम् ।।

[That flower-weapon god (i.e. the god of love-Kāmadeva) conquers the three worlds single-handed whose prowess could not be destroyed by Shambhu while He was taking away his body.]

In the present verse there is enough cause for the destruction of the prowess of Kāmadeva in the form of Shiva who burnt to ashes his body with the fire from his third eye and yet Kāmadeva conquers all the three worlds even today. Clearly, the desired destruction, which could not be effected, remains in the domain of mystery. The verse, under review, in effect, is an excellent example of "Acintyanimitta Viśeṣokti"

An English example of the figure is to be found in the following lines from Shakespeare's sonnet no. 65:

O none, unless this miracle have might,
That in black ink my love may still shine bright

Here the cause of the destruction of Mr. W.H. and his beautiful form is available in the form of all-destroying Time before which all are helpless–none can prevent the decay and destruction of Mr. W.H. except black ink, which apparently may be regarded as an accomplice of Time but which, strangely and bafflingly, can ensure imperishability and immortality to Mr. W.H. through the poems of the poet on him, written in it. It is indeed rather miraculous and incomprehensible but a fact nobdoy can dispute. Clearly, the lines of Shakespeare are an example of 'Acintyanimitta Viśeṣokti'.

अजहत्स्वार्था (Ajahatsvārthā)

The term denotes a form of 'Laksaṇā', one of the three powers of words, the other two being 'Abhidhā' and 'Vyanjanā'. This form of 'Lakṣaṇā' is also known as 'upādānalakṣaṇā'. Normally, 'Lakṣaṇā' consists in words' power to connote meanings other than their literal or primary meanings. For example, in the Hindi sentence–'लाल-पीला होने से कोई फायदा नहीं होगा', the connotational meaning is: 'no use getting angry'. But this connotational meaning has left the primary sense of the expression 'लाल-पीला होना' in its entirety. But when some words or expressions, while connoting something other than their primary meanings, retain the residual primary meanings owing to the law of inclusion, we have 'Ajahatsvārthā Lakṣaṇā'. For example, in the Sanskrit sentence 'कुन्ताः प्रविशन्ति', the connotational meaning is: 'Spear-wielding soldiers are entering (the battlefield)' but in this connotational sense of the sentence, the primary sense of the 'Lākṣaṇic' word 'कुन्ताः', namely, 'spears' is clearly retained. Please note that the word 'अजहत्' means 'while not abandoning altogether' and the word 'स्वार्थ' means: 'its own primary sense (i.e. Abhidheyārtha). Thus the whole expression means 'a lakṣaṇā in which the primary sense of the word has been retained and not abandoned altogether'. The Hindī poet Rāmadhārīsingha 'Dinakara' has used

'Ajahatsvārthā lakṣaṇā' very beautifully in the following lines:

विद्युत् की इस चकाचौंध में देख दीप की लौ रोती है।
अरे हृदय को थाम महल के लिये झोपडी बलि होती है।।

[See, the flicker of the (earthen) lamp weeps in this dazzle of electricity. O, hold your heart, my friend! the hut is sacrificing itself for the sake of the palace!]

In the second line of the verse, cited above, the two words 'महल' and 'झोपडी' have 'अजहत्स्वार्थालक्षणा' The first word connotes 'the rich people owning palaces' and the second word implies 'poor men of villages living in huts'. The poet is commenting on the evil consequences of industrialization in which the poor villagers, living in huts, are compelled to leave their huts so that rich people could erect their palatial buildings in place of those huts. Please mark that in both examples the primary sense remains intact.

English poetry can supply beautiful examples of 'अजहत्स्वार्था लक्षणा'. Keats uses this wonderfully well in the last two lines of the third stanza of his 'Ode to a Nightingale':

Where Beauty cannot keep her lustrous eyes,
Or new Love pine at them beyond tomorrow.

In the first line the word 'Beauty' means 'beautiful ladies' and the word 'Love' in the second line connotes 'Lovers' and in both cases the residuum of the primary senses of the words concerned have been retained. Both the words are clearly examples of 'Ajahatsvārthā Lakṣaṇā', subsuming as they do the primary senses that they normally carry.

अज्ञातयौवना (Ajnātayauvanā)

This is a variety of the category of heroines called 'मुग्धा' (Mugdhā) in the section of Indian poetics called 'Nāyaka-Nāyikābheda'. The term denotes a fond, young maiden who is unconscious of her youth that has descended on her suddenly. Look at the following verse cited by Bhānudatta in his *Rasamanjarī* 5:

नीरात्तीरमुपागता श्रवणयोःसीम्निस्फुरन्नेत्रयोः
श्रोत्रे लग्नमिदं किमुत्पलमिति ज्ञातुं करं न्यस्यति।
शैवालाङ्कुरशंकया शशिमुखी रोमावलीं प्रोच्छति

श्रान्ताऽस्मीति मुहुः सखीमविदतश्रोणीभरा पृच्छति ।।

[(Some onlooker is remarking on the behaviour of a maiden, bathing in a pond): "having come to the bank out of the water (of the pond), the beautiful one places her hand on her eyes, touching the vicinity of her ears, out of sheer doubt, to find out if some lotus has clung to them (i.e. her ears). The moon-faced one has started rinsing the line of hair on her abdomen above the navel, suspecting it to be the sprouts of the green moss (Śaivāla) and owing to the weight of her buttocks but being unconscious of it, asks her female friend again and again why she (the moon-faced one herself) is feeling tired".]

The heroine of the verse, cited above, has developed into a fully bloomed young lady, but she does not realize the changes that have taken place in her. Such a type of heroines is known as 'Ajnātayauvanā'. Most of the Hindī poets of the period called 'Rītikāla' dealt with this type of heroines on a grand scale. Most notable among these poets were Keśavadāsa, Matirāma, 'Deva', 'Padmākara' and 'Bihāri'.

The father of Western poetry, namely, the Greek poet Homer, had created an 'Ajnātayauvanā Nāyikā' in the person of Nausisca in his epic *Odyssey* Book V where the fully bloomed maiden does not shy away from the naked Odysseus and provides him shelter out of compassion. And the English poet Shakespeare's creation Miranda, the heroine of the *Tempest* is clearly an 'ajnātayauvanā'. The character of Miranda as an 'Ajnātayauvanā' is fully revealed in the following speech of the lady, addressed to Ferdinand:

I do not know
One of my sex! no woman's face remember
Save, from my glass, mine own; nor have I seen
More that I may call men than you, good friend
And my dear father; how features are abroad
I am skillless of; but, by my modesty,
The jewel in my dower, I would not wish
Any companion in the world but you.
Nor can imagination form a shape,
Besides yourself, to like of.

Tempest III.i. 48-60

That Miranda is an 'ajnātayauvanā' is clear from her confession 'how features are abroad I am skill-less of' (ll. 5-6 of the citation) where the word 'features' stands for the physical changes wrought by the youth that has overtaken her suddenly. The state of her being unconscious of her youth and sex as distinct from the male sex also contributes to her claim as an 'ajnātayauvanā'.

अतद्गुण (Atadguṇa)

This is a figure of speech existing when despite all favourable circumstances, something, living in the proximity of another thing, superior to itself, does not take on the virtues of that thing, though it ought to, according to logical reasoning. Literally, the word means: 'not taking on the qualities of that thing (in the proximity of which the thing, under discussion is placed). In a normal case, inferior objects take unto themselves the virtues of the superior object in whose proximity they are placed and when this norm is violated, we have the figure of speech called 'Atadguṇa'. Ācārya Mammata is credited with having invented this figure. But according to Panditaraj Jagannātha, it cannot be regarded as an independent figure for it can be subsumed in 'Viśeṣokti'.

A Sanskrit example of 'Atadguṇa' is the following verse:

गाङ्गमम्बु सितमम्बु यामुनं कज्जलाभमुभयमत्रमज्जतः।
राजहंस! तव सैव शुभ्रता चीयते न च नचापचीयते।।

[O Lordswan! your whiteness remains the same (though) you bathe in both–the white water of the Ganges as well as the blackish water of Yamunā; it neither increases nor does it decrease.]

Here the constancy of the whiteness of the Lordswan is being highlighted by the poet. The Hindu public regards the water of the Ganges as white in colour and that of the sister-river Yamunā as blackish. The swan wades in the waters of the two rivers without being affected by either whereas in the normal course it should be whiter after it bathes in the Ganges and less white or blackish after it wades through the water of Yamuna. But the unique feature of the whiteness of the swan is that it is not affected–neither by the Ganges, nor by Yamunā and remains as white as ever. Since the swan does not take on the quality either of the two rivers in spite of its contact with both, the verse, under question, is an example of 'Atadguṇa'.

An English example of 'Atadguṇa' is to be found in Shakespeare's sonnet no. 53:

And you in every blessed shape we know
In all external grace you have some part,
But you like none, none you, for constant heart

Here the poet is describing Mr W.H. in Platonic/mystical terms. All the beautiful forms of nature are, according to the argument of the sonnet concerned, subsumed in the single Reality called Mr. W.H. Though he is present in all beauties of the world–Adonis, Helen, Spring–he transcends them all, and remains the least affected by them; his constancy of heart has no influence or effect of any beautiful object of the world. Clearly, the figure involved is 'Atadguṇa'.

अतिकरुण (Atikaruṇa)

Some Hindī theorists like the poet 'Deva' and the essayist Bābu Gulāba Rai have conceived of five varieties of Karuṇa Rasa–Karuṇa, Atikaruṇa, Mahākaruṇa, Laghu Karuṇa and Sukhakaruna but this classification failed to find favour with the learned experts. When the poet tries to make the audience or reader shed extra-tears, we have 'Atikaruna'. However, this is regarded not as a virtue but as a blemish, pure and simple. In Bhavabhūtis's *Uttararāmacaritam* Rāma in the state of his separation from Sītā faints again and again. Evidently, the poet had intended the play to extract extra-tears from his spectators by depicting his hero most pathetically. This authorial weakness, it must be mentioned, could not find favour with Aristotle who strongly condemns poets like Euripides for indulging in excessively tragic scenes (Vide *Poetics* XIII). Evidently, Euripides, like, Bhavabhūti, suffered from the 'Atikaruṇa'. Even Shakespeare in *King Lear* has been charged with exulting in extra-pathetic scenes, especially in the closing scene of the play. Dr. Samuel Johnson, as he himself maintained, could not bear a second reading of *King Lear* until he was forced by the editorial responsibility to do so when he was asked to edit the plays of the master-dramatist. Likewise, Charles Dickens has been attacked by critics like David Cecil in his essay on that great novelist in his critical work entitled *The Early Victorians* for his having tried to draw extra-tears from the eyes of his readers by focussing their attention on the excessively pathetic scenes in his novels.

Evidently 'Atikaruṇa' is a short-coming rather than a virtue in a literary work where the writer fails to keep his emotion under control. अति सर्वत्र वर्जयेत् ('Excess must be avoided everywhere') is a principle not confined to ethics; it should govern the working of aesthetics as well.

अतिकल्पना (Atikalpanā)

This is a term of recent origin, invented by Hindī critics to designate a class of radio-plays which are absolutely imaginary and have no real substance, having events, implausible and impossible. But the term 'Atikalpanā' can be used in reference to any literary piece which is wholly fantastical with no basis in real life. Most of the mythological stories from the 'Puraṇas' are fantastical, the product of 'atkalpanā'. To the same category belong the American and British serials based on what is known as 'star-war' or stories concerning some superman such as Mr Phantom. Robert Southey's *Curse of Kehama*, too, can be called the product of 'Atikalpanā' because here also, quite like the stories in the 'Puraṇas' events of fantastic nature have been described, having no basis in real life. A modern western critic Tzvetan Todrov has classified Henry James' work entitled "The Turn of the Screw" as an instance of fantastic literature. (Vide *The Fantastic: A Structural Approach to a Literary Genre*, trans. Richard Howard). It should be made very clear here that literature, by its very nature, depends on things imaginary or things imagined but literary works, that have the admixture of reality, alone make universal appeal whereas literature, falling under the category of 'Atikalpanā', has only ephemeral value. Its fate can be compared with that of "citrakāvya" which seldom finds favour with the connoisseurs of fine arts.

अतिशयोक्ति (Atiśayokti)

This is a figure of speech which is famous in the West as 'Hyperbole'. The literal meaning of the word is: 'a statement that is based on excessiveness'. Ācārya Bhāmaha, the author of the earliest of the known and extant treatises on the art of poetry as distinguished from drama, defines it in his poetics called काव्यालंकार (2nd 'Pariccheda', kārikā 81) in terms of some extraordinary thought, meant for some wonderful poetic effect (camatkāra) and he asserts in kārikā 85 of the second 'Pariccheda' of his treatise that 'Atiśayokti' is the basis of all figures of speech–कोऽलंकारोऽनया विना (Is there a figure without some kind of अतिशयोक्ति?). His near successor Ācārya Dandī reiterates his position:

विवक्षा या विशेषस्य लोकसीमातिवर्तिनी।
असावतिशयोक्ति स्यात् अलंकारोत्तमा यथा।

(काव्यादर्श 2/214)

[The intention of stating the special feature of something in a manner that crosses the limits of the world is 'Atiśayokti', the best of all figures.]

The figure has several varieties; the following 8 varieties have finally been recognized:

1. रूपकातिशयोक्ति (Rūpakātiśayokti)

This is a figure in which the minor term (i.e. 'upameya' or the thing which is to be compared with some other thing) is suggested through the major term (i.e. 'upamāna' or the standard of comparison) which is clearly mentioned. A Sanskrit example is the following verse:

कथमुपरि कलापिनः कलापो
विलसति तस्य तलेऽष्टमीन्दुखण्डम्।
कुवलययुगलं ततो विलोलं
तिलकुसुमं तदधः प्रवालमस्मात्।।

[(Somebody is praising the beauty of some lady, treating her as a picture): "How at the top of (the picture) is fluttering the peacock's feather? Below it (the peacock's feather) is the moon-disc of the eighth night (Aṣtamī) below which is the shivering duo of blue lotus. Below that is Til-flower and then Coral."]

In the verse, cited above, we have a list of some major terms, recognized in the Eastern tradition as patterns of excellence for different parts of the female beauty. The parts of the lady's body that the onlooker seeks to glorify have not been mentioned at all but we can infer them from their major terms which alone have been clearly mentioned. The peacock-feather suggests the lady's lock of hair because it is regarded as the best pattern of shine and luxuriance and precisely these are the marked qualities of beautiful locks. The moon disc of the eighth night (aṣtamī) is regarded as the standard of elevation and width; so it is the established 'upamāna' or standard of comparison for the foreheads of ladies. Similarly, the standard of comparison for the eyes of ladies is the blue lotus ('kuvalaya')–merely by mentioning the duo of blue lotus, the poet suggests the pair of the lady's eyes. In like manner the Til-flower suggests the lady's nose and Coral her lips.

A Hindi example of the figure "Rūpakātiśayokti" is the 'Pada' of 'Sūradāsa' which begins thus:

अद्भुत एक अनूपम बाग।
युगलकमल पर गजवर क्रीडत तापर सिंह करत अनुराग।

[(Some onlooker is describing the body of Rādha): "Oh! there is a marvellous matchless garden (in which) king Elephants are playing their tricks on a duo of lotus over which the lion is making love..."]

The physical frame of Rādhā has been presented here as a unique garden with very strange phenomena. In this garden there is a pair of lotus-flowers over which the duo of king-elephants is playing and over these kingelephants is a lion making merry. The garden is the physical frame of Rādhā. The duo of the lotus-flower suggests the feet of Rādhā and the pair of king-elephants suggests the thighs of the lady and the lion her waist. We must note that ladieś feet are normally compared with the lotus-flower, thighs with elephants and waist with the lion in the literary tradition of India.

An English example of 'Rupakātisayokti' is to be found in Keats's famous sonnet entitled 'On First Looking into Chapman's Homer':

Much have I travelled in the realms of gold
And many goodly states and kingdoms seen;
Round many western islands have I been
Which bards in fealty to Apollo hold.

Here Keats is presenting his wide reading of great poets and their classics in terms of his long journey of various states ruled over by bards in perfect loyalty to the emperor of poetry-called Apollo. 'Realms of Gold', 'goodly states and kingdoms', and 'western islands' are all 'upamānas' for 'first-rate poems', 'comic, satirical and tragic poems' and 'literatures of the western world'. Thus only by mentioning certain 'upamānas' the poet suggests the 'upameyas'. The extract is no doubt an example of 'Rūpakātiśayokti'.

I believe that 'Rupakātiśayokti' is full of great potentiality. Allegories like *The Faerie Queene, Pilgrim's Progress* and the *Animal Farm* can be considered as long-drawn examples of 'Rūpakātiśayokti' and symbolist poems like Yeats's 'Byzantium' can also be brought within the range of the figure.

2. भेदकातिशयोक्ति (Bhedakātiśayokti)

This variety of 'Atiśayokti' consists in making the subject on hand unique and matchless or far superior to its normal 'upamāna' or standard of comparison. How this all is done can be available to a serious reader-who realizes the beauty of the logic put forth by the poet. Let us consider the following Sanskrit example:

> अन्यदेवाङ्गलावण्यमन्याः सौरभसम्पदः ।
> तस्या पद्मपलाशाक्ष्याः सरसत्वमलौकिकम् ।।
>
> [(Some lover of a lady is reflecting on her beauty:" The loveliness of the limbs of that lady with eyes like lotus-leaves is rather different and the riches of her fragrance are different altogether and her elegance extraordinary indeed".]

The loveliness of a lady is usually compared to that of the leaves of a lotus. The lady of the present piece has her eyes as lovely as the lotus leaves but beyond this apparent resemblance, there exists no similarity between the two, the loveliness of the lady's limbs being entirely different from those of the lotus and her sweet smells, too, being all different. Thus there is some similarity between the 'upameya' (i.e. the lady of the piece) and the 'upamāna' in the form of lotus-leaves but that similarity is confined to the shape of the lady's eyes which look like lotus leaves. Beyond this so-called similarity, the differences are vast indeed, the lady's limbs being far lovelier than the limbs of the lotus-flowers and her fragrance, too, being entirely different from the fragrance of the lotus-flowers and her inner charms being divine. Thus since the verse brings into limelight that which distinguishes the subject of the verse (upameya) from its usual standard of comparison (upamāna), in the present case (lotus-leaves), through the use of the 'vācakas' (signs) like 'anyat', 'anyāḥ' and 'aloukika', the figure is 'Bhedakātiśayokti'.

An excellent English example of the figure is the following passage from P.B. Shelley's lyric "To a Skylark":

> Sound of vernal showers,
> On the twinkling grass,
> Rain-awakened flowers,
> All that ever was
> Joyous, and clear, and fresh, thy music doth surpass.

To bring home to the reader the joyousness, clearness, and freshness of the music of the Skylark, the poet refers to some standards of comparison-'vernal showers on the twinkling grass' and 'rain-awakened flowers' but finds them all insignificant before the song of the skylark which surpasses not only these two 'upamānas' but all possible 'upomanas' noted for their 'joyousness', 'clearness' and 'freshness'.

Here we should remember that there is a figure called व्यतिरेक ('vyatireka') in which the 'upameya' is shown through a tour-de-force to be superior to the 'upamāna' and thus there is the chance of confusing 'Bhedakātiśayokti' with 'Vyatireka'. But readers should note that in 'vyatireka' the 'upamāna' is held in contempt and the 'upameya' is praised on certain points whereas in 'Bhedakātisayokti' the 'upameya' is just shown to be far ahead of the 'upamāna' merely by assertion.

3. सम्बन्धातिशयोक्ति (Sambandhātiśayokti)

Where there is no plausible relationship between two objects and even then some relationship is artfully established, we have the figure of speech called 'Sambandhātiśayokti'. Consider the following verse of Sanskrit:

सौधाग्राणि पुरस्यास्य स्पृशन्ति विधुमण्डलम्

[The tops of the palaces of this city are touching the orb of the moon.]

There is no conceivable relationship between the buildings and the round of the moon but here the tops of the palaces (of the city concerned) touch the orb of the moon and clearly a very intimate relationship has been established between the tops of the palaces and the orb of the moon. Thus the verse is an excellent example of 'Sambandhātiśayokti'.

An English example of the figure is the following passage from Doctor Faustus by Christopher Marlowe:

Was this the face that launched a thousand ships
And burnt the topless tower of Iliam?

There cannot be conceived any relationship between the face of a lady and the burning of the highest tower of a city. But here the face of Helen has been credited with having launched a thousand ships and burnt the highest tower of Iliam (Troy). The 'atiśayokti' here lies in a relationship being established where, in point of fact, there was no relationship of any kind; it is 'sambandhātiśayokti', pure and simple.

'Sambandhātiśayokti' sometimes exists where some relationship between the 'upameya' and 'upamāna' is established by means of a Conditional Clause. The following Sanskrit verse is an example:

असितगिरिनिभं स्यात् कज्जलं सिन्धुपात्रे
सुरपुरतरुशाखा लेखिनी पत्रमुर्वी ।

लिखतु यदि गृहीत्वा शारदा सर्वकालं
तदपि तव महिमानमीश! पारं न याति।।

[Should the sea be the inkpot, some black mountain of soot the black ink, some branch of Kalpavṛkṣa assume the shape of a pen, the whole-earth that of a paper and the goddess of learning Śāradā start writing for ever, even then, O Lord! your glory will never come to an end!]

Here the glory of the Lord is impossible to be counted by man. But some divine counter (in the present case Śāradā) in some special circumstances, was first thought to be able to accomplish that impossible task but later found to be inadequate. Thus a kind of relationship, however inadequate it may be, has been established and so the figure called 'Sambandhātiśayokti' stands justified.

A very beautiful and famous Hindi example of "Sambandhātiśayokti" based on some condition is available in the following extract from the *Rāmacaritamānasa* of Goswamī Tulasīdasa:

जौं छविसुधा पयोनिधि होई। परमरूपमय कच्छप सोई।
सोभा रजु मन्दरु सिंगारु। मथै पानि पंकज निज मारू।
एहि विधि उपजै लच्छि जब, सुन्दरता सुखमूल।
तदपि सकोच समेत कवि, कहहिं सीय समतूल।।

("बालकाण्ड", near दोहा 247)

[If the nectar of beauty were the ocean, the mythical turtle were granted some extremely beautiful form, prettiness were the rope and the sentiment called "Śrīngāra" incarnate were the mountain Mandarācala and Cupid or Kāmadeva himself could do the churning act and in this way if some Luxmī or goddess of beauty were born as the source of happiness and beauty then only can poets compare it with Sītā and that, too, quite hesitatingly.]

Here an almost impossible condition has been laid down and on the fulfilment of that condition alone the resultant object could come close to the subject on hand (i.e. Sītā) and that, too, quite marginally. We can cite the following stanza from "To a skylark" of P.B. Shelley as an example of this variety of "Sambandhātiśayokti":

Yet if we could scorn
Hate, and pride, and fear;

If we were things born,
Not to shed a tear,
I know not how thy joy we ever should come near.

Here humanity as a whole has been conceived of as some thing to be described as a peer of the joyous skylark and then a condition is laid down at the fulfilment of which mankind could come close to the Skylark rather marginally and not fully.

4. असम्बन्धातिशयोक्ति (Asambandhātiśayokti)

This figure exists where the age-old recognised relationship between a major term (upamāna) and a minor term (upameya) is clearly denied though it is, to all intents and purposes, quite plausible and valid. The following Sanskrit verse is an example:

त्वयि दातरि राजेन्द्र! स्वर्द्रुमान्नाद्रियामहे।

[(Some brahmin is praising the charitable behaviour of some king:) "O Lord of kings! we do not pay any heed to heavenly trees (such as 'Kalpataru', Pārijāta etc.) there being a donor of your nature."]

Heavenly trees like 'Kalpavṛkṣa' and 'Pārijāta' are recognized in the Hindu tradition as the greatest fulfillers of human wishes but the admirer of the king in question slights them and purports to state that the heavenly trees are nothing in respect of donation before a donor like the king.

A Hindī example of this figure is to be found in the following verse of Tulasīdāsa:

जेहिं बर बाजि राम असवारा। तेहि सारदउ न बरनै पारा।।

[Even Śāradā, the goddess of learning, cannot describe full-well the horse Rāma was riding.]

In the Hindu tradition Śāradā is the goddess of learning; nothing is beyond her power of description. And yet the poet says that even She could not describe the beauty of the horse that Rāma was riding during His wedding procession.

A very beautiful English illustration of the figure is available in the following stanza of Shelley's lyric entitled "To a Skylark":

Chorus Hymeneal
Or triumphal Chaunt,
Matched with thine would be all
But an empty vaunt,
A thing where in we feel there is some hidden want.

Joy and happiness are expressed best in wedding songs and in songs of victory and indeed these two are the specimens of the expression of joy. But the joy that the Skylark is experiencing is, according to the poet, beyond the reach of the group-songs of marriage as well as of the songs sung during the celebration of some victory, regarded as the last words in the matter of the expression of joy. No doubt, the passage is an excellent example of "Asambandhātiśayokti".

5. अक्रमातिशयोक्ति (Akramātiśayokti)

Normally, cause precedes its effect but when the poet cleverly describes both cause and its effect as taking place all at once, we have the figure "Akramātiśayokti". A Sanskrit example of the figure is the following verse:

आलिङ्गन्ति समं देव! ज्यां शराश्च पराश्च ते।

[(Some bard is praising the prowess of his master:) "Lord, thy arrows and enemies embrace "Jyā" (the string of the bow and the earth) simultaneously".]

In the normal course of the world, if you want to kill your enemies, you will first place your arrow on the string of your bow and throw it and only then can the arrow kill the enemies. But here the touching of the string of the bow by the arrows and the touching of the earth by the enemies are described as happening all at once without any interval or gap. The Biblical statement from "the Book of Genesis" in the "Old Testament", namely, 'God said light and there was light' affords an illustration of 'Akramātiśayokti' for here, too, God's command (cause) and the birth of light (effect) have been described as taking place at one and the same time.

6. चपलातिशयोक्ति (Capalātiśayokti)

When effect takes place the moment the cause is mentioned or heard, we have the figure of speech called "Capalātiśayokti". A Sanskrit example is the following verse:

यास्यामीत्युदिते तन्व्या वलयोऽभवदूर्मिका

[The lover-husband having said 'I shall depart', the ring of the lady became an armlet.]

The hero of the verse has not yet gone abroad–he has just mentioned his future plan–and yet his lady became so frail that her ring started serving as an armlet–she could wear it on her arm, so frail it had become.

A similar Hindi example is the following couplet:

सुनत पयान-मुहूरत पी को। दरकूयो मुकतहार तचि तीको।।

[The moment the lady heard of the departure-hour of her lover, her pearl-string burst (presumably owing to the heat of agony, caused by the prospective separation).]

The heroine of the verse has hardly been separated from her lover when she starts burning with the agony of separation and the result is clear from the bursting of the pearl-string on her breast.

This is indeed the limit of the lady's sensitivity and delicacy.

An English example of 'Capalatiśayokti' is found in the closing two stanzas of "The Scholar Gypsy" by the Victorian poet Matthew Arnold:

Then fly our greetings, fly our speech and smiles!
-As some grave Tyrian trader, from the sea,
Descried at sunrise an emerging prow
Lifting the cool-hair'd creepers stealthily,
The fringes of a southward-facing brow
Among the Aegean isles;
And saw the merry Grecian Coaster come,
Freighted with amber grapes, and Chian wine
Green bursting figs, and tunnies steep'd in brine,
And knew the intruders on his ancient home,
The young light hearted Masters of the waves;
And Snatched his rudder, and shook out more sail,

Here the flight of the Tyrian trader (effect) has been described by the poet as taking place at the mere sight of the Grecian Coaster when the invasion by the latter (cause) has hardly happened. A better English example is the following extract from the 3rd stanga of Shelley's "Ode to the West Wind":

For whose path the Atlantic's level powers
Cleave themselves into chasms, while far below
The sea-blooms and the oozy woods which wear
The sapless foliage of the ocean, know
Thy voice, and suddenly grow grey with fear,
And tremble and despoil themselves; oh, hear!

Here the "growing grey with fear" (effect) of the "sea-blooms and the oozy woods" has been described as taking place at their mere hearing of the voice of the West Wind which has hardly visited them. No doubt, we have "Capalātiśayokti" here.

7. अत्यन्तातिशयोक्ति (Atyantātiśayokti)

When effect is described skilfully as happening much before the cause, we have "Atyantatiśayokti". Consider the Following Sanskrit verse:

प्रागेव हरिणाक्षीणां चित्तमुत्कलिकाकुलम् ।
पश्चादुद्भिन्नबकुलरसालमुकुलश्रियः ।।

[The heart-buds of the dear-eyed became ecstatic and the buds of 'Bakul' and Mango blossomed forth in their full glory afterwards.]

In the literary tradition of India the spring season is distinguished by its congeniality to love-making when 'Bakul' and 'Mango' blossom forth and arouse erotic desires in the hearts of lovers, especially female lovers. But the poet of the verse on hand wants to highlight the extraordinarily passionate nature of the heroines of his conception who grew full of passionate desires even before the blooming of 'Bakul' and 'Mango' by reversing the natural order of cause and effect. In the normal course of Nature 'Bakul' and 'Mango' bloom first and as a result of their blooming, ladies become full of passionate desires but in the poetic world of the verse concerned, the ladies became passionates prior to the blooming of 'Bakul' and 'Mango'. An English example of 'Atyantātiśayokti' is to be found in *The Rape of the Lock* Canto III ll. 149-52:

Ev'n then, before the fatal engine clos'd,
A wretched sylph too fondly interpos'd;
Fate urged the Sheers, and cut the Sylph in twain,
(But Airy Substance soon unites again.)

Here we find that the Sylph was cut into two parts (effect) first and the two blades of the scissors closed later (cause) whereas in the normal course the Sylph could have been cut into two parts only after the closure of the blades of the scissors. Clearly, the verse cited contains the figure "Atyantātiśayokti".

8. सापह्नवातिशयोक्ति (Sāpahnavātiśayokti)

This is actually a special form of "Rūpakātiśayokti" in which minor terms ("upameyas") are inferred from the use of major terms ("upamānas"), employed profusely in the piece. "Sāpahnavātiśayokti", however, differs from "Rūpakātiśayokti" proper; it invariably has an element of denial stated or implied. A Sanskrit example is the following verse:

त्वत्सूक्तिषु सुधा राजन्, भ्रान्ताः पश्यन्ति तां विधौ ।।

[The nector, O king, lies in thy good speeches; the misguided ones look for it in the moon.]

The moon is traditionally regarded as the storehouse of nectar; indeed, one of its synonyms is 'Sudhākara' (literally the treasure of nectar). And it is the established major term wherewith to compare the countenance of beautiful ladies and gentlemen. Here it has been used as an 'upamāna' of sweetness. Through the verse some poet is paying a tribute to his patron-king's voice by saying that the real nectar is to be found in the beautiful statements of his master rather than in the moon. Thus the claim of the moon to the ownership of nectar is implicitly denied and that of the king's statements is asserted. Evidently, the verse contains 'Sāpahnavātiśayokti'. Shakespeare has made a profound use of this figure in the following speech of Biron in *Love's Labour's Lost Act* IV Scene III. 350:

From women's eyes this doctrine I derive:
They sparkle still the right Prometh fire;
They are the books, the arts, the academes
That show, contain, and nourish all the world.

In the western tradition, the fire that Prometheus had stolen from the gods and given to mankind was the "upamāna" of all arts and refinements. Here Biron is paying a rich tribute to the women of the world by denying the source of arts and skills to the Promethean fire and attributing it to the eyes of beautiful ladies. Thus the whole speech of Biron is informed by the figure "Sāpahnavātiśayokti", indicated by the epithet "right" employed to qualify the expression "Promethean fire".

अत्यन्ततिरस्कृताविवक्षितवाच्यध्वनि (Atyanta-Tiraskṛtāvivakṣita-vacya-Dhvani):–This is a kind out of numerous forms of 'Dhvani', formulated by ācārya Ānandavardhana. In this kind of 'Dhvani' or 'Suggestion', the primary dictionary meaning is ignored completely, giving rise to an entirely new meaning which, to all intents and purposes, has nothing to do with the literal meaning of the word or statement concerned. The following lines of the Hindi poet Sumitranandana "Panta" has "Atyantatiraskṛtāvivakṣitavācyādhvani", based on a word:

तुम्हारी आँखों का आकाश, सरल आँखों का नीलाकाश।
खो गया मेरा खग अनजान, मृगेक्षणि! इनमें खग अज्ञान।

[O doe-eyed one!, my innocent bird, my fond bird, has been lost in the sky of thy eyes, the blue sky of thy clear eyes.)

The speaker of the above lines–the lover-poet, is no keeper of birds [literally, goers (ग) to the firmament (ख)]. So he cannot be supposed to be in possession of a bird. No doubt, the sense of the word 'खग' is hampered because the literal meaning of the word, namely, 'bird' and even its etymological meaning–'goer to the firmament' does not convey any sensible meaning. But from the context of the poem–a human lover, admiring the eyes of his lady-love–we realize that what has actually been lost in the firmament of the eyes of the lady-love is the 'heart' of the lover, the speaker of the lines, his मनस् (manas). Thus in arriving at this sense of the word, the primary meaning of the word, which is not adequate in the context, has been ignored completely.

An excellent example of the second variety of the "dhvani" concerned (i.e. sentence-based as opposed to the word-based) is to be found in Angada's speech in the "Lankākānda" of *Rāmacaritamānasa* of Tulasīdāsa:

नाक-कान बिनु भगिनि निहारी। छमा कीन्ह तुम्ह धर्म बिचारी।
धर्मसीलता तव जग जागी। पावा दरस हमँहु बड भागी।।

(before Doha No. 22)

[Witnessing your sister (Sūrpaṇakhā) bereft of nose and ears you forgave (the perpetrator of the act, namely, Rāma and Lakṣamana) in view of the law of righteousness. Indeed your righteousness is known to the whole world. I, too, am indeed very lucky to have your 'darśana' (sight).]

In the above extract, Angada, the peace-envoy of Rāma to the court of Rāvaṇa, who has abducted Sītā, Rāma's wife, is retorting to the remark of Rāvaṇa to the effect that he has tolerated so long the harsh words of Angada because he abides by the principles of right conduct. Angada's reply to Rāvaṇa's claim to righteousness, appears, to all intents and purposes, very positive and appreciative but, in point of fact, it is a statement of clear condemnation. It implies the opposite of what it says and this implied sense of the whole statement is dictated to us by the context, including the identities of the addresser and the addressee. The first sentence means that Rāvaṇa must be a coward rather than a tolerant man if he bore patiently the sight of his own sister bereft of her nose and ears and did nothing to punish the perpetrators of that offence. The second line mocks Rāvaṇa's claim to righteousness by implying his abduction of Sītā through treachery and fraud. And Angada's admission that he regards himself as a very lucky man to have the 'darśana' of Rāvaṇa is actually his statement of regret that he has had the 'darśana' of evil incarnate and thus it is his great misfortune that he has come to the court of an utterly wicked and cowardly man. Clearly, in arriving at this implied sense of the passage, we have ignored its plain sense completely. The extract is thus illustrative of 'Atyantatiraskṛtāvivakṣitavācyadhvani'.

An English example of 'Atyantatiraskṛtā-vivakṣtta-vācya-dhvani' based on a single word or expression is to be found in the following line from Shakespeare's sonnet no. 18:

'But thy eternal summer shall not fade'

In the sonnet concerned the poet is trying to prove the superiority of Mr. W.H. over 'a Summer's Day'. We find the line, cited above, a little baffling when we bear in mind the fact that he is a man and not a year, having seasons like summer, winter, spring etc. Thus the sense of the expression 'thy summer' causes some problem: its true sense is hampered. Naturally, the reader is forced to interpret the expression in terms of the youthfulness, beauty, liberality and other qualities of head and heart of Mr W.H.–qualities that have nothing to do with the literal/primary meaning of the word 'summer' regarded as a season of the year. Since the primary meaning has been completely lost in arriving at the implied sense of the expression, the expression is an example of 'Atyantatiraskrtāvivaksita-Vācya-Dhvani' residing in a word or an expression.

An example of the second kind of 'Atyantatiraskṛtāvivakṣita-Vācya-Dhvani' is found in the repeated statement, namely, 'But Brutas is an honourable man' in the famous speech of Mark Antony in Shakespeare's Roman play *Julius Caesar* Act III scene II. In the said speech Antony is actually refuting Brutus's charges levelled against the murdered Caesar. In that context the literal meaning of the sentence makes no sense; it becomes meaningful only when we take it in in the opposite sense of what it states, namely, Brutus is the most dishonourable man on earth. Chaucer's "General Prologue" to his *magnum opus* the *Canterbury Tales* is full of examples of "Atyantatisaskṛtāvivakṣita-vācya-Dhvani".–For example, in his portrayal of the character of the Monk, the poet remarks:

'And I seyde, his opinioun was good'.

This statement of the poet, in its context, is baffling. The Monk flouts all rules, set down by Church-fathers like St. Maure and St. Benedict. Clearly, the intended meaning of Chaucer is that the Monk was a most un-Christian, unholy and wicked man whose views on religious practices were devilish and abominable; the poet detested them. In arriving at this desired meaning of the statement, the apparent, primary meaning of the remark, has been ignored altogether. The line is evidently an excellent example of 'Atyanta-Tiaskṛtāvivakṣita-Vācya-Dhvani'.

अत्युक्ति (Atyukt):–What the Western critical tradition calls 'Hyperbole' (Over-shooting) is denoted in the Eastern tradition by the term अत्युक्ति (Atyukti) rather than the more popular term 'Atiśayokti' which is somewhat different from 'Hyperbole' as the discussion of that term in the entry concerned makes amply clear. When something is described in patently false and highly exaggerated terms, we have the figure called 'Atyukti'. To ācārya Pīyusavarṣī Jaideva goes the credit of having invented and popularized the term. Jaideva declares:

अत्युक्तिरद्भुतातिथ्यशौर्योदार्यादिवर्णनम्

(चन्द्रालोक 5/116)

['Atyukti' is the description of astonishing hospitability, prowess, liberality etc. which is not true to facts.]

Consider the following Sanskrit verse from *Bhojaprabandha,* glorifying the brilliancfe of king Bhoja:

भोजप्रतापं तु विधाय धात्रा
शेषैर्निरस्तैर्परुमाणुभिर्किम्।
हरे करेऽभूत पविरम्बरे च
भानुर्पयोधेरुदरे कृशानुः।।

> [After the prowess of Bhoja was formed, what was (created) by the Creator by means of the remaining atoms? (From the remaining atoms) was born bolt in the hand of Indra, the sun in the sky and the fire (Vadavāgni) in the belly of the ocean.]

Here in praising the prowess and brilliance of king Bhoja, the bard seems to have gone wild. He says that the Creator first used all his skill and resources in creating the brilliance of Bhoja and then with the help of the remaining elements on His palms, He formed Indra's bolt, the Sun and the fire in the womb of the ocean–all the three noted for their brilliance. This is clearly a false account on its very face because Bhoja was not in existence before the creation of all the three potentates–Indra's bolt, the Sun and "Vadavāgni".

An English example of "Atyukti" is the following passage from Marlowe's *Doctor Faustus*

> Had I as many souls as there be stars.
> I'd give them all for Mephistopheles.
> By him I'll be great emperor of the world
> And make a bridge through the moving air
> To pass the ocean with a band of men;
> I'll join the hills that bind the Afric shore,
> And make that country continent to Spain
> And both Contributory to my crown.
> The Emperor shall not live but by my leave
> Nor any potentate of Germany.

The passage, cited above, records the ambitions of a Renaissance man who plans to accomplish things humanly impossible–projects like joining Spain and Africa. The proposed projects bespeak the future prowess of the speaker. Since the prowess is not true to the domain of possibility, the speech is clearly "Atyukti" of Jaideva's formulation.

It must be borne in mind that a few Sanskrit theorists are not in favour of allotting the status of an independent figure of speech to "Atyukti"; according to them it is subsumed in the figure called "Udātta". Most important names in the list of such theorists are those of Nāgeśa and Viśveśvara Pandita.

अद्भुत रस (Adbhuta Rasa):–This is one of the 9 sentiments or aesthetic attitudes recognized by the Sanskrit theorists. This sentiment is evoked where there is a description of some extraordinary, wondrous and awe-inspiring object or event. Naturally, "Vismaya" or the sense of wonder is its "Sthāyībhāva" or basic mood. Its 'Ālambana Vibhāva', the component aesthetic surface, consists of objects or beings of some extraordinary or supernatural proportions; the performers of miracles performed can serve as the 'Ālambana' of this sentiment. The discussion or analysis of the miracles or miraculous acts concerned serves as the "Uddīpana-Vibhāva" of "Adbhuta-Rasa". Stupification, perspiration, horripilation, speechlessness and torpor of the witnesses constitute its "Anubhāvas" or consequents or bodily reactions. "Vyabhicārī" or "Sancārī bhāvas" (i.e. fleeting feelings) of "Adbhuta-Rasa" are: doubt, recollection, delight, curiosity etc. The colour of this sentiment has been declared "yellow" and "Gandharvas" are regarded as the presiding deities of this "Rasa". The eleventh chapter of the *Bhagvad-Gītā* where Lord Krishna reveals his universal Form to Arjuna is the classic example of "Adbhuta Rasa". Tulasīdāsa's *Rāmacāritamānasa* provides examples of "Adbhuta Rasa" on numerous occasions. Pārvatī's encounter with the different manifestations of Lord Rāma in all directions while she was trying to test the divinity of the Lord; Kausalya's witnessing of the child Rāma in the Cradle as well as in the courtyard at one and the same time and Kākabhuśundī's experience with the omnipotence of the infant Rāma whose extended hands pursued Jayanta and no god intervened to help him out of sheer fear until he sought shelter in the feet of the Lord who forgave his offence–all these episodes are excellent examples of Adbhuta Rasa. If we want a single verse invocative of 'Adbhuta Rasa' we can cite the following verse from *Bhagwad-Gītā:*

> रूपं महत्ते बहुवक्त्रनेत्रं
> महाबाहो बहुबाहूरुपादम् ।
> बहूदरं बहुदंष्ट्राकरालं
> दृष्ट्वा लोकाः प्रव्यथितास्तथाहम् ।।

> [O large-armed one! witnessing thy magnificent form, having many countenances and eyes, countless arms, thighs and feet, many bellies and numeous jaws, making it look terrible, all the worlds and I are perturbed excessively.]

Here the largest conceivable form of Lord Krishna is the "Ālambana Vibhāva", the detailed account of the multiplicity of Krishna's limbs are the "Uddīpana Vibhāva"; the feeling of being shaken terribly felt by Arjuna and others is the "Anubhāva", त्रास (or fear), वितर्क (or doubting and questioning) etc. are the "Vyabhicārī bhāvas" and "Vismaya" (or sense of wonder) is the "Sthāyībhāva". Augumented and supported by the Ālambana, Uddīpana, "Anubhāvas" and "Sancari-bhavas", the 'Sthāyibhāva Vismaya' gets transformed into the sentiment called "Adbhuta".

There is no dearth of "Adbhuta Rasa" in the literary tradition of the West. Mystery and miracle plays of England can supply ample examples of "Adbhuta-Rasa" and so can the treatment of the supernatural by Shakespeare and others. Besides, plays, poems and novels, dealing with Christ's resurrection, can furnish excellent examples of the sentiment, under review. The first two scenes of the First Act of the *Tempest* provide "Adbhutrasa" abundantly; here Prospero causes the ship of Alfonso, Sebastian, Antonio, Ferdinand, Gonzalo etc. to sink in the sea by means of his magic wand and later saves it miraculously through the spirit Ariel. Keats provides "Adbhut-Rasa" in his "Lamia" where the serpent-woman disappears at the sight of the sage Apollonius. The third section of Coleridge's "Kubla Khan", however, can be cited as illustrative of "Adbhuta-Rasa", located in a single stanza:

Could I revive within me
Her symphony and song,
To such a deep delight't would win me,
That with music loud and long,
I would build that dome in air,
That sunny dome! those caves of ice!
And all who heard should see them there,
And all should cry: Beware! Beware!
His flashing eyes, his floating hair!
Weave a circle round him thrice,
And close your eyes with holy dread.
For he on honey-dew hath fed
And drunk the milk of Paradise.

Here the music-loving persona with "flashing eyes" and "floating hair" of the poem is the "Ālambana-Vibhāva"; "dome in the air", "sunny dome" and "caves of ice" constitute the "Uddīpana-Vibhāva" (the excitants); people's cry: 'Beware', 'Beware' is the "Anubhāva" along with their thrice circling round the persona of the poem; people's closing of the eyes (सुप्ति) and fear (भय) are the "Sancāris". With the help of these constituents, the "Sthāyī-bhāva Vismaya" felt by the people (onlookers) gets transformed into a "Rasa" called "Adbhuta", manifested in the thrill and ecstasy that the reader of the poem undergoes when he bursts into the last two lines:

For he on honey-dew hath fed
And drunk the milk of Paradise.

It must be placed on record that the romantic style of poetry is most congenial to our "Rasa" whether it is English, German, French or American Romantic poetry or even the "Ccāyāvādī" poetry of Hindi, for the sense of wonder is the very basis of romanticism. Shakespeare, the most romantic of poets, has given expression to the power of romantic vision in the first scene of the 5th Act of his comedy *A Midsummer Night's Dream:*

The poet's eye, in a fine frenzy rolling,
Doth glance from heaven to earth, from earth to heaven,
And as imagination bodies forth
The forms of things unknown, the poet's pen
Turns them to shapes, and gives to airy nothing
A local habitation and a name.

Indeed, the romantic poets tend to see 'the light that never was on sea or land', as Wordsworth says in his poem entitled 'Elegiac Stanzas' and this is the essence of "Āścarya-Rasa", better known as "Adbhuta-Rasa".

It must also be mentioned that श्ृंगार, वीर and भयानक "Rasas" are quite friendly to "Adbhuta"; these can intensify it.

अधमा नायिका (Adhamā Nāyikā):–Sanskrit theorists have conceived of a kind of the heartless heroine who does harm to her hero who despite her heartless behaviour always seeks to do good to her. Such heroines have been called "Adhamā" (wicked). These heroines are always indifferent to the advances of the hero and treat them cruelly. Kaikeyī of the *Rāmacaritamānasa* is a superb example of "Adhamā Nāyikā". The following verses will serve the purpose of illustration, though Tulasīdāsa describes the heartlessness of Kekayī at great length in his epic:

केहि हेतु रानि रिसानि परसत पानि पतिहि नेवारई।
मानहुँ सरोष भुअंग भामिनि विषम भाँति निहारई।।
दोउ वासना रसना दसन वर मरम ठाहरु देखई।
तुलसी नृपति भवितव्यता बस काम कौतुक लेखई।।

['O Queen! Why should you be annoyed?' saying this when (King Daśaratha) tries to touch (Kekayī) (the latter) pushes his hand off and looks at him as if she were an angry female snake. The aspirations born out of (the two boons) were like

> the two tongues and the boons themselves like the fangs of the female snake, looking for the proper place (on the person of the king) to bite. Tulasīdāsa says that the king (under the influence of the Fate) regards this behaviour of the queen as the sport of Kāmadeva (the god of Love and sex)]

Here the heroine called Kekayī is clearly being very cruel to her lover, King Daśaratha, who is all love for her and despite that the heroine does not respond favourably to his advances but rather intends to cause positive harm to him. No doubt she deserves to be called 'Adhamā' (wicked).

Olivia in Shakespeare's *Twelfth Night* comes quite close to the notion of "Adhamā Nāyikā" in so far as she is unkind to the messages of love from Duke Orsino. Viola (in the garb of a boy called Cesario) has to call her "the cruellest she alive" and casts the following curse on her:

> 'Love make his heart of flint that you shall love,
> And let your fervour, like my master's be
> Place in contempt.
>
> (Act I, Scene V)

Thus at least in the eyes of Viola, Olivia is an "Adhamā Nāyika", maltreating as she does, Duke Orsino who loves her heartily, not directly but by proxy.

अधिक (Adhika)

This is a figure of speech belonging to the type called "Atyukti". The theorist Rudrata is the first to have recognized and given currency to it and later theorists like Mammatha and Viśvanāth also approved its independent existence. It resides where the contained, technically called "Ādheya" or "Āśrayī" is skilfully described as exceeding the container (Ādhāra). Consider the following verse from the epic *Śiśupalavadham* by Māgha:

> युगान्तकालप्रतिसंहृतात्मनो जगन्ति यस्यां सविकाशमासत।
> तनौ ममुस्तत्र न कैटभद्विषस्तपोधनाभ्यागमसम्भवाः मुदः।।
>
> [The happiness caused by the arrival of the sage Nārada could not be contained in the body of Lord Krishna, the enemy of the demon Kaitabha–the body that absorbs all the worlds at the time of the Deluge ("Pralaya").]

Here the body of Krishna, an incarnation of Vishnu is the container and the contained is His happiness at the sight of sage Nārada. The contained has been depicted as exceeding the container (the Lord's body) which is capacious enough to contain all the 14 worlds and absorb them at the time of Total Destruction (Pūrṇa-Pralaya); that is to say that the volume of Krishna's happiness is far larger than the volume of His body, capable of containing all the 14 worlds ("Bhuvanas").

The reverse of the above condition constitutes the second variety of "Adhika"; this happens when the contained is skilfully shown to be the contained of something, usually regarded as the container of all. Consider the following Hindi verse by Matirāma, a poet of the Rītikāla:

> जाके कोस भीतर भुवन करतार ऐसो,
> जाके नाभिकुण्ड में कमल विकसत हैं।
> राव भावसिंह तेरी कहाँ लौं बड़ाई करौं,
> ऐसो बडो! प्रभु तेरे मन में बसत हैं।।

> [O king Bhāvasingh! I do not know how I should praise thy devoutness for in thy heart resides the Great God (Viṣṇu) in whose navel-pond blooms the lotus having a thelmos in which resides the creator of all the worlds!]

Here the heart of King Bhāvasingh has been depicted as the container of Viṣṇu in the thalmos of whose navel-lotus resides Brahmā, the Creator of the universe. Viṣṇu's nave, which is just a very small part of the body of the Lord, contains Brahmā, the Creator of all worlds. And since that God Visnu resides in the heart of King Bhāvasingh, the largeness of the heart of the king can very well be imagined.

As an English example of the first variety of "Adhika" we can cite the following lines of Pope's *Rape of the Lock:*

> Sol through white curtains shot a timorous ray
> And oped those eyes that must eclipse the day.
>
> (Canto I,ll. 11-12)

Sol (the sun), to all intents and purposes, is an infinitely large object and can contain numberless eyes. But Belinda's eyes have been skilfully described as the container of 'sol' (the sun) because thy are capable of eclipsing him (the day or the sun) and thus can be described as the container and the sun the contained.

Wordsworth's lyric "The Solitary Reaper" has "Adhika" in the following lines:

O listen! for the vale profound
Is overflowing with the sound.

The reaper, as a matter of fact, is singing in her field–an area of a few square metres. But a valley contains hundreds and thousands of such fields. And yet the poet suggests that the song (the contained) was far larger than the container (the valley).

The second variety of "Adhika" can be illustrated from Donne's lyric "The Canonization":

You, to whom love was peace, that now is rage;
Who did the whole world's soule contract, and drove
Into the glasses of your eyes...

Here the sceptical onlookers, who had been the adversaires of the lovers, have turned admirers and devotees because the lovers have been canonized (i.e. have achieved the status of saints). The above speech is that of the adversaries, turned into admirers, who are paying tributes to the pair of lovers by saying that their union has drawn together the soul of the whole world (i.e. the universal soul) and has transformed it into the glasses of their eyes because those eyes have exhumed its inherent divinity. Here we find that the soul of the whole world stands contained in the eyes of the lovers and thus the lines clearly have the figure "Adhika" (the second variety).

अधिकपदता (Adhikapadatā):–When a poem uses words which are unnecessary and redundant, we declare the poem as suffering from a poetic defect called "Adhikapadatā". It is present where we could easily dispense with a word or words. In other words, "Adhikapadatā" is present where the presence of a single word or many words are not justifiable by any means, or wherever those words are unfunctional. Look at the following Hindi verse of "Bihārī", noted for his brevity and precision:

लपटी पुहुप पराग पट सनी स्वेदमकरन्द।
आवत नारि नवोढलौं, सुखद वायु गतिमन्द।।

[The pleasant slow-pace wind is coming (i.e. blowing) like a newly-wed lady, drenched with sweat in the form of fragrance and wrapped up in silken clothes of pollengrains of flowers.]

The word 'पुहुप' meaning 'flowers' is unnecessary in the verse, cited above, because the word 'पराग', used soon after that word, carries the sense of 'pollengrains' and "pollen grains" belong to flowers and to nothing else. Thus the word 'पुहुप' is unfunctional and redundant and its use makes the verse defective; it should have been dispensed with and a word like 'पीत' should have been used instead without any damage to the metrical arrangement of the verse.

The western theorists have a term 'Pleonasm' for what the Sanskrit theorists call 'अधिकपदता'. Consider, for example, the sentence: 'He hurried in haste to the bus-station'. The sentence suffers from "Adhikapadatā" because the verb "hurried" inheres the sense of 'haste'; thus the adverbial expression 'in haste' is redudant and should be dispensed with : 'He hurried to the bus-station' is the fairly correct and flawless sentence. A literary example of 'Adhikapadatā' is the expression 'deceiving elf' in Keats's 'Ode to a Nightingale' l. 74. Since elves, by their very nature, are deceitful, the epithet 'deceiving' used by Keats for the noun 'elf' is unwarranted and superfluous and makes the line suffer from 'Adhikapadatā', or 'Pleonasm'. However, Professor K.G. Srivastava of the University of Allahabad, in opposition to Kingsley Amis, has very ably defended the use of the epithet "deceiving" for the word "elf" by arguing that only the elves of the Scottish tradition are mischievous and decitful; the elves of the Teutonic tradition are good and helpful to man. (Vide Professor Srivastava's article on the subject in *The Explicator (1982)*

अधिकार and अधिकारी (Adhikāra and Adhikārī)

These are the terms of dramaturgy. The first signifies the central fruit or objective of the dramatic action. Ācārya Vishvanātha beautifully defines it in the following words along with his explanation of the other term, i.e. 'अधिकारी':

अधिकारः फले स्वाम्यमधिकारी च तत्प्रभुः ।

(साहित्यदर्पण 6/43)

> [The hero's mastery or authority over the fruit of his own action is his 'adhikāra' and he himself is the 'adhikārī' or owner of that fruit.]

Evidently, "Adhikāra" is what the West calls 'the outcome of the action' and the term "Adhikārī" is what the West calls 'the protagonist' The outcome of the action in Kalidāsa's *Abhijnānaśākuntalam* is the rediscovery of Śakuntalā and the discovery of Bharata and the person who would own and enjoy this fruit (i.e. the union with Sakuntalā and

Bharata) is king Duṣyanta, the protagonist of the play or "Adhikārī" of the fruit of that action. In Shakespeare's *Twelfth Night* the "adhikāra" or the outcome of the action is the discovery by Duke Orsino of the fact that the page-boy Cesario is actually the lady Viola who sincerely loves him and the "Adhikārī" is the Duke himself who enjoys the fruit of this outcome of the action by marrying Viola.

अधीरा (Adhīrā)

The term "Adhīrā" denotes a kind of legally wedded wife, technically called "Svakīyā" who goes into a rage at discovering her husband's passion for and attachment with some other woman. Such a heroine gets easily annoyed with her philandering husband and ridicules him harshly. There are two sub-varieties of "Adhīrā":–मध्या (Madhyā) and प्रौढा (Prauḍhā). The first variety consists of heroines who scold in harsh words their husbands for their mis-conduct whereas the second consists of heroines who punish their erring husbands by boxing their ears and even by beating them.

The following Sanskrit verse depicts a "Madhyā Adhīrā":

सार्धं मनोरथशतैस्तव धूर्त! कान्त!
सैव स्थिता मनसि कृत्रिमहावरम्या।
अस्माकमस्ति नहि कश्चिदिहावकाश-
स्तस्मात्कृतं चरणपातविडम्बनाभिः।।

[O trickster! there stands in thy heart that very beauty, having hundreds of desires, rendered elegant by means of artificial gestures of love, There is no scope for us here (i.e. in thy heart). The displays of thy falling (at my feet) are due to that very (misconduct) of thine."]

Here the aggrieved heroine is scolding her erring husband in fairly harsh words. She is, therefore, a "Madhyā Adhīrā Svakīyā Nāyikā".

An English example of this variety is to be found in Dryden's *All For Love* Act IV where Antony's legally wedded wife Octavia ridicules her misled husband quite harshly:

'Tis not well,
Indeed, my lord, 'tis much unkind to me,
To show this passion, this extreme concernment,
For an abandoned, faithless prostitute.

No doubt Octavia is a "Madhyā Adhīrā Svakīya Nāyikā" who takes her husband Antony to task verbally in harsh words.

The second variety of "Adhīrā", i.e. the "Prauḍhā Adhīrā" is artfully exemplified in the following Sanskrit verse:

प्रतिफलमवलोक्य स्वीयमिन्दोः कलायां
हरशिरसि परस्या वासमाशंसमाना।
गिरिशमचलकन्या तर्जयामास कंप-
प्रचलवलयचंचत्कान्तिभाजा करेण।।

[Seeing her own reflection in the disc of the moon, located on the forehcad of her husband–Hara (i.e. Shiva), Pārvatī slapped the dweller on the Kailāśa (i.e. her own husband) with her hand, shining like the lustrous armlet, under the suspicion that some other woman had taken possession of her husband's head.]

Pārvatī's impateince with and intolerance of her husband's association with another woman makes her slap the Lord (i.e. Shiva) with her hand, entitling her to be called प्रौढा अधीरा नायिका. The literature of the West is not devoid of this variety of heroines. However, the punishment meted out by the Western heroines to their husbands for their infidelty is very violent and tragic. The greatest example that comes to mind is that of Media, the heroine of a tragedy by the Greek dramatist Euripides, bearing that name. She was a sorceress and was the wife of Jason. When Medea came to know of Jason's affair with Glauce or Creusa, she went into a frenzy and killed her two sons by Jason and thus punished him for his betrayal. Thus she emerges as an example of प्रौढ़ा अधीरा नायिका.

अध्यवसान (Adhyavasāna):–The process through which the minor term called 'upameya' assumes the attributes of the major term or 'upamāna', is known as 'Adhyavasāna'. The term is normally employed in the discussion of सारोपा लक्षणा and the figure of speech called रूपक. There is 'Adhyavasāna' when the major term takes possession of the minor term completely so much so that the difference between them disappears completely. For example, in the expression रात्रिकापालिकी, the fundamental difference between the night (रात्रि) (which is the minor term) and the 'female' skull-worshipper (कापालिकी) (which is the major term) has disappeared, making the two identical, we have "Adhyavasāna". Similarly, in Tennyson's expression 'black bat night', the minor term is 'night' and the major term is 'black bat'; the latter has possessed the former so completely and absolutely that there is hardly a difference between the two–the major term has subsumed and absorbed the minor term to such an extent that they have become one, the minor term losing itself in the major term. This is the 'Adhyavasāna' of the minor term in the major term. A synonym of 'Adhyavasāna' is 'Tirohaṇa' –the process of getting lost.

अनन्वय (Ananvaya):– When with a view to stressing the extraordinariness of an object, the poet makes that object itself its 'upamāna' (major term or standard of comparison), implying that nothing in the world is like it save itself, we have a figure of speech called अनन्वय (Ananvaya). The theorist Bhāmaha defines it in the following words:

यत्र तेनैव तस्य स्यादुपमानोपमेयता।
असादृश्यविवक्षातस्तमित्याहुरनन्वयम्।।

(काव्यालंकार 3/45)

['Ananvaya' exists where an object is compared with itself, with a view to stressing the point that its standard of comparison is not available.]

Let us consider the following Sanskrit verse:

न केवलं भाति नितान्तकान्तिनितिम्बिनी सैव नितम्बिनीव।
यावद्विलासायुधलास्यवासास्ते तद्विलासा इव तद्विलासाः।।

[It is just not that that lady with most lustrous buttocks is shining forth like a lady having buttocks, comparable to herself; even her exciting gestures are comparable to the exciting gestures of her own, which are the dwelling place of the dance called 'Lasya' performed by the wielder of the weapons in the form of all possible exciting gestures (i.e. the god of Love called Kāmadeva).]

Here the lustrous lady with beautiful buttocks is her own standard of comparison and so are her exciting gestures their own major term (upamāna). The sense is that the lady concerned cannot be compared with any other lady, past, present or future save herself and her gestures, too, are their own standard for these are not to be found anywhere else. Clearly, the verse is an excellent example of "Ananvaya".

Christophor Marlowe's line: 'And none but thou shalt be my paramour' can be cited as an English example of 'Ananvaya', if we read the line as follows:

'And none but thou thyself art thy own compeer' and in point of fact, the purport of the whole speech is that Helen is her own standard of comparison. We are talking here of the beautiful passage in *Doctor Faustus* where Faustus exclaims: 'Was this the face that launched a thousand ships?' and continues:

O, thou art fairer than the evening's air,
Clad in the beauty of a thousand stars.
Brighter art thou than flaming Jupiter
When he appeared to hapless Semele:
More lovely than the monarch of the sky,
In wanton Arethusa's azured arms,
And none but thou shalt be my paramour.

In the last line of the passage we have "Ananvaya" if we read it as 'And none but thou shalt be thy own compeer' and that precisely is the chain of thought of the speaker (i.e. Faustus).

It must be noted that in a simile something (minor term) is compared with some other thing (major term) which is normally its superior. But in "Ananvaya" the thing being described is at once the minor term as well as major term–'upameya' and 'upamāna' all at once.

अनुकर्ता and अनुकार्य (Anukartā &Anukārya)

These are the critical terms of dramaturgy and refer to the actor on the stage and the role of the character he has been assigned by the director of the play. For example, the famous actor of the 18th century English theatre–David Garrick (1717-1779) was noted for the tragic roles he specialized in. He had played the lead-roles of Shakespeare's tragedies like *Hamlet* and *King Lear*. In respect of *Hamlet* he was the "anukartā" and the character whose role he played was the 'Anukārya': The success of a play largely depends on how closely the 'anukartā' performs the role of the "anukārya" and the question of "how closely" will be determined by the response of the spectators. If the "anukartā" of the role of Duṣyanta in Kālidāsa's *Abhigyānaśakuntalam* convinces the spectators by means of his faithful representation of Duṣyanta's role and compels them to forget for the time being the difference between the actor as a fellow man on the one hand and the character whose role (i.e. Duṣyanta) he is playing, the play will be deemed as fairly successful as an "anukṛti" or *mimesis* (imitation or representation). The costume, weapons, ornaments, manner of speech and gestures–all play their roles in this effect. The "Anukartā" must live the life of the "Anukārya" for the success of his own performance and also for the success of the play as a whole.

अनुकूल (Anukula) I

This is a term from "Nāyaka-Nāyikā-Bheda" of Sanskrit poetics. The term denotes a hero (Nāyaka) who is devoted to his wife and keeps all other women at arm's length, remaining contented with his lady-love, under all circumstances. The theorists like Dhananjaya and Vishvanātha extend it to cover a lover who is devoted to a single lady: 'अनुकूलः एकनिरतः', as ācārya Vishvanātha puts the case. The following Sanskrit verse suggests all the essentials of an "anukula" hero through the words of his beloved, addressed to her female friend:

> अस्माकं सखि! वाससी न रुचिरे, ग्रैवेयकं नोज्ज्वलं
> नो वक्रो गतिरुद्धतं न हसितं, नैवास्ति कश्चिन्मदः।
> किन्त्वन्येऽपि जना वदन्ति सुभगोऽप्यस्याः प्रियोनान्यतो
> दृष्टिं निक्षपतीति विश्वमियता मन्यामहे दुःस्थितम्।।
>
> [Both of my garments (lower as well as upper) are, by no means, fascinating, nor is my necklace white (i.e. it is not of pearls). There is nothing artful about my gait, nor is there any abandonment in my laughter nor is there any intoxication in me whatsoever. But even my enemies say that this lady's lover, notwithstanding the fact that he is so beautiful, does not cast his glance anywhere else. Friend, from this very fact. I infer that the whole world is full of sorrow except me!]

Here the lover has been presented as a genuine and sincere lover whose love for his lady-love is absolute and unconditional, irrespective of the fact that she is a plain and simple woman, having nothing special to attract men towards her. All the famous romantic tales of the world in all traditions can supply examples of "Anukula" lovers–Majnoo, Romeo, Rānjhā, Leander etc. can be cited as "Anukula" lovers. Hardy's Gabriel Oak also belongs to the same category, devoted as he is under all circumstances to Bathsheba Everdene. And so far as the concept of 'Anukula' husband is concerned, it is best exemplified by Rāma who loves his wife Sītā unconditionally and absolutely under all conditions. Bhavabhūti has made an immortal picture of Rāma as an "Anukula" husband in his masterpiece *Uttararāmacaritam*, especially in the verse beginning with the words: "अद्वैतं सुखदुःखयोरनुगतं सर्वास्वस्थासु यत्". And for an English example of "Anukula" husband we can cite the King of France, the husband of Cordelia in Shakespeare's *King Lear,* for he continues to love his wife even when Lear deprives her of her share in his kingdom, rendering her a pauper. The following speech of the King of France bears testimony to his claim to the title of an 'Anukula' husband:

> Fairest Cordelia, that art most rich being poor,
> Most choice, forsaken; and most lov'd, despised.
> Thee and thy virtues here I seize upon:
> Bet it lawful, I take up what's cast away.
> Gods, gods! 'tis strange that from their cold'st neglect
> My love should kindle to inflam'd respect.–
> Thy dowerless daughter, king, thrown to my chance,
> Is Queen of us, of ours, and our fair France:
> Not all the dukes of waterish Burgundy
> Can buy this unprized precious maid of me.

And the King of France remains true to his words, stated above, unto the last. He is no doubt an excellent example of the 'Anukula' husband in the Western tradition.

अनुकूल (Anukūla) II: The term 'Anukula' also signifies a figure of speech. The credit of having discovered this figure goes to the theorist ācārya Vishvanātha who defines it in the following words:

अनुकूलं प्रातिकूल्यमनुकूलानुबन्धि चेत्

(साहित्यदर्पण 10/64)

> [If unfavourableness (is managed skilfully) to turn out to be favourable, we have the figure called "Anukula".]

Thus the figure 'Anukula' consists in the unfavourable situation's turning out to be quite favourable and welcome. Consider the following Sanskrit verse:

कुपितासि यदा तन्वि! निधाय करजक्षतम्।
बधान भुजपाशाभ्यांकण्ठमस्य दृढं तदा।।

> [(Some culpable lover is supplicating to his lady-love:) "O frail-bodied, in case thou art angry, then tie firmly the neck of this man (i.e. the lover) with the rope of thy arms after causing nail-wounds".]

If somebody's lady-love gets angry–that is really a very unfavourable situation. But here that apparently unwelcome situation has been suggested to be the source of an ultimately beneficial and therefore favourable one when in the form of punishment the lover will get sweet embraces and nail-wounds from his sweet-heart.

Kālidāsa in the first part of his *Meghadutam* makes a very beautiful use of the figure "Anukula":

अम्भोविन्दुग्रहणचतुरांश्चातकान्वीक्षमाणाः
श्रेणीभूताः परिगणनया निर्दिशन्तो बलाकाः।
त्वामासाद्य स्तनितसमये मानयिष्यन्ति सिद्धाः
सोत्कम्पानि प्रियसहचरीसम्भ्रमालिङ्गितानि।।

[(The Yakṣa in exile on the hill of Rāmagiri, is telling his Cloud-messenger that on his way to Alakā, he will pass through many regions having beautiful sights, including that of the demigods called Siddhas, embracing their women:)] "While observing the cātaka-birds, expert in catching the water-drops (of rains in the sky itself) and pointing at the cranes, assembled in rows, keeping count of them, the demigods called Siddhas, coming across thee, will honour thee on obtaining at thy thundering the sudden embraces from their ladyloves, full of perturbations".]

The thundering of the cloud is very fearsome indeed and is unfavourable by any standard of reckoning. But the same unfavourable circumstance proves to be a blessing in disguise by providing the Siddhas the most-sought-after embraces from their ladyloves. Thus the verse of Kālidāsa is illustrative of the figure "Anukula".

For an English example of this figure we can cite Robert Browning's lyric in the form of a dramatic monologue entitled "Prospice" in which the lover-poet regards the most unwelcome event of life called 'Death' as a source of perfect bliss for it would provide him everlasting union with the soul of his late wife–Elizabeth Barret Browning, resting in the lap of God. Consider the closing lines of the poem and see how they exploit the figure "Anukula" very artfully:

The black minute's at end,
And the elements' rage, the fiend voices that rave,
Shall dwindle, shall blend,
Shall change, shall become first a peace out of pain,
Then a light, then thy breast,
O thou soul of my soul! I shall clasp thee again
And with God be the rest.

अनुक्तनिमित्ता (Anuktanimittā)

This is a variety of the figure of speech called विशेषोक्ति (Viśeṣokti), the other variety of that figure being "uktanimittā". In "Anuktanimitta Viśeṣokti" the reason of the unproductiveness of the action notwithstanding the presence of production-friendly factors, is skilfully allowd to remain unstated. The following Sanskrit verse is an excellent example of this figure:

> निद्रानिवृत्तौ उदिते द्युरत्ने सखीजने द्वारपदं पराप्ते।
> श्लथीकृताश्लेषरसे भुजङ्गे चचाल नालिंगनतोऽङ्गना सा।।
>
> [Slumber having disappeared and the gem of the sky (i.e. the sun) having risen (in the sky) and the female friends having arrived at the threshold as also the paramour having lessened the pleasure of embracing, that lady with beautiful limbs did not swerve from the embracing (of her lover).]

In the normal course of life, any sensible woman would cease embracing her lover the moment she learns of the arrival of someone at her doorstep, if not at the sun-rise itself. But here 4 causal factors of the cessation of the act of embracing have been stated and yet the effect has not been produced. However, the reason for this strange phenomenon has not been stated. Clearly, the verse, under discussion, is an example of "Unuktanimittā Viśesokti"; the charm lies in the suggestion that the lady is abnormally passionate and that her libido is insatiable.

An English example of "Anuktanimittā Viśeṣokti" is to be found in "The Rime of Ancient Mariner" by S.T. Coleridge:

> Water, water, everywhere,
> And all the boards did shrink;
> Water, water, every where,
> Nor any drop to drink.
>
> (Part II ll. 118-122)

In the last two lines of the stanza, cited above, enough causal factor for the satisfaction of the human requirement of thirst being available notwithstanding, the satisfaction of the thirst is ruled out. But why so? No explanation has been provided. Thus the lines contain "unukta-nimitā-Viśeṣokti". The poet very artfully suggests the mysterious and eerie atmosphere of the situation described by means of the employment of the figure concerned.

lion vis-a-vis Samson was like a kid vis-a-vis a lion. But the very use of the word 'kid' takes away a lot of grandeur from the description of Samson's prowess. Had the poet used the word 'elephant' or 'bison', the analogy would have been in place. Can a lion be called a brave animal if it tears off some 'kid' into pieces? Absolutely not; even an ordinary man can do that, leave aside a lion. No doubt, Milton's line suffers from 'Anucitārthadoṣa'.